D0301596

GENDER AND THE GARDEN IN
EARLY MODERN ENGLISH LITERATURE

Women and Gender in the Early Modern World

Series Editors: Allyson Poska and Abby Zanger

In the past decade, the study of women and gender has offered some of the most vital and innovative challenges to scholarship on the early modern period. Ashgate's new series of interdisciplinary and comparative studies, 'Women and Gender in the Early Modern World,' takes up this challenge, reaching beyond geographical limitations to explore the experiences of early modern women and the nature of gender in Europe, the Americas, Asia, and Africa. Submissions of single-author studies and edited collections will be considered.

Titles in this series include:

Masculinity and Emotion in Early Modern English Literature
Jennifer C. Vaught

Oral Traditions and Gender in Early Modern Literary Texts
Edited by Mary Ellen Lamb and Karen Bamford

Women, Space and Utopia 1600–1800
Nicole Pohl

Genre and Women's Life Writing in Early Modern England
Edited by Michelle M. Dowd and Julie A. Eckerle

Women's Letters Across Europe, 1400–1700
Edited by Jane Couchman and Ann Crabb

Gender and the Garden in Early Modern English Literature

JENNIFER MUNROE
University of North Carolina at Charlotte, USA

ASHGATE

Published by
Ashgate Publishing Limited
Gower House
Croft Road
Aldershot
Hampshire GU11 3HR
England

Ashgate Publishing Company
Suite 420
101 Cherry Street
Burlington, VT 05401-4405
USA

Ashgate website: http://www.ashgate.com

British Library Cataloguing in Publication Data
Munroe, Jennifer
Gender and the garden in early modern English literature. – (Women and gender in the early modern world)
1. English literature – Early modern, 1500–1700 – History and criticism 2. Gardens in literature 3. Gardening in literature 4. Sex role in literature 5. Gardens – Social aspects 6. Group identity in literature
I. Title
820.9'364

Library of Congress Cataloging-in-Publication Data
Munroe, Jennifer.
Gender and the garden in early modern English literature / by Jennifer Munroe.
p. cm.—(Women and gender in the early modern world)
Includes bibliographical references.
ISBN: 978-0-7546-5826-9 (alk. paper)
1. English literature—Early modern, 1500–1700—History and criticism. 2. Gardens in literature. 3. Gardening in literature. 4. Sex role in literature. 5. Gardens—Social aspects. 6. Group identity in literature.
I. Title.

PR428.G37M86 2008
820.9'364—dc22

2007042076

ISBN: 978-0-7546-5826-9

Printed and bound in Great Britain by MPG Books Ltd, Bodmin, Cornwall.

Table of Contents

List of Figures

Acknowledgements

The modest garden of my own making presented here grew out of the patient dedication and commitment of many people for whom I am eternally grateful. Thanks first to Carol Neely, who spilled much ink pouring through the draft pages of this text. I am grateful for her words of encouragement as well as her painstaking critique. Thanks, too, to Lori Newcomb, who one might say planted the seeds of this project by turning me on to the beauty of the Renaissance garden in her graduate seminar in the spring of 1999. My work on gardens is no doubt better from the many hours spent in her backyard sipping tea with fresh mint from her garden. Achsah Guibbory, who inspires me in countless ways and is a dear friend; and Michael Shapiro, who read drafts of this book early-on and gave me books about Shakespeare's gardens. Other generous readings of drafts came from Chuck Conaway, Kim Woosley-Poitevin, Elizabeth Klett, Chung-In Im, Stephen Hamrick, and members of the Early Modern Workshop in the English Department of the University of Illinois; and Kirk Melnikoff and Helen Hull at the University of North Carolina at Charlotte graciously offered commentary that in no small ways strengthened my argument. And finally, to Ilona Bell, whose comments at a late stage in this project helped me to trim unnecessary weeds; and Rebecca Laroche, in whom I have found a kindred spirit in Flora's court.

The work in this book was only possible because of time spent with musty books found in various archives in London. A Travel Grant from the University of Illinois and a Faculty Research Grant and money from the Small Grants Program from the University of North Carolina at Charlotte provided funding that allowed me to pour through manuscripts at the British Library and assisted with permissions and reproductions fees. I also want to thank the American Association of University Women, the PEO, and the English Department at the University of Illinois for fellowship funding that contributed to the early work on this project, and the University of North Carolina at Charlotte, which provided me with a research grant and much-needed leave that allowed me to bring it to a close. I thank in particular the staff at the British Library, who provided critical assistance at various moments.

Finally, I am well aware of the sacrifices made by those who love me for this project to happen. First, to my children, Jamie and Schuyler, whom I suspect thought it would never end; your patience and words of encouragement kept me going, and you make me proud. And to Alan, whose steadfast support makes me feel as if there is nothing I cannot accomplish.

Introduction

Laying the Groundwork

Each spring, countless men and women take shovels in hand and move outside to transform the landscape, whether that involves tackling a small flower plot in their backyards or a planting a community vegetable garden to share with friends and neighbors. No matter the scale of their gardens or their experience as gardeners, these enthusiasts proceed with a vigor unsurpassed by so many other kinds of household "work." Botanical gardens attract visitors from far and wide to spend a few hours, or perhaps the entire day, strolling in the well-kept beds of flowers both common and exotic. What is it about gardening that has captured the interest of the laborer and admirer alike for centuries, though? Just as they are today, early modern English gardens were sites of particular interest for men and women at least in part because they were spaces for growing things. Yet they were also ideologically-charged spaces that conveyed social meaning. *Gender and the Garden* reconstructs how gardens functioned as such spaces, how they typified what geographer Denis Cosgrove terms historically-contextualized and geographically-specific "ways of seeing" the world (xxix).[1] The book argues that early modern gardens, both actual and imagined, provide a window into how early modern social space—and of particular interest here, the gendered power relationships in it—was shaped and reshaped by people as they made and remade the places they inhabited. As such, this book understands the early modern English garden to be a site where men and women transformed the look of the natural world, but the garden was also a space where they could manipulate their position in society, too.

Looking at the relationship between gardens and gendered social identity reveals how gardens were imagined as complex and often contradictory sites of ideological struggle, where one could conceive of renegotiating social position as much as one

---

1   Cosgrove's work has been influential not only for geographers but also for scholars in a variety of disciplines who study landscapes. Scholars have critiqued Cosgrove's claim that "a landscape is a way of seeing that has its own history, but a history that can only be understood as part of a wider history of economy and society" (xiv), citing the ways that such a thesis might draw attention to already-discussed groups of people who are foregrounded as part of dominant discursive systems, such as men and the aristocracy. The work since accomplished in Geography and other fields has shown, however, that the fundamental problem with Cosgrove's thesis was not his historicizing of landscape study but rather the range of people he studied as part of that history. Even though Cosgrove repeatedly posits the relational qualities of landscapes—as depending on both imagination and actual properties— he tends to emphasize the imagined characteristics more so than the actual ones. As should be clear from my emphasis on DeCerteau's and Lefebvre's work (as I discuss later in this Introduction), I believe that landscapes, and for the purposes of this book, gardens, are both.

might imagine fitting in.[2] In *The Description of England* (1577), for example, William Harrison suggests some of the garden's unspoken meanings when gardening was understood to be an artistic endeavor rather than as a subsistence practice alone:

> How art also helpeth nature in the daily colouring, doubling, and enlarging the proportion of our flowers, it is incredible to report; for so curious and cunning are our gardeners now in these days that they presume to do in manner what they list with Nature, and moderate her course in things as if they were her superiors…For mine own part, good reader, let me boast a little of my garden, which is but small and the whole area thereof little above three hundred foot of ground, and yet, such hath been my good luck in purchase of the variety of simples that, notwithstanding my small ability, there are very near three hundred of one sort and other contained therein, no one of them being common or usually to be had. If therefore my little plot, void of all cost in keeping, be so well furnished, what shall we think of those of Hampton Court, Nonsuch, Theobalds, Cobham Garden, and sundry other appertaining to divers citizens of London, whom I could particularly name if I should not seem to offend them by such my demeanor and dealing? (265, 270)

Harrison's observations reinforce how gardening marked human artistic superiority over a postlapsarian, or "fallen," natural landscape, even as it was simultaneously seen as and used to mark social differentiation too. Harrison, that is, does more than describe the gardens he saw. He also details their social significance: how the gardener's skill earns him admiration; how the aristocratic gardens at Theobalds and Nonsuch, for example, are paragons that other gardeners might aspire to; and how, even his own "small skill" helped him make a "little plot" that was "well furnished" enough to call to mind the gardens on England's great estates. At the same time, his description of gardening and the relationship between (masculinized) art and (feminized) nature together suggest an underlying gendered tension inherent to gardening. His phrase "as if they were her superiors" articulates anxiety about the extent to which those (male) gardeners to whom he refers *are* the superiors of (feminized) nature; and, the way that Harrison describes his "small plot" and the "simples" it contains aligns his garden (and his gardening practice) with women, who were admonished by male writers in printed gardening books to plant smaller scale gardens than men because women inherently had, like Harrison ironically claims of himself here, "small ability." Harrison certainly reiterates the familiar gendering of nature and art that underlies men's claim to superiority over women and their gardening, but at the same time his deferent position relative his own superiors in the art aligns him with women and destabilizes such otherwise easily gendered dichotomies.

As Harrison's and others' similar descriptions remind us, landscape practices are rooted in ideologies that penetrate the surficial or articulable signs registered by users, and ideologies have a direct bearing on the physical environment. Different kinds of gardens (kitchen versus aesthetic) and their specific purposes (subsistence versus show) each resonated ideologically in different ways.[3] While most kitchen gardens

---

2   See Chapter 8, "Dominant, Residual, and Emergent" in *Marxism and Literature*.

3   See also the recent work of geographer Alan R.H. Baker, who sees landscapes as "expressive of authority" and bearing the signs of ideologies (5).

contained vegetables and herbs routinely found in household cooking and medicinal recipes, and the status of those who planted them was relatively equal, aesthetic pleasure gardens bore signs of differentiation and specialization—both among their growers and users and in the plants they selected for display. Aesthetic gardens in elite households often featured manicured hedges to create boundaries between the garden space and the rest of the physical landscape and within these gardens one likely found branches crafted into arbors for banqueting, topiaries that transformed small trees and bushes into geometrical designs, and hand-selected plants artfully shaped into knots, parterres, and labyrinths. These displays evinced what William Lawson described in *A New Orchard and Garden* (1617) as the way "Art restoreth the Collectrix of Nature's faults" by taking a disorderly landscape and making it beautiful. Even as these gardens represented the desire to order nature through human art they established a different hierarchical ordering among household members and garden laborers: aesthetic gardens might well be designed by the owner or his wife, overseen by a professional gardener, and planted by day laborers, the same men and women who may well have farmed their own piece of land as tenant farmers before the period of mass reallocation.[4]

Still, aesthetic gardens were not strictly the domain of dominant groups alone. In fact, garden landscapes often represented competing interests in realigning authority, for the marginalized as well as the elite. I qualify Roy Strong's claim in *The Renaissance Garden In England*, then, that the formal, aesthetic garden during this period was "a symbol of pride and an expression of royal and aristocratic magnificence; *man* conquered the earth, tilled and planted it, subjecting it to *his* will" (11, my emphasis). Such a claim, albeit supported by the preponderance of examples in Strong's book, suggests that gardens were almost exclusively the domain of the male elite. True, formal gardens were almost exclusively the domain of royalty and aristocracy (and arguably, men) early on, but by the middle of the sixteenth century this changed. We know, for example, that the social status gained by land ownership and gardening extended beyond just the elite to the upwardly mobile middle class men and women as the sixteenth century progressed.[5]

4　For more information on the widespread land reallocation and enclosure movement in England during the sixteenth century, see Joyce Youings, *Dissolution of the Monasteries*; Joan Thirsk, *The Rural Economy of England*; Richard Schlatter, *Private Property*; Mark Overton, *Agricultural Revolution in England*; G.E. Mingay, *A Social History of the English Countryside*; and Leonard Cantor, *The Changing English Countryside, 1400–1700*. I also discuss this topic more at length in Chapter 1.

5　Most marked changes in land use stemmed from the privatization of land, which took many forms throughout the period. First, monastic land was seized by the State and redistributed among a relatively small number of wealthy well-connected aristocratic families. Palliser calls this redistribution in the mid-sixteenth century the "greatest transfer of land since the Norman Conquest" with parcels of land sold, granted as gifts, or otherwise exchanged by Henry VIII, Edward XI, and Mary Tudor (Palliser 90). In fact, by the time Elizabeth took the throne mid-century, three-quarters of the monastic land was considered "alienated" and either lay in the hands of private landowners or was otherwise held by the crown (Youings 118). Consequences of the new land acquisition and the emphasis placed on private ownership as a mark of social status included landowners "indulging in conspicuous

Different uses of the garden intersected and catalyzed one another throughout the period in an ongoing refashioning of the landscape and the self through a combination of gardening practice, the different gendered social relationships gardens represented, and the gardens men and women might imagine in their writing. The story that surfaces is one of mobility and limitation, disenfranchisement and belonging. The characters featured in this story include men from the middling sort who drew from their (sometimes failed) experiences as husbandmen to enable claims to literary status and authority on gardening; a geographically displaced middle-class courtier who used his metaphorical gardens to gain favor with the queen, substitute her female authority for male, and amass wealth and land; a middle-class woman who sought a sympathetic connection with other women who were marginalized and disinherited as she was, whose garden served as an ideal site to imagine recouping their losses, finding community and redemption; and an aristocratic woman who evoked socially-appropriate avenues for women's creativity (needlework and gardening) and showed how published writing might be an acceptable creative outlet for women too. The men and women whose texts I study all saw themselves as disenfranchised figures, seeking inclusion in domains from which they either participated marginally or were openly excluded, and they extended this inclusion to others like them as well.

Gender and the Garden challenges the alignment of the garden with just men or just the elite by pointing to "fissures" related to shifting gardening practices and meanings in actual gardens, and isolating how they are made manifest in the gardens imagined in texts.[6] Such moments appear historically, as, on the one hand, the presence of rare flowers in one's garden attested to the privilege and status of the upper class, while common and easily-accessible flowers and plants were aligned with the "common sort" in whose gardens they grew. John Gerard, contemporary herbal writer, suggested as much when he identified the perceived link between flower rarity and social status when he declared, "Far fetched and dear bought is best for ladies" (Qtd. in Thomas 232). On the other hand, as more members of the middling sort could afford to plant aesthetic gardens, gardens signaled moments of rupture and functioned as highly manipulable indicators of social status for a range of men and women, not just those of the aristocracy. For instance, when William Lawson insists on the connections between the garden and social status in *A New Orchard and Garden* (1618), saying that one might make a knot-garden because "the eye must be pleased with the forme," he addresses not just those of the elite or those in their employ who might read his book, but also a developing readership of persons from the middling sort. Therefore, his admonishment that "the better sort may use

---

consumption, and borrowing heavily at high rates of interest...[as well as] an exceptional fluidity among landed families and estates" (Palliser 90). From 1550 to 1850, private property rights were established on almost all of the arable land in England, but most of the change in land ownership took place among the upwardly-mobile gentry, not the aristocracy. In fact, some historians have estimated that the percentage of land owned by the "middling and lesser gentry" nearly doubled from the middle of the fifteenth through the late seventeenth centuries—from 25 per cent to 45–50 per cent—and yeoman family farmers and other small owners grew from 20 per cent to 25–33 per cent. These increases make this demographic the largest growing group of landholders during the early modern period in England (McRae 14).

6   For further discussion and theorizing of fissures, see Alan Sinfield, *Faultlines*.

better formes, and more costly worke" shows how such status from gardening was no longer limited just to the most wealthy and privileged in England (11).

Flowers were a particularly *changing* fashion, and the garden became a way to mark "distinction" among its practitioners and authorities.[7] "As each flower went out of fashion," writes Keith Thomas, for instance, "it lost its commercial value and descended the social scale" (231–32). More complicated types of blooms, such as "double-blooms" and "out-of-season" flowers, were often cultivated by lower class men and women, who were more likely to give their blooms the constant attention and care that the hired gardeners of the aristocracy were not motivated to provide. Once men and women from diverse backgrounds incorporated formal gardens and claimed this "art" for themselves, the specific contents of their gardens, it signified upward social mobility (and social status) for a more varied group of people. For example, while members of the aristocracy and gentry earlier in the seventeenth century identified gillyflowers and carnations as "most prized," once these flowers became prolific enough that those from the lower classes could buy and plant them, tulips and auriculas (flowers virtually unknown to people in England until then) became the newly desirable fashion instead.

Men and women from the lower ranks of society could appropriate status markers simply by purchasing and planting in their own gardens the plants once deemed exotic and rare but that had since become less expensive, more abundant through cultivation over time. Those from lower classes could use their employment as garden laborers or their own gardens to destabilize the very status boundaries the elite tried so hard to demarcate; and members of the elite in turn sought new ways of differentiating status in response to the always-present potential for destabilization. In fact, some who labored in the gardens of the elite could even catalyze the transition from rare to common by pocketing imported bulbs and seeds to plant in their own gardens.[8] As the first commodity market, the tulip trade made wealth and status a possibility for individuals who would otherwise have earned only modest incomes (Goody 195–99).[9] For instance, success in the tulip trade allowed a poor farmer to purchase the largest house in the township and become a highly respected city official, only to lose it all when the bottom dropped out of the market.[10]

As the work of landscape architects has demonstrated, gardens, both then and now, also bear the signs of particularly gendered power relations negotiated by

---

7   In *Distinction* Bourdieu discusses how, as the bourgeousie established itself, a new kind of competition arose between members of the middle class and the elite. The developing (or developed, as is the case in Bourdieu's study) middle class could acquire goods and obtain elite status, or marks of "distinction," formerly obtained only by members of the elite by using wealth and prestige they gained through professions.

8   See Goody, 182–205 for a discussion of the iconic significance of flowers and gardens in the period, which includes "tulipomania" and the importation of other exotic plants. See also Thomas, 226–41.

9   Goody describes not only the impulse to import and plant exotic flowers, but also the Puritan counter-impulse to reject such indulgences.

10   See Dash for a more lengthy account of how the tulip trade developed as well as what led to its downfall.

those who make them, use them, and imagine them.[11] The publication of William Lawson's *A New Orchard and Garden* in 1618 suggests one way that the garden was understood in gendered terms, as it includes separate books for male and female gardeners with quite different instructions for and purposes in planting the garden for each. As Lawson (and others like him) suggest, men were to plant comparatively larger-scale gardens for profit and pleasure, while women were to engage their skills in planting modest flower and herb gardens that reflected their relatively less-developed skill set. Still, numerous women, particularly those of the elite, were known for their extensive garden displays, as was the case of Elizabeth Shrewsbury and Lucy Harrington, who were instrumental in the design and planting of elaborate gardens on their personal estates at roughly the same time Lawson's manual appears. Moreover, by the mid-seventeenth century, women had established themselves in the realm of aesthetic gardening, and were cited as such by male writers on the topic, as was true in Hugh Plat's *Garden of Eden* (1652) and Nicholas Bonnefons's *The French Gardiner* (1658).[12] Despite such noteworthy successes in women's gardening during this period, the value of such activity and its products stood in tension with the gardening associated with their male counterparts. Therefore, while the gendering of the garden may have circumscribed women's involvement and the extent of their gardening in some ways, it also offered new possibilities for women to catalyze their own social mobility or assert agency over their social status.[13]

In the same way gardens signified a gardener's ability to "fashion" her/himself, they suggest how we might theorize the dynamic process of *gendered* self-fashioning in the early modern period. Just as the gardener's art that shapes and marks the boundaries of a given piece of land is limited to some degree by the inherent qualities of the land he or she cultivates, so too is the artful shaping of the (gendered) self at once challenged by as it challenges the limits of that shaping. In both cases, these different examples of fashioning—of land and of the self—necessitate a repeated stylization that calls to mind Judith Butler's now familiar formulation of gendered identity, which involves the "repeated stylization of the body" and is "neither a single act nor a causal process initiated by a subject and culminating a set of fixed effects" (*Gender Trouble* 33, *Bodies that Matter* 10). Both the stylized garden, constituted by artful practice, and the stylized body that "performs" gender produce the appearance

---

11   See, for example, Riley, whose article comes from a special issue on women and landscape. Riley further questions whether there might even exist what he calls a "gender-neutral" landscape and argues instead that "Women have no choice but to use male-biased landscapes" (162). For similar questions, although related to modern landscape design, see Masden and Furlong.

12   See also Hannah Woolley's *The Accomplisht Ladys Delight* (1675 ed.) as an early domestic manual for women by a woman with an interest in gardening for women. The 1675 and 1720 editions include a short section titled, "The Ladys Diversion in Her Garden," most likely written by Thomas Harris. It is unclear whether Woolley played a role in the inclusion of this short section on gardening, but the fact that it was included in her longer text nevertheless associated a woman writer with expertise on this topic. Harris was an unknown writer, while Woolley's books sold well; therefore, the inclusion of Harris's section would more likely have been to help Harris capitalize on Woolley's successes rather than the other way around.

13   See Harris, Lazzaro, Merchant, and Keller.

of a finished product (the gendered self or the garden plot), but both are always in the process of changing or potentially changing. That gendered self is neither strictly a product nor agent of such gendered identity. Likewise, anyone who has ever gardened knows that fashioning a garden is never fully in one's own hands. Regardless of what one intends to make grow, weeds perpetually threaten to overtake the cultivated space; or climatic conditions, such as changing positions of the sun or too much or too little rain, for example, make it impossible to control completely how quickly or well plants will produce. Garden images in poetry may well evoke the idea of the garden in general terms, but the odds of each reader imagining exactly the same garden space must be astronomical.

We might well ask ourselves, then, what kind of gendered authority relationships did gardens, and the way men and women imagined them in texts, reflect in late sixteenth- and early seventeenth-century England? To this end, I evoke the work of geographers Alan R.H. Baker and Gideon Biger, who remind us that cultivated landscapes are "social constructions," signaling with "non-verbal" cues and "powerful visual signs, conveying messages forcefully" (Baker and Biger 2, 5). What men and women planted in gardens in early modern England, how they arranged their gardens, and the type of planting practices that went into making them collectively (en)gendered the social relationships among their users and inhabitants and generated symbolic meaning. As I discuss more fully in Chapter 1, when men and women grew kitchen gardens for subsistence purposes, and especially before aesthetic gardens were available to them, gardens represented the relatively egalitarian social relationships among family and community members who labored in them to meet the household's basic nutritional needs. As more men and women used kitchen gardens to generate surplus income for market purchases, or when men and women grew plants for sale (and, especially, profit) at the market, these gardens represented differently, and the social relationships among men and women in them became more stratified, since there was more at stake in the act of planting and in the yields from their production. A still greater reorganization of these relationships and revaluing takes place when men and women—first from the aristocracy but later from the middling sort—planted aesthetic flower gardens, sometimes just small-scale flower designs for decoration, and other times large-scale displays with elaborate statuary, grottoes, banqueting houses, and automata. These different types of gardens and the different ways they signified social status therefore in turn also signified a realignment of authority.

Such multiple signification underlies this book's interest in the garden as both a real and imagined space and as a site for the production of (gendered) social space. As such, I draw in part from the work on everyday practices by Michel De Certeau, whose interest in "spatial practices" informs my own. My own analysis of this phenomenon is informed by De Certeau's discussion of "stories" that articulate these practices, representations that reflect even as they influence the practices themselves. Yet, in trying to isolate the social as well as the physical aspects of space I also turn to the work of Henri Lefebvre, who sees the "production of space" as collectively constituted by three related categories: spatial practices, representational spaces, and representations of space. Though Lefebvre does not discuss gardening as such or literature at length, his model proves useful in understanding the relationship between gardens, writing, and gendered social identity in that it allows us to consider the three aspects of "space" as interconnected and mutually contributive to cultural production. As such, Lefebvre diverts our focus from *just* texts or *just* gardens as discrete cultural and/or material objects. *Spatial practices*, as he theorizes them, involve individuals' perceptual experiences of the spaces they occupy, the everyday activities they engage in that occur in physical space. *Representational space*, by contrast, is "lived through its associated images and symbols, and hence, is the space of 'inhabitants' and 'users'…[the] space which the imagination seeks to change and appropriate" (39). Comprised of "non-verbal cues," representational spaces are the product of spatial practices, and they encompass the dynamic collective of social relationships that go into that production. *Representations of space* depict how individuals identify with lived and perceived spaces; they are filtered through the intellect and imagination, and they "tend toward a system of [linguistic] (and therefore more intellectually worked out) signs" (39).

As a spatial practice, gardening was perceived through the bodily experiences of the men and women who wielded the hoe and dug in the dirt to plant a garden, and the gardens they made represented the social relationships relevant to its planting and display. As more people planted gardens during the mid-to-late sixteenth century for aesthetic purposes, gardens functioned as a new kind of space that marked social status and helped facilitate social mobility for men and women of the middling sort who had the expendable income to supplement their regular household, or kitchen, gardens with attractive displays of flowers and other decorative plants. At the same time, gardens in texts early in the sixteenth century represented the social relationships in gardens planted for household consumption; and the kinds of representations later in the period emphasized differently hierarchized social (and increasingly gendered) relationships in market and aesthetic gardens for profit and pleasure.

As Chapter 1 shows more at length, practical gardening books show how representations of gardens influenced social signification even as they prescribed ways to adapt the material conditions of one's garden. The men who wrote gardening books tied their credibility as writers to their practical expertise as gardeners and husbandmen. John Fitzherbert concludes his *The boke of husbandry* (1533)[14] by saying that he regards his writing about husbandry as a civic duty, stemming from his long experience as a husbandman. He calls his book the "seede" he has "sowen" and frames his textual garden as a type of cultivation for future generations of husbandmen to employ as they, too, wield hoes and shovels to transform their own yards. Readers should accumulate enough experience to "amende it [his book] in places, where as is need" and should remember that Fitzherbert wrote his instructions "of charytie and good zele that he bare to the weale of this mooste noble realme, whiche he dydde not in his youthe, but after he had exercysed husbandry, with great experience, [40] yeres" (125). William Lawson similarly frames his book, *A New Orchard and Garden* (1618), as the culmination of many years of trial and error

---

14   The STC ascribes authorship of this book to John Fitzherbert, though it is not certain that he wrote it. It is possible that Sir Anthony Fitzherbert wrote the book instead, since it reads "By Master Fitzherbert" on the title page. Therefore, the STC also ascribes alternative authorship to Sir Anthony.

(more successful than not, he argues): "When in many yeares by long experience I had furnished this my Notherne Orchard and Country Garden with needfull plants and vsefull hearbes, I did impart the view thereof to my friends, who resorted to mee to conferre in matters of that nature, they did see it, and seeing it desired, and I must not deny novv the publishing of it" (A2). As we might expect given Lefebvre's way of understanding the relationship between representational space (here, the garden) and representations of space (garden images and settings) in texts, such practical books also shaped ways of thinking about the garden itself. Even as male writers used their experience to legitimate their practical advice, these books simultaneously mobilized a gendered discourse about gardening tied to the practical activities one was to carry out in the garden itself. These books increasingly suggest, for example, how men should plant large-scale orchards and gardens with profit and pleasure in mind and how men, not women, would be the professionals whose labor might adorn the grounds of country houses and estates of the nobility; and they admonish women to plant more modest gardens for their delight that should be, like the women themselves, subordinate to their male counterparts.

It is here that I want to adapt Lefebvre's tripartite model, though. Lefebvre's understanding of representations of space in texts, like the preponderance of scholarship on early modern gardens, relies on published sources alone. Such emphasis on print as a primary means of cultural reproduction prioritizes select modes of representation that, by virtue of certain period prohibitions and simple necessity, excluded women in general and some men in particular. Looking only at print sources reinforces a skewed version of how men and women may actually have gardened or how those gardens signified to them and to others. In particular, these printed books tend to name men as the authorities and professionals in gardening, women as amateurs and subordinate to their male counterparts as the women were to be to their husbands, brothers, and fathers. Therefore, in Chapter 1, I turn to manuscripts written by women themselves as a counterbalance to printed evidence to illustrate how women readily engaged in and were considered authorities in different kinds of gardening throughout the period, even if their own voices did not typically appear in print. Looking at manuscripts as alternative sources of representation repositions women as co-producers of social space, whereas in printed books they remain largely recipients of men's advice, or they disappear altogether. If, as Lefebvre suggests, representations of space seek to change the conditions of the spaces they represent, then bringing together *both* manuscript sources by women and print sources by men illuminates how both men and women, sometimes in accord, sometimes in conflict, mutually shaped (and altered through active engagement) the meanings of the garden spaces they both imagined and inhabited.

Much as a landscape historian might, I study one type of "built environment," the garden, in its physical and cultural contexts to identify the contestatory nature of the gendered power relationships it embodies.[15] Such a study of gardens from several centuries ago, however, has its limitations and though I seek to isolate traces of real gardens as much as possible, I readily acknowledge that any gardens I identify are to some degree always going to be representational—due in large part because

---

15 See Harris (16) for further theorizing about gardens as "built environments."

of their inherently ephemeral nature. While caretakers at some estates, such as those at Penshurst in Sussex (the family home of Lady Mary Wroth), have recently turned to architectural plans or archaeological evidence to reconstruct gardens from earlier periods, such efforts to recreate an ephemeral phenomenon can only at best be speculative. And, most of the plans that remain only reach back to the later seventeenth and eighteenth centuries, not earlier. Moreover, the Puritan impulse to strip England of its ostentatious "impurities" left many of the gardens from the early seventeenth century and before without display or artifice, or, as was often the case, as a pared down plot of land. As a result, this book reflects a mindful approach to the various degrees and representational qualities of the gardens that remain, almost entirely recorded in writing but that presume a greater or lesser direct connection to the actual gardens thus represented.

To this end, *Gender and the Garden* elucidates the links between the garden as a built environment and another, the text, which offers representations of gardens that convey ways of seeing the world, embedded in the physical landscape and charged with social meaning. As a kind of built environment, actual gardens are predicated on the notion that the inherently wild landscape be shaped into a cultivated space to grow flowers, vegetables, and fruit. English gardens are notorious for their ability to function as extensions of the house, another built environment.[16] But gardens in texts are yet another kind of built environment that depended on the imagination to reconstruct them. In practical manuals published during the late sixteenth and early seventeenth centuries, for example, writers often included woodcuts and designs for knots and parterres that depict what the finished garden might look like; and even if no woodcut was included, a reader might well have imagined how his or her finished garden might look based on detailed descriptions of the height, color, and scent of certain plants or the promise of bountiful harvests that would undoubtedly follow if the gardener was only patient enough to persist. Poetic texts from the period are a different kind of built environment still, in that they are highly ordered, formalized types of linguistic packages, arguably typified by George Herbert's shaped poetry or the Elizabethan sonnet. Poetry, that is, depends on the manipulability of language on the printed page, a constructed environment, even if two-dimensional, with words as its materials; and those words create an image of the garden evocative of the actual built garden spaces familiar to men and women readers.

The poets whose work occupies a majority of this book appropriated the representational currency of gardening practice and actual gardens when they wrote about gardens and displaced their representational meaning onto other domains to imagine social reform in them. Chapter 2 studies two bodies of work by Edmund Spenser, *A View of the State of Ireland* (1633) and the Bower of Bliss and Garden of Adonis episodes from *The Faerie Queene* (1590). As Chapter 1 shows, the gendering of gardens and garden discourse in the period generally cast men as superior in intellect and talent as the "real" gardeners, while women were constructed as amateurs in need of special guidance. The gardens in Spenser's texts, likewise, reinforced the preeminence of male authority over Irish subjects, and over the Irish landscape the

---

16   See Mark Girouard, *Life in the English Country House* and Roy Strong, *The Renaissance Garden in England.*

male colonizers sought to make "English." Guyon's multiple temptations in garden spaces throughout Book 2 and his destruction of the Bower of Bliss, an infertile, unproductive space under Acrasia's authority, prepare the garden for "reform" and "replantation" represented by the perpetually (re)productive Garden of Adonis in Book 3. But Spenser's revision of the garden space in these episodes also enables his critique of Elizabeth's authority over the (male) English subjects in her employ in Ireland. The context of early modern gardening may have enabled Spenser's imagined gardens as instituting male authority over a would-be colonized Other in his Irish text and epic poem, but Spenser nevertheless had to negotiate his inferior position as subject to a female monarch in very real terms. Such a negotiation is manifest in these books: as they point to two alternatives for female rule, these garden episodes represent either the destructive seductress, such as Acrasia or Phaedra, whose fertile yet unproductive gardens must be destroyed, or the chaste yet powerful woman, such as Belphoebe, whose power and very being ripens like fruit from within the male poet's well-ordered garden.

The two chapters that follow focus on poetry by women, one from the middling sort and one elite, and demonstrate how the parameters of reforming the gendered terms of spatial domains is quite different for women. Despite their class differences, Aemilia Lanyer and Lady Mary Wroth share something in common: their writing evinces an interest in using gardens to isolate gender inequity, proposes certain circumstances by which parity might be possible, and yet acknowledges the material limitations of making substantive changes to women's material conditions. Whereas it would be in Spenser's best interests to have gardens in his texts that reinforce the notion of male authority inherent to early modern garden spaces, the writings by the women poets I study utilize some of the ways that such gendered authority relationships proposed at the level of discourse often stood in tension with women's actual experience. As manuscript writings show, the way women actually gardened or used their garden plants in early modern England demonstrated them not to be the inferiors of men, but rather in many cases their equals if not their superiors. If we look beyond the printed representations by men to manuscript sources (many of which were by women), gardens frequently signified in ways that did not necessarily demarcate strictly gendered boundaries in everyday contexts. The women poets I study here imagined gardens that drew on the relative parity that characterized many women's everyday experiences with and in their gardens to argue for gender parity in other spatial domains where they were otherwise disenfranchised.

Aemilia Lanyer's *Salve Deus Rex Judaeorum*, the subject of Chapter 3, depicts gardens where women might take possession of the land and real property they are denied in actual terms in early modern England. In her dedicatory material, Lanyer appeals to specific female patrons who have all been disinherited by fathers, husbands, and brothers. In the long religious poem, "Salve Deus," Lanyer challenges men's right to disinherit women and offers representations of gardens and garden imagery in which women identify with Christ and men encounter alienation. In the Garden of Gethsemane, for instance, Christ delivers the salvation that brings "inheritance" and "lands" in heaven for women, while Christ's male disciples abandon him and are thus cast out of his inner circle. Finally, the garden in Lanyer's appended country house poem, "To Cooke-ham," mobilizes a broader critique of restrictive inheritance laws (of immediate import in the dedicatory material) and recreates an idealized, Edenic space (by virtue of their connection with Christ and other women) in which she, Margaret, and Ann (and by extension, other women too) enjoy freedom and community and recoup their losses, even if only temporarily, on earth.

The final chapter shows how Lady Mary (Sidney) Wroth appropriates the creative positions women already have in gardening (and needlework) to show that women could also display creativity and femininity in a practice otherwise off limits to them—writing. But Wroth's sequence also foregrounds how these spatial practices presented a double-bind for women: they could develop their creativity and independence in socially-appropriate domains, but such involvement reinforced dominant ideologies about appropriate feminine behavior prescribed by men as familiar to early modern scholars today as they were several hundred years ago. Wroth's interwoven representations of gardening, needlework, and writing reflect this double-bind by emphasizing that women who engage in these practices can use them as creative outlets yet acquire only limited mobility. In the labyrinth— which represents all three domains at once and typifies this double-bind—Wroth's Pamphilia wanders through the maze articulating her unrelenting desire for self-expression at the same time she insists that such desire meets only obstacles, leading her to question perpetually, "In this strang labyrinth, how shall I turne?"

Gender and the Garden thus positions written representations, or texts, as just one among other aspects of a dynamic system of social change as well as recipients or transmitters of it. In so doing, it may focus on texts, but it de-prioritizes the text as a primary means of cultural production and emphasizes instead how the social conditions men and women may imagine in their writing always lies in tension with the everyday practices and the spaces men and women occupy and make. In the course of unpacking the dense contextual layers of what we might characterize as alternative, even if recognizable, "built environments." I offer a revised history of the early modern English garden and readings of early modern English texts that incorporate it. Hence, the book has implications not only for literary studies, but also for the fields of landscape and garden scholarship more broadly; it underscores how different cultural domains work together in ways that potentially traverse disciplinary, cultural, and geographic boundaries.

My interest in the relationship between physical and social space in early modern England necessarily takes me into territory that overlaps with other recent scholarship interested in early modern material and literary culture. Patricia Fumerton and Simon Hunt, Lena Cowen Orlin, Wendy Wall, and Susan Frye and Karen Robertson, for example, all examine the relationship between literature and material practice in architecture, clothing, and food preparation and that draw on Michel de Certeau's theoretical work on the "everyday."[17] These scholars do more than just situate literary texts in such material contexts as the nunnery, the marketplace, the bedroom, the drawing room, and the kitchen; they also resituate the contexts themselves, citing

---

17   See, for example, Orlin, ed. *Material London*; Fumerton and Hunt, *Renaissance Culture and the Everyday*; Frye and Robertson, ed. *Maids and Mistresses, Cousins and Queens;* and Wall, *Staging Domesticity*. See also DeCerteau, *The Practice of Everyday Life*.

them as evidence of "common" or ordinary ways of identifying with early modern culture.

Early scholarship on gardens in literature sought to contextualize gardens in texts historically, yet these studies tended to cast the garden more in symbolic terms than in practical, and such studies typically relied largely on a history penned by purveyors of dominant cultural values. As a result, works by such scholars as Stanley Stewart and Terry Comito typically reconstitute men as agents, women as objects in the garden. Stanley Stewart, for example, argues that images of the enclosed garden throughout seventeenth-century poetry are archetypes for paradise, tied to a primarily symbolic "primeval event, an archetypal fact of life" that reproduce a "shared linguistic culture" from previous historical and cultural contexts (xiii). Terry Comito similarly shows how gardens in poetry might represent "man's attempt to possess an external world" that stemmed from post-Reformation tensions arising from a split between secular and spiritual domains (52).

Rebecca Bushnell and Andrew McRae, on the other hand, examine more directly the link between practical gardening and the literary imagination.[18] Bushnell and McRae both analyze class relationships in gardening as they look at how practical gardens and gardening books soared in popularity among the middling sort and represent what Bushnell calls, "green desire," or the potential to use gardening expertise for social advantage. However, neither scholar considers at length either the gendered implications of either these practical books or aesthetic gardening practice. Nor do they acknowledge the extent of women's participation in these discourses, either as writers or as gardeners. Bushnell, for example, does include a chapter in *Green Desire,* in which she shows how women did indeed work in gardens throughout the period; however, her analysis tends to focus on how women either were undervalued in or disappeared from gardening practice altogether, invariably silenced in our contemporary scholarly dialogue as one might argue they were by the men who wrote about them four hundred years ago.[19]

Gender and the Garden, on the other hand, focuses on how the developing discourse both McRae and Bushnell examine was specifically gendered, which becomes most apparent as the transition from subsistence (and amateur) to aesthetic (and professional) gardening takes place during the second half of the sixteenth and early part of the seventeenth centuries. Because I cite this transition as key to a developing gendered gardening discourse, I devote much of the book to the signification of gardens as utilitarian and aesthetic objects and to literary texts that are also self-consciously aesthetic objects, poems. My work seeks to resolve the problem Bushnell raises in her book when she acknowledges that printed books may have admitted that women worked in gardens, but their gardening work "ceased to be represented" (127). By reading manuscripts that provide evidence of women's gardening alongside printed books (as I do in Chapter 1) and poetry by women (Chapters 3 and 4), I trace a history of women's gardening told by the

---

18   See Bushnell, *Green Desire* and McRae, *God Speed the Plough.*

19   For instance, Bushnell writes, "The country housewife and her plants were recognized only to be discarded from the print record, because they and their gardens were without 'value'" (127).

women themselves that exemplifies their centrality not just in performing garden duties prescribed in printed books for them, but also in finding alternative ways to identify with their gardens. And yet, as I show in Chapter 2, the notion that men were the authorities and valued players with respect to gardening was understood at a broader discursive level, even if the variety of garden representation (textual versus manuscript, for example) reveals anxieties about the extent to which such notions stood in tension with practical circumstances.

Throughout this book, I emphasize how women, like men, made gardens, and in so doing, they were also co-producers of early modern social space. Likewise, women shared in cultural production when they wrote about their gardens, even though what they wrote often did not become a book for public consumption. To be sure, women like Lady Mary Wroth and Aemilia Lanyer wrote poetry in which they represented women as active producers and users of gardens, but women whose specific identities have long faded from historical record also wrote about their gardens, which they kept in manuscript books they often passed down to daughters, sisters, and friends. The fact that men were understood to be the primary producers of gardens and writing did not necessarily equate with their gendered power position being inherently secure or stable. As these manuscripts readily show, women made gardens and wrote about them in ways that helped them negotiate their place in early modern English social space relative men and each other. Expanding a study of literary texts as much as possible to explore how they interrelate with the everyday practices and spaces people made at any given moment in time makes it possible to see texts as dominant modes of production that are still dependent on the ideas and experiences of men and women not necessarily identified as significant in dominant or strictly public modes of representation. This book asks us to revalue the experiences of a wider range of men and women than we would if we interpreted early modern social space through the lens of texts (especially published) alone, and we can then reevaluate what we consider texts, and who we value as producers of early modern social space.

Chapter 1

Gardens, Gender, and Writing

Gardening books printed during the sixteenth and early seventeenth centuries in England documented the shifting meanings of the garden at the same time they mobilized the differentiated positions among those who designed, worked, and owned them. Directly tied to practical methods and design, these manuals shaped a developing discourse about how to garden, who planted gardens, and what people sought when they planted them; in the process, they also cultivated the gendered relationships relevant to gardening practice and the garden spaces that people made. As such, these books have much to teach us about the interrelationship between the garden as a physical *and* a social space. But what, more precisely, is the nature of this interrelationship in these books? As prescriptive texts for everyday activities, these books certainly taught people how to plant the food they would later eat and how to grow the flowers they would later enjoy. At the same time, as Rebecca Bushnell rightly reminds us, these books also represented imagined relationships, what "ought to be," as much as what arguably was to be found in the average household's working garden (109).

The manuals studied in this chapter establish a context for the remaining chapters of this book; at the same time, their significance is more than contextual. They are, as scholars have recently argued, themselves texts worth studying as such.[1] As the motivation for planting turned more to earning social and economic capital, gardens increasingly functioned as contested sites where men and women from different classes vied for positions in a reconfigured and dynamic system of growing things. If men from the middling sort sought status as writers about gardening, then what they wrote also helped men and women achieve status in gardening, whether that meant designing the gardens of the elite or arranging the parterres and knots, or even more modest plantings, in their own yards. Printed books by such popular writers as Gervase Markham, William Lawson, and others suggest how planting an artful flower garden might function as a means of asserting one's social position. One of the most prolific writers on husbandry and gardening, Markham writes, for example, "I say, to behold a delicate, rich, and fruitfull Garden, it shewes great worthinesse in the owner, and infinite art and industry in the workeman, and makes mee both admire and love the begetters of such excellencies" (*The English Husbandman*, 1635 ed., 192).

A growing emphasis in artistic and specialized methods, plants, and roles in the garden thus demarcated boundaries between those who worked in and those who might assert dominion over the garden space. Men from the middling sort acquired social status as professional gardeners and as landowners, while women and lower

---

1   For examples of such studies, see Wall, "Renaissance English Husbandry," Leslie and Raylor, McRae, and most recently, Bushnell.

generally speaking at least, relegated to positions of less authority
urse, there were exceptions to this rule). Establishing creativity and
rdening became more acute as gardening was seen increasingly as
rm accessible to members of the non-elite as well as the elite, which
rated new points of conflict between men and women. Publishing
rdening manuals served as one way to translate gardening experience
into au.. ity, as was the professional claim to have mastered the art of gardening
itself. Only select men may have published practical manuals, though, and only
men were permitted the professional status of "gardener." By the early seventeenth
century, these relationships became subdivided more transparently along gendered
lines, with women increasingly associated with smaller-scale decorative and kitchen
gardening and men linked to larger-scale pleasure and profit-oriented gardening and
orchard management.

I begin this chapter by tracing the shift in gardening from a subsistence to an
artistic and profit-oriented endeavor, the effects of which left their mark on both the
physical *and* the social landscape in England; specialized ways to garden, that is, went
hand in hand with hierarchized roles for gardening practitioners. Specialized forms
of gardening practice were increasingly understood in gendered terms—professional
and profit-oriented gardening for men, and amateur gardening for women—and they
are the subject of the second section. Printed books, all written by men, may well give
the impression that women became, like the flowers they planted, silent recipients
of pruning and shaping, but such is the case only if we exclusively consider printed
representation. Manuscript writings, on the other hand, offer concrete evidence of a
thriving gardening practice conceived of and recorded by women who understood
their garden work to be active and of consequence. The chapter concludes,
therefore, with an elaborated consideration of manuscript evidence by women as
a counterbalance to printed books on the topic by men. These unpublished texts
reveal how women sometimes used their gardens in the ways prescribed for them by
male writers, but at other times, their practice deviated considerably from discursive
norms; and women were by no means passive vessels for men's use, as suggested by
Shakespeare's "Sonnet 3," in which the woman is the field to be tilled and in whose
womb (the field) the man plants his seed. Rather, women were in their own right
creative agents who implemented, adapted, and shaped gardening practice in ways
that defied simply characterized gendered dichotomies.

Dividing Plots: Specialization and the Art of Gardening

This section focuses on how profit, pleasure, and the art of gardening together
compelled people to rethink the boundaries between skillful and amateur gardening
and the gardens people made. As printed books posited a transition from primarily
subsistence to aesthetic gardening they simultaneously qualified the specific duties
of those who gardened. Rather than devoting exclusive attention to planting methods
and plant varieties, manual writers concerned themselves as much or more with
how to organize a household around the practical aspects of growing, harvesting,
and using garden plants. One reason for this might be that available plant varieties

remained mostly the same during the first half of the sixteenth century as they had been in the past—typically just barley, oats, wheat, rye, peas, and beans. Therefore, male and female audience members for these books were more than likely already familiar with planting practices for these crops and probably relied on common knowledge instead of institutionalized practices for their information. At the same time, throughout this period, there was an increasing interest in codifying a discourse about gardening, possible in part by the work of published gardening books, that stood in tension with (or at times even openly contradicted) routine common knowledge practices regularly practiced by men and women, literate or illiterate, from different classes and geographical areas of the country.

The transition from utilitarian to aesthetic planting was also aided by the widespread trend of converting previously communal land to enclosures, which sparked controversy across the countryside. Conceiving of land as private property led to individuals redirecting the use of that land for personal (or individual family's) gain, which typically took the form of enclosing or engrossing land for the purposes of maximizing productivity and yield. While the move to enclose land was definitely present long before the dissolution of the monasteries under Henry VIII, the scale and motivation for doing so changed during the sixteenth century.[2] Whereas in the later Middle Ages, enclosed land allowed small-scale tenants a piece of property to lease and farm for household subsistence, by the mid-sixteenth century (and increasingly), enclosed land served several different purposes, all related to increasing profits and maximizing productivity: 1) landlords sought to maximize the productivity on the land they controlled by evicting tenants and hiring day laborers so that the profits would remain in the primary (landholding) household instead of being shared with the tenants who farmed the land. This land could be turned into large-scale commercial farmland, which yielded greater profits through market sale than through shared cultivation on commons; 2) private landowners might convert arable land into sheep pasture, which eliminated the overhead of having to hire farm labor and made the land more profitable per acre; and 3) a landlord could turn common fields into enclosed fields that he could divide up and rent to small-scale tenant farmers. Although there was an increase in small tenant farming families, especially during the first half of the sixteenth century, the amount of land they farmed was in most cases large enough only to sustain their individual household not to turn a profit (Overton 147).

---

2   While I am paraphrasing the general motivations for enclosing land, historians are not necessarily in complete agreement about the extent to which privatizing land use altered the landscape or the motivations for doing so. Generally, though, most historians seem to agree that humanist attitudes about private property rights and the secularization of land ownership after the dissolution of the monasteries reoriented the way people thought about owning and using land. Historian Mark Overton cites "changes in the ways in which land was held, the move from communal to individualistic farming, [and] the reorganization of farms and the establishment of private property rights" as having the most widespread impact on planting practices (168). Leonard Cantor articulates four major changes in the way land was held and used during this period: the total area of cultivated land expanded; agricultural productivity increased; planting became an increasingly commercial activity to service the growing markets; and agricultural specialization developed (23).

The enclosure movement sparked controversy both in early modern England and with scholars today about how widespread the impact of this practice was on the working poor and the effects it had on the population shifts from the rural to urban areas. Viewing land use as a profitable enterprise instead of a subsistence activity enabled some members of the merchant and gentry classes (as well as upper class landowners) to gain wealth and social status along with property while those at the lowest end of the social scale suffered the greatest losses. In *The Country and the City* Raymond Williams argues that the enclosure movement had devastating effects on the rural countryside, which caused urban populations to soar, families to starve as they sought work in cities without ready employment, and agricultural productivity to shift from small-scale farming to large-scale planting for market consumption. Historians more optimistic about the impact enclosures had on the English social and physical landscape suggest that these changing land practices may have displaced rural families at the expense of some of the poorer ones, but these were a necessary trade-off that enabled other gains, such as the development of markets and a more defined middle class. At best, land privatized and put into the hands of the so-called morally responsible (and financially-viable) men of England might be envisioned as a system by which those who held land were good stewards and took care to ensure that both the land and the poor who worked it might thrive. At worst, though, enclosures were portrayed as a nefarious system by which land passed from the church to the state and then to a (still) relatively small cross-section of England's families, even if that number was larger than before and included part of the population previously more marginalized.

The up-and-coming gentry and merchant families, who, as a group, accumulated the most total land during this period, comprised the primary audience for husbandry and gardening manuals. Attesting to their widening and secular audience, these manuals first appeared in the vernacular early in the sixteenth century and increased in numbers throughout the period as the number of landholding families who could potentially use them multiplied too. Practical manuals engaged with contemporary debates about the effects of enclosing land but were marketed for the group most likely to benefit from this practice, we find, not surprisingly, that early manuals in particular idealize enclosure methods as the best means possible to maximize productivity and profit for the private landowners who might buy these books.[3] Enclosed land, John Fitzherbert insists in the first vernacular husbandry manual in England, is the great social equalizer; it keeps everyone fed, rich and poor alike: with enclosed land, he argues, "then shall *not* the ryche man over-eate the poore man with his cattel" (77, my emphasis). Though Fitzherbert encourages enclosures for better sheep health and as the means to generate the most profit from land use, he frames enclosures as part of a community system of agriculture and husbandry, with the assumption that land enclosed for pasture does not detract from potentially arable plots but rather supplements them for the good of all (44). In effect, Fitzherbert frames enclosures as a utopian method of land use, focusing still on using that land

---

3   See Fitzherbert 42, where he argues that enclosed land for pasture is more economically viable, since a landowner can earn more profit from a herd of sheep than from the crops grown on the same plot of land.

for the greatest good, while later in the period, and even by the time Thomas Tusser makes his own argument for enclosures thirty-four years later, the motivation for enclosing land was shifting more toward private use and private profit.

Like Fitzherbert, Thomas Tusser concedes in his *Fiue hundreth points of good husbandry* the potential abuses of the enclosure system, but he still praises its potential to spawn relatively egalitarian social systems by which men earn their own living through hard work—ideals in line with a developing market economy. On the one hand, for example, Tusser writes:

> The poor at enclosures do grutch,
> Because of abuses that fall;
> Lest some man should have but too much,
> And some again nothing at all. (182)

But he nevertheless reassures his readers that enclosed land for pasture is ideal for maximizing agricultural productivity and individual profit:

> More profit is quieter found,
> (Where pastures in severall be;)
> Of one seely acre of ground,
> Than champion maketh of three.
> Again what a joy it is known,
> When men may be bold of their own? (181)

Though Tusser here promises a three-fold return on enclosures for grazing pasture, he elsewhere promises the same return on enclosures as sectioned off plots of arable land for planting. In his section titled, "Concerning Tillage," Tusser contends, "Good land that is severall, crops may have three, / in champion country, it may not so be" (1580 ed., 112); "severall," or enclosed, land makes it possible to diversify the farm, to plant different varieties at once and therefore increase the likelihood of having at least one crop survive if the climatic conditions are unfavorable for growing another. John Hales similarly defends enclosures as safeguarding the productivity of England's landscape: "Experience sheweth that tenauntes in common be not so good husbandes as when every man hath his part in several."[4] Sir Thomas More's *Utopia*, on the other hand, satirizes the way greedy landowners enclosed and converted their arable land to pasture because pasture land was more economically profitable; in *Utopia*, sheep dominate and quite literally consume the covetous gentry who were unsympathetic toward tenants they evicted to enclose their land for pasture.

Cases brought to the Star Chamber for state intervention reflect the most extreme impact of enclosures on English families and confirm concerns such as those voiced by Hales and More. One such case pitted displaced tenants against their landlord (and new private landowner) typifies the disputes involving this kind of land enclosure practice from the early years of the Protestant Reformation onward:

> John Palmer beynge a man of great power, Immediately after his first entre in to the premisses by and thorowe his extorte powre toke from your said poore Subdiates their

---

4   Both Hales and More are quoted in Thirsk, "Making."

pastures houlden by copie as is aforesaid and enclosed thiem, and the same pastures together with other landes hath lately Imperked convertinge the same to his owne proper use and commodite…and through lyke powre toke ffrom your said poore Subdiates all their Commons and made of thiem ffyshepondes converting the same to his proper use as is aforesaid. (Tawney and Power 29)

Citing unethical enclosure practices, the plaintiffs in the suit argued that John Palmer, their landlord, displaced copyholding tenants for the purpose of redistributing their holdings and turning arable land into grazing land for "his owne proper use and commoditie." The tenants further alleged that Palmer took "ther mansion howses, groundes, landes, tenementes and Orchardes perforce ayenst ther willes, and them hath spoyled, distroyed, and pulled downe some of the howses of your said poore subdiates and the tymbre hath geven awaye, some of the howses hath burned and dryven some of your said poore subdiates owt of the said lordeshipp by force and violence" (Tawney and Power 20). Disputes over unfair enclosure practices constituted the largest organized uprisings before the English Civil War. Kett's Rebellion in 1549 stemmed from tenants' outrage over landlords' overgrazing on privatized, enclosed pasture land; and the Midland's Revolt in 1607 pitted tenants against landlords once again, centered around disputes over private enclosure practices that converted previously arable farmland into pasture.

By the late sixteenth century, widespread enclosure practices had indeed increased the number of families dependent on markets for food, and with a number of devastating years of bad weather and bad crop production, prices had escalated to extreme levels, and production dropped to levels such that starvation and poverty had become chief concerns not just for townships but for the state. Depopulation and decreased agricultural production made it necessary to import the products that would otherwise have been produced on English farm land, a situation that directly resulted from the engrossing of such land for private use by gentlemen landowners who put their own wealth above that of the state, or the "common" wealth. Such greed, some argued, constituted crimes against the "Commonwealth," which indicates an overlapping concern with both economic stability and self-sufficiency and the strength of the "realm" as it derives from a balance between individual prosperity and the production for the common good of England. These crises prompted Parliament's intervention in 1597, issuing The Tillage Act, which was intended to maximize the total acreage of land farmed by mandating that arable land converted into private grazing pasture during Elizabeth's reign be converted back to arable farmland (Tawney and Power 84–85).[5] The Tillage Act proposed that individuals should strive to balance the good of the "Commonwealth" (by which Parliament meant the "realm" and the suffering masses who comprised the realm's subjects) and the individual wealth of the comparably small number of "gentlemen" who benefited from enclosure for pasture or who were driving prices higher by evicting tenants and forcing them to move to the cities to find work and rely on the markets for their foodstuffs (Tawney and Power 89).

---

5   The Tillage Act of 1597 was the only instance of parliamentary intervention in gardening and land use practices until the eighteenth century.

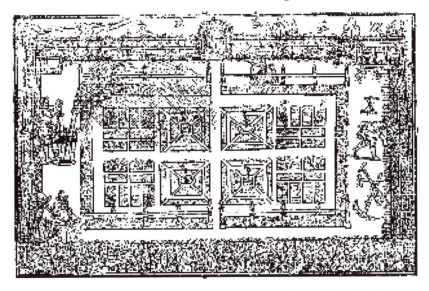

Fig. 1   Woodcut, Thomas Hill's *The gardeners labyrinth* (1577)

Throughout the course of these changes in the way land was used, the garden for profit and as art object begins to permeate the pages of printed books, as exemplified in the use of illustrations and the gardens people made following writers' advice, such as we see in Fig 1 from Thomas Hill's *The gardeners labyrinth*. Taken from one of Thomas Hill's best selling gardening books, this woodcut illustrates some of the ways that a move toward artful gardening brought with it an interest in the segregation of both plants and people in the garden. The wall that surrounds the garden isolates this space from the uncultivated landscape outside; the raised beds throughout protect the plant species from mixing, as each contains what appears to be only one, or possibly two, plant species; and the parterres in the center define the garden's symmetry as they simultaneously enclose still more varieties of plants and contribute to the overall spectacle of the garden. Likewise, the people in this garden each have a different purpose and are, like the plants, prevented from intermingling, lest they lose sight of the status boundaries that demarcate them here. Pictured on the far right and far left center, two laborers work to maintain the garden as they function to balance the woodcut visually. Garden admirers are isolated from such work and pictured in the far left bottom and upper right, in conversation or, perhaps, focused on the garden's beauty, seemingly not noticing that anyone labors there at all.

This and other books by Thomas Hill exemplify how emphasizing pleasure and profit in the context of artful gardening generated new ways of seeing the people who practiced this art in hierarchized terms too.[6] Though Hill explains planting methods in very practical terms, such as planting seeds in the waning or increase

---

6   Hill's books were quite popular. They were modified somewhat and published at least thirteen times between 1558 and 1608, either under that title or as similar tracts titled, *The profittable arte of gardening, A most briefe and pleasaunte treatise* and *The gardeners*

of the moon to maximize the propagation, he incorporates advancements in gardening technology and employed the terminology that had come to differentiate its practitioners in practical ways in England at the same time. Although Hill at times uses terms like "husbandman," "Gardener," and "owner" interchangeably, as if to suggest overlapping identities, he more often than not partitions the duties, for example, of the owner and the (paid, professional) gardener, the first time we see such articulated distinctions in print.[7] Unlike earlier writers on husbandry and subsistence farming,[8] who generally used the term "husbandman" in the broadest sense of the word to include individuals from a variety of social and class backgrounds, Hill differentiates between the "owner," who owns the land where the garden is located and who manages labor, and the "Gardener," who is in the owner's employ and who might oversee some of the laborers, but who still labors himself.[9] In Hill's book, for instance, the owner and his guests are the recipients of the delights the alleys and walkways provide and the gardener the one who orchestrates their display:

> The commodities of these Allies and walkes, serve to good purposes, the one is, that the owner may diligently view the prosperity of his herbs and flowers, the other for the delight and comfort of the wearied mind, which he may by himself or fellowship of his friends conceive, in the delectable sights and fragrant smells of the flowers, by walking up and down, and about the Garden in them…Thus briefly have I touched the benefit of Walks and Allies in any Garden ground; which the Gardener of his own experience may artly tread out by a line, and sift over with sand, if the owner will. (*The gardeners labyrinth* 47)

---

labyrinth (the most commonly issued title and written under the pseudonym "Didymous Mountain").

7   See especially 23–25, 32, 35, and 46, though Hill does so throughout.

8   See Fitzherbert, *The boke of husbandry* (1533) and Tusser, *A hundreth good pointes of husbandrie* (1557) and *Fiue hundreth points of good husbandry* (1573).

9   By asserting quantifiable differences in this way, Hill's text misrepresents the proportion of rural English households who might actually hire a professional gardener instead of having the gardening performed by amateur gardeners, men and women who gardened as part of their everyday practices. Only the wealthiest landed families could have afforded to employ someone practiced in the art of gardening. If it is true, as G.E. Mingay argues, that only 7.5–10% of the population left property and wealth totaling over £250, while over half of the population left less than £50 at death, then only a small minority of families would have had the income available to pay someone to do the gardening for them (89). During the sixteenth century, especially after the dissolution of the monasteries, very few laborers had more than 4 or 5 acres of land, and two out of every three laborers "probably had little more than a garden, perhaps a small close or two attached" (90). Husbandmen and other laborers, who constituted as much as 11–15% of the population, had on average somewhere between £50 and £99 in personal holdings, and yeoman farmers, perhaps 12–16% of the population, might have had property totaling between £100 and £249 (89). Hill's text appears oriented more toward those with ready money to pay a gardener and save themselves the trouble of doing the planting, which automatically excluded a majority of men and women in England. And, by framing the gardener's duties as somehow different from an amateur gardener's, Hill appeals to the group most likely to identify with a desire and the ability to hire a gardener and shapes discourses about these duties as different, whereas in many cases they were not.

Hill's Gardener "artly tread[s] out" his alleys and covers them with sand, while the owner "diligently view[s]" his "prosperity": one labors, that is, while the other enjoys labor's fruits.

Imagining gardening as encompassing specialized spaces using specialized labor introduced class distinctions and paved the way for gardening to develop as a profession. Hill, for instance, likens gardening to one of the "noble Artes" of the same rank as "Physicke and Surgerie," which places it squarely in a developing discourse about specialization in the context of professional versus amateur endeavor.[10] At roughly the same time, that is, formal distinctions emerged in England for the first time between "Gardeners" and those who simply planted gardens.[11] "The one word gardener for several hundred years did duty for many men of various skills and often diverse social standing," explains John Harvey, but during the sixteenth century, and as Hill's text manifests, the word "gardener" came to apply more readily to someone specially trained in the skills of gardening and employed in this profession, and this term was associated with profit-making activity such as market gardening (1). Hill's *The profittable arte of gardening* (1579), for example, hails the gardener's skill as superior to any of his predecessors, owing jointly to his unique talent and the landowner's beneficence.

With potentially substantial profits at stake, men in London formed the Gardener's Company (formerly, the Guild of Gardeners) and formally requested its recognition by the Crown in 1605. As was typical of guilds, participation in the Guild of Gardeners included both men and women, and their trade was understood to include a range of gardening duties. The request to form the Gardener's Company, however, privileged men over women as members at the same time it delineated distinct boundaries between the different types of gardening. The application sought to codify professional gardening as "the trade crafte or misterie of gardening, planting, grafting, setting, sowing, cutting, arboring, rocking, mounting, covering, fencing and removing of all plantes, herbes, seedes, fruites, trees, stocks, setts and of contriving the conveyances of the same belonging" (Steele 2–3). The Company itself likely included "10 garden designers, 150 noblemen's gardeners, 400 gentlemen's gardeners, 100 nurserymen, 150 florists, 20 botanists, and 200 market gardeners" (Harvey 6).[12] Though the request does not explicitly exclude women, the various positions available would not likely have been ones that women could hold, which means that women were, whether directly or indirectly (in this case), systematically disenfranchised from the more status- and profit-oriented professional gardening. Establishing gardening as a profession was, in other words, a process of exclusion. The Company's charter renewal in 1616, for instance, stipulated exclusive rights

---

10 Contextualizing gardening in this way also calls to mind the gendered boundaries that in turn develop relative professionalization, as I discuss later in the chapter. Surgery, physic, and later gardening, when understood as professions simultaneously marginalize women from participation; in the context of amateur endeavors, on the other hand, women were ready participants.

11 See also Thomas, 192–241.

12 See Harvey for a thorough discussion of this early stage of professionalization. Harvey catalogues the number of those associated professionally with gardens and early nurseries as part of his Introduction,1–13, especially 5–7.

to the organized practice of gardening and "prohibited any person inhabiting the City or within six miles thereof ('other than such of our subjects as shall garden for their own household use and private spending') from using or exercising the Art or Mystery of Gardening within that area 'either in places privileged or unprivileged' without the licence of the Company." Furthermore, it "forbade any person not a member of the company from selling garden produce except at such accustomed times and places" as designated by the Company (Steele 4).

At roughly the same time, the nursery trade in England was flourishing, making a commercial activity out of what was otherwise a primarily utilitarian practice, so too was interest in seeing gardening as something to which one might aspire. Growing up in response to the changing and specialized markets in plants, professional nurseries were a "new form of business, practically unheard of in the Middle Ages... [which] was an offshoot of the age of discovery, of exploration, of world trade, of colonial expansion and of imperialism" (Harvey 9). Professional nurseries and the gardeners who used them directly served the interests of aesthetic gardening, which had gained widespread popularity by the end of the sixteenth century among members of the middling sort and elite alike. As John Harvey elaborates in *Early Nurserymen*, although nurseries were "in part concerned with plants of utilitarian importance, the whole phenomenon of plant exploration and plant raising depended mainly on aesthetic factors in garden design and appreciation of nature, as well as on the instinct for collecting" (9).

Manuals published from the early seventeenth century onward, like the Gardener's Company, the nursery trade, and the professionalization of gardening more broadly, establish a distinct interest in categorizing both plants and those who would plant them. A fine example of this categorization is Gervase Markham's *Maison Rustique or, The Countrey Farme* (1616), which reinforces notions that those who work the garden, like the plants they attend to, each have a proper place:

> At the one side of this House, even just in the place whereupon the Sunne riseth, and in one part thereof wee will place the household garden, which neere unto the borders of this quick-set hedge shall containe a frame of Railes in forme of an Arbor for Vines to runne upon, for the furnishing of our household with Veriuice [verjuice], and other necessary hearbes for the house: and we shall not altogether neglect or forget to provide and plant in the same place hearbes fit for medicine. And yet furthermore in this garden also you shall plant things to make your profit upon, as Saffron, Teazill, Woad, red Madder, Hempe, and Flaxe...In the other part wee shall make a garden for flowers and sweet smels, with his ornaments and quarters, garnished with many strange Trees. About the hedge we shall set, for to make pottage withal, Pease, Beans, and other sorts of Pulse, as also Melons, Citrons, Cucumbers, Artichokes, and such like. (Sig. B)

The garden Markham describes in painstaking detail seemingly has every square inch organized into an orderly array of abundant plants and flowers, subdivided by their specific uses: medicinal and cooking herbs, profitable crops, decorative flowers, and pottage vegetables. In fact, Markham (among others) articulates a particular interest in tailoring the garden to growing conditions in England rather than other climates or regions and argues that doing so creates a sense not just of horticultural import, but also collective national identity.[13] The very structure of his book similarly emphasizes stratification. Part I includes the practical "Knowledge of Husbandly Duties," while Part II promises "the Art of Planting, Grafting, and Gardening, either for pleasure or profit; together with the use and ordering of the Vine, the Hop-garden, and the preservation of all kind of Fruit."[14] Along with these subdivided categories, Markham defines the "Office of Husbandmen," the "Office of the Fruiterer," and the "Office of the Gardener," in such a way that links the identities of the garden laborers to the specific type of gardens they make.

Like Hill and Markham, William Lawson emphasizes differentiation among garden space users in *A New Orchard and Garden* (1618), yet he represents still more differentiation in the garden space, as he more overtly links specialization (of garden labor and the gardens themselves) and social status. Lawson's *A New Orchard* contains the first example of clearly defined differences between the owner, the (professional) gardener, *and* the waged laborers hired to attend to the estate gardens. His books establish for the first time in print, that is, a clear top-down hierarchy from the owner, to the gardener, to the "unskilful servant." Always in the third person in the manual, the gardener is clearly the social inferior of the owner but the superior of those "unskilful" men and women below him. Yet those "unskilful" laborers are still vital to the success of the garden or orchard, since, as Lawson puts it, "the Gardiner cannot doo all himselfe" (5).

The Gendered Art of Gardening

As suggested by The Gardener's Company charter and the general trend in professionalization and specialized gardening, a specifically gendered tension developed among perceived authorities on the topic, practitioners, and laborers, and the way that labor would be divvied up among them. Manuals printed from the later sixteenth century onward demonstrate a collective effort to separate the male and female gardener and the different ways each should apply her/his gardening skill to transform the untamed landscape into an artistic masterpiece. These printed books, for example, imagine men as specialized laborers, whose "husbandry" attested to their virtuous manhood. Gervase Markham articulates as much in *The English Husbandman* (1613), in which his definition of "husbandman" incorporates an earlier use of the term, one who works the fields: "A Husbandman is he which with discretion and good order tilleth the ground in his due seasons, making it fruitful to bring forth Corne, and plants, meete for the sustenance of man. This Husbandman is he to whom God in the Scriptures giveth many blessings, for his labours of all other are most excellent, and therefore to be a Husbandman is to be a good man" (Sig. A3). However, the husbandman Markham describes is also one whose labor

---

13   See also Wall, "Renaissance National Husbandry" for a more lengthy discussion of the relationship between Markham's book and a burgeoning nationalism in England at this time.

14   Reginald Scot published the first manual on growing hops in 1574, *A Perfite Platforme of a Hoppe Garden*. Other manuals began to appear around the same time that focused on a specific crop, such as Hugh Plat's *The nevve and admirable arte of setting corne* (1600).

is associated specifically with profit and professional specialization: "The labour of the Husbandman giveth liberty to all vocations, Arts, misteries and trades, to follow their severall functions, with peace and industry, for the filling and emptying of his barnes is the increase and prosperitie of all their labours. To conclude, what can we say in this world is profitable where Husbandry is wanting, it being the great Nerve and Sinew which houldeth together all the joynts of a Monarchie" (Sig. A3). In fact, as Markham emphasizes, "for it [husbandry] of all things is he most profitable, then of all things it must needs be most necessary, sith next unto heavenly things, profit is the whole aime of our lives in this world" (Sig. A3–A3r). Profit, for Markham, is matched only by skill in the art, designed and executed by men, as he insists that success in artful gardening results from "the industry of mens braines" and the "bringing forth such new garments and imbroadery for the earth" (110).[15]

Gardening as a masculine enterprise is further evidenced by numerous books printed throughout the period, such as Richard Gardiner's *Profitable Instructions for the Manuring, Sowing, and Planting of Kitchin Gardens* (1608), Thomas Hill's *The profittable arte of gardening* (1568), Leonard Mascall's *The Country-mans Recreation, or the Art of Planting, Grafting, and Gardening in Three Books* (1640), and, later, Leonard Meager's *The English Gardener: or a Sure Guide to young Planters and Gardeners* (1670) and Carew Reynell's *A necessary companion or, The English interest discovered and promoted in the advancement of most trades and manufactures with infallible rules for the attainment thereof. Together with the emprevement of orchards, vine-yards, medows, pasture lands, &c.* (1685). "English" gardening, as these books suggest, and profit-oriented gardening, whether it be vegetables or flowers, was understood to be men's domain and conceived as a distinctly manly exercise. Scholars have recently turned to gardening manuals as evidence of the uniting of profit, professionalization and masculine (English) identity.[16] Andrew McRae discusses, for instance, how gardening, like surveying and chorography, were tasks for men.[17] The profession of gardening itself, as we saw earlier in this chapter, was conceived largely as a male endeavor, and it was articulated even more clearly as such when the Worshipful Company of Gardeners sought to revise its charter in the early eighteenth century. In *Adam Armed* (1700),

---

15 Markham's use of "imbroadery" here is particularly telling. Embroidery at this time was understood to be an activity that evidenced women's proper feminine behavior. Gardening was imagined as a kind of embroidery on the landscape, as Lord Burghley also describes the gardens on his estate, and some of the same people who drew garden patterns also made pattern books for women's embroidery. At the same time, by incorporating the notion of gardening as embroidery on the landscape, Markham is appropriating what is typically understood as a woman's activity into something for the "industrie of mens braines." See Chapter 4 on Lady Mary Wroth's poetry for a more lengthy discussion of the significance of embroidery and gardening.

16 See especially Wendy Wall, whose article "Renaissance National Husbandry" explores constructions of nationalism as it was linked to masculinity in Markham's books. See also Michael Leslie, Timothy Raylor, and Andrew McRae. See also Alexandra Sheperd and Will Fisher, both of whom link manhood in the period to these and other discursive modes.

17 See especially Chapter 6, "'To know one's own': the discourse of the estate surveyor" 169–97 and Chapter 8, "Chorography: the view from the gentleman's seat," 231–61.

the Company argues that it should remain true to what it saw as its original purpose of being a "well-regulated Body of *Men*, able to Educate a Succession of Gardeners to serve the Kingdom" and that, in so doing, they might prevent "interlopers," or the "Pretenders" who are "unskilled" in the art from usurping profits from the learned professionals (1, 8, my emphasis). Who these "interlopers" were is not clearly defined in *Adam Armed*, but it is reasonable to conclude that they might have been amateur gardeners (or at least those not formally recognized by the Company as "gardeners"), a group that would have included all women, whose art and profit-oriented gardening work may have especially threatened the economic and social privileges the (male) professionals would have otherwise enjoyed exclusively.

A shift toward professional and profit-oriented growing may have benefited (or potentially benefited) men in general, but it arguably marginalized women from positions of authority and power and made them more dependent on men.[18] When household members toiled together in the garden to subsist, that is, women were highly valued and necessary members of the labor force, as was the case in earlier manuals, such as John Fitzherbert's *The boke of husbandrie* (1533) and Thomas Tusser's *Fiue hundreth points of good husbandry* (1573).[19] Fitzherbert and Tusser's households reflected how women, as well as men, shared in the backbreaking tasks—preparing, sowing, planting, and harvesting beds for household consumption and market trade on a smaller scale. As Sara Mendelson and Patricia Crawford explain, "The basic work of women farmers in the countryside," for example, "was the production of food, drink, and clothing for their households...They planted kitchen gardens, and processed the fruit from orchards. From their kitchens farm labourers and servants were fed; without women's labour, cash for the purchase and preparation of food and clothing would be needed" (306). Much more so than in books that followed, Fitzherbert's husband and housewife share many of the duties outside, including the plowing and harvesting, and his housewife takes her turn bringing the harvest to the market. In fact, Fitzherbert admonishes the husband to have the utmost trust in his wife, since her ability to negotiate at market has a direct bearing on the household's sustenance.

Tusser's book, on the other hand, is directed to a subsistence household, but one that begins to show signs of understanding its purpose as profit-oriented too. In the book, Tusser prescribes duties for the husband and housewife that suggest a shifting, though not yet firmly established, discourse about gendered household roles as the household adapted to shifting socio-economic conditions that moved women into the domain of the kitchen and men into the marketplace.[20] Tusser's husband

---

18　Cahn identifies a number of tasks traditionally associated with women's unpaid domestic tasks that also became professionalized during the sixteenth century, such as textile production and dairy farming (48).

19　While this is generally true in Fiztherbert's manuals, an obvious exception is the section he titles, "Ten Properties of a Woman," which characterizes a woman's desirable qualities in much the same way he characterizes the cattle and horses on the pages that precede it. The ideal woman in this section has a broad forehead, ample childbearing hips, etc.

20　Tusser's *Five hundreth points of good husbandry* was a much more lengthy (as the title suggests, roughly four hundred more points) volume that expounded on the advice he gives in the earlier edition. The changes Tusser makes to his original manual illustrates the increased

receives directions in the form of almanac "abstracts," in which the husband plows, splits logs, plants wheat, barley, oats, and hemp, repairs the retaining wall around the house, drives hogs into the woods, gelds bull calfs and rams, and mows the pasture (among other duties). In "Good Huswife's Duties," though, Tusser makes it clear that the housewife also does some of these same duties, even if many of her tasks are to be done indoors. At the same time, Tusser includes demarcated sections for the husband and housewife in which their duties are clearly different from one another's. The housewife in Tusser's text labors for 16-18hrs per day in summer (14–16 hours per day in the winter), including duties that range from plowing, planting, and trading seeds to spinning flax for clothing, churning butter and making cheese, to making candles. She supervises the servants and manages many of the practical workings inside of the house, especially the kitchen (79, 176). While Andrew McRae mentions the husbandman and housewife having different chores, he says little about the significance of such differentiation in broader social terms or its effects on shaping the way discourses about gardening would develop over time.[21] On the one hand, Tusser singles out the husband's and housewife's duties and begins to designate them as "different" from others' in the household. Her duties relate more to domestic chores inside the house than to the outside labor required for the economic viability of the household, a move that later leads to a devaluation of the housewife's social position as she is associated with the domestic sphere. On the other, isolating the housewife's duties lends a singular authority to her work that others do not have. Tusser's distinction (and seemingly unrealistic list of chores) places her in a position of preparing the garden stuffs and using the hemp, wool, flax, and grain from planting instead of doing the planting herself. He moves her from the plow to the kitchen, a spatial relocation that many have cited as foundational to developing ideologies of femininity.

By the time Thomas Hill publishes *The gardeners labyrinth* (1577), devoted exclusively to gardening (as opposed to husbandry or household management), we begin to see more clearly defined gendered divisions in the garden than were present in earlier manuals. While situated in a Classical context, Hill's "history" of gardening more accurately reflects, even as it helps construct, contemporary modes of English gardening; he links, for example, subsistence gardens with the housewife and the "common sort" and aesthetic gardens with the "reformed" and "skilful" (and, implicitly, with men):

> Columella reporteth that the ancient husbandman so slenderly looked unto (or rather forced of) Gardens, that they in furthering the grouth and yield of their fruits and herbs, bestowed small travel and diligence. And as they appeared negligent in their labours of the Garden, so were they well pleased with a mean living, insomuch that the common sort fed and lived willingly on grosse and simple herbs...The Garden plots at length grew so common among the meaner sort, that the charge and the chiefest care of the same, was

---

interest in differentiating tasks, which stems from the changing orientation to gardening by later in the period.

21   See McRae, "While the country farm tradition takes only passing notice of women, Tusser appreciates the interdependence of the gendered labours of husbandman and 'huswife'" (148).

committed unto the wife, insomuch that these accounted not the wife of the house to be a huswife indeed, if she bestowed not paines and diligence, as Cato reporteth, in the weeding, trimming, and dressing of the Garden. (*The gardeners labyrinth* 24–25)

The gardens tended by the "meaner sort" in Hill's assessment are of a substandard quality when compared with those of the "reformed" in that the "reformed" (and improved) gardens focus on the sensual pleasures gardening could provide and depend on "skilful" hands and careful planning:

But after the age and people were reformed, and brought by the instruction of Epicure, to a more delight of themselves in coveting to feed on dainty herbs and sallets, with meats delectable, and taking an earnester care for the pleasing of their mouths, they laboured then to become skilful, and to use a greater care about the ordering and apt dressing of Garden plots. (24)

By aligning men's gardening labor with the "skilful," and women's with the "common," Hill's book portrays gardening in such a way that punctuates what many historians have identified as the devaluation of women's labor more broadly during the period relative an interest in demarcating professional status for men.[22]

As Hill's and others' books represent, the turn toward specialization in gardening "tended to de-skill women's work" (Cahn 49). What Hill described, though, also manifest in practical ways, as was the case when the sickle replaced the scythe as the implement of choice for weeders (Overton 188). By replacing the sickle, a tool light enough for women to use, with the scythe, a tool that was seen as almost exclusively for men, women were more restricted in their options for garden labor, and they tended to be relegated to jobs in the garden perceived as less taxing and, therefore, meriting lower wages. In a subsistence context, as exemplified by the housewife in early books, such as those by Fitzherbert and Tusser, women had relatively more authority and "were engaged in much the same tasks as men, with the exception of some of the heaviest farm work like ploughing. Women were usually solely responsible for looking after the dairy, the pigs and poultry, the vegetable garden and orchard" (188). As the tenant farm became increasingly a thing of the past, women had to seek employment outside of the home, so that they could afford to purchase foodstuffs and other household goods they previously planted or made themselves. However, as such work became more commercially (or professionally) oriented, what were previously regarded as skillful contributions by women in the garden were revalued and understood to be of less import to the workings of the large-scale gardens, and many women became day laborers for modest wages (and then had to use their wages to buy food at the market). And when women worked as weeders alongside lower class men, they earned wages equal only to half of their male counterparts for the same work.[23] Ironically, then, women may have been able to use their gardening skills to forge an income for themselves and their families,

---

22 See especially Cahn, Overton, and Mendelson and Crawford.

23 "If it was normally through the family that women participated in economic production," argues Martha C. Howell, "then only through family units of this sort would women have achieved high labor status in market production, and it is likely that with the

but their entry into the workforce in this context served to reaffirm their subordinate position in concrete economic as well as other, more broadly discursive ways.

Rather than characterizing such gendered divisions as mobilizing a clear and straightforward *devaluation* of women's labor, though, I am suggesting that this tension catalyzed a *revaluation* of it. The publication of Markham's *Countrey Contentments* (1615) exemplifies the complex the negotiation of gendered power inherent to imagining separate gardening duties for men and women.[24] Manuals like Markham's, for example, reinforce a gendered division in areas related to gardening, such as herbal medicine. Markham contends that women's knowledge in this realm is limited, and that they should leave the real work to the specialists, the (male) professionals:

> Indeed we must confess that the depth and secrets of this most excellent art of physic is far beyond the capacity of the most skilful woman, as lodging only in the breast of the learned professors; yet that our housewife may from them receive some ordinary rules and medicines which may avail for the benefit of her family, is (in our common experience) no derogation at all to that worthy art. (8)

Just as women's gardening becomes subordinated to men's gardening in Markham's and others' published manuals, so too does Markham here relegate women's involvement in herbal medicine to "ordinary" and "common" knowledge, leaving the "art of physic," like the "art of gardening" to the "learned professors." At the same time, his admonition betrays an anxiety about how what is at once common could indeed become artful and that the line between the "learned professors" and the "ordinary" housewife is articulated perhaps less clearly in actual ways than in imagined ones. In the first comprehensive herbal written in English, *The Herball* (1597), John Gerard makes a similar move when he combines classical wisdom with his experiences as an apothecary to claim authority and status and lend credibility to his book. Those who published materials on herbal medicine monopolized this knowledge for men, although knowledge about herbal remedies actually derived in the most everyday contexts from women's direct experience and authority.[25]

However, Markham's book for housewives also demonstrates how the artistic use of garden plants in the delicate dishes that adorned the tables of even the more modest households still helped women make space for themselves in artistic realms and establish positions for themselves in domestic spheres. Markham's housewife prepares "Sallats for show only" and elaborate meals that "will not only appear delicate to the eye," but will "invite the appetite with the much variety thereof" adorn the pages of Markham's book (*The English Housewife* 121). And Markham's housewife also learns how to prepare sagewater, rosewater, water of cloves, and other

---

disappearance of this family production unit, as it was replaced by other methods of production, women lost labor status" (201–2).

24   Markham's *Countrey Contentments* (1615) indicates an interest in separate manual for men and for women. In it, he includes *The English Housewife* as its penultimate part. The section was published on its own as a separate book numerous times, beginning in 1631.

25   For further discussion of the gendering of early modern herbals, see Rebecca Laroche, "'This Manlike Worke of Herbes': The Gendering of the English Herbal." unpublished.

distillations that cure ailments and perfume the house and those who dwell there. As gardening becomes more an art form in England, so too does the housewife's use of her garden plants.[26] Just as Markham claims that men's orchards and gardens will bring him pleasure, so too does he suggest that women's banquet tables will bring "contentment to the guest, and much pleasure and delight to the beholders" (124). The housewife's feast comes off as a culinary performance, with its stage the table, its actors the foods she has prepared and adroitly assembled—the marzipans, dried fruits, sliced citrus fruits, and wafer cakes she arranges and keeps secretly in her cabinet until such time as they are needed. But when the moment arrives, she ushers each out in succession so as to enhance her meticulous choreography:

> But when they go to the table, you shall first send forth a dish made for show only, as beast, bird, fish, or fowl, according to invention: then your marchpane [marzipan], then preserved fruit, then a paste, then a wet sucket, marmalade, comfits, apples, pears, wardens, oranges, and lemons sliced; and then wafers, and another dish of preserved fruits, and so consequently all the rest before: no two dishes of one kind going or standing together, and this will not only appear delicate to the eye, but invite the appetite with the much variety thereof. (121)

Markham's housewife is hardly the passive recipient of rules for food preparation; she orchestrates a masterpiece, creating what appears to be a living show. But Markham's housewife is more than just a director and choreographer: she also does the sowing, planting, and gathering that makes such a show possible. The country housewife, according to Markham, should "have knowledge of all sorts of herbs belonging to the kitchen...know the time of year, month, and moon, in which all herbs are to be sown; and when they are in their best flourishing, that, gathering all herbs in their height of goodness, she may have the prime use of the same" (60).[27]

Women's tasks in the kitchen could certainly be backbreaking work, but, as Fig 2 suggests, the kitchen was also a site of creative agency and women's networks.[28] The two women standing at the pot just left of center may be hard at work preparing the day's meal, but their presence serves as a reminder that the kitchen is a space where women related with one another too. They stand with their bodies poised almost in an embrace, suggestive of an empathetic connection between them. Even though the woman at the table in the rear of the woodcut sits alone, as does the

---

26 Markham's *The English Housewife* was one of the books most commonly recorded in ships' logs on transatlantic trips to The New World. Ironically, though, because Markham emphasized so stringently growing conditions and the plants one might find (or plant) in England, the housewives in North America probably found themselves imagining how they might implement his advice more than they could do so in actual terms in such different conditions. For an excellent discussion of Markham's *The English Housewife* and the transatlantic book trade, see Jennifer Mylander, "Early Modern 'how-to' Books: Impractical Manuals and the Construction of Englishness in the Atlantic World" (forthcoming).

27 Published at roughly the same time as Markham's manual, Hugh Plat's *Delightes for Ladies* (1609) offers similar helpful hints and recipes for preparing and preserving food in ways that please the eye and the palate.

28 For groundbreaking and solid scholarship on women's alliances, see Frye and Robertson.

Fig. 2   Women working together in kitchen. From Nicholas Bonnefons's
              The French Gardiner (1672)

woman at the very center stirring the pot over the fire, the visual emphasis of the woodcut draws the reader's eye to the way the women are clustered along the center of the piece. One cannot help but get the impression that, while these women toil away at their daily tasks, their labor creates a kind of community among them.

As suggested in books like Markham's, when women's work moved from outside at the plow to inside the house, they lost power in some respects but they also forged viable positions for themselves as creative agents in the more decorative areas of gardening and plant use.[29] By the early seventeenth century, manuals addressed to women identify these positions as key to women's roles within the "art" of gardening, and entire booklets appeared for the first time that contained designs for knots and mazes to be used in the garden.[30] That is, a woman's increased involvement in aesthetic instead of subsistence or even market gardening both helped and hindered their ability to develop social status. As was true in other domains traditionally associated with women, such as textile production, the shift in women's positions relative the household economy required that they found new ways of identifying themselves relative the family and other women (Cahn 53–6).[31] Rather than vanishing from the landscape, we must remember, women simply found new ways to situate themselves in relationship to gardening, new ways to distinguish themselves as authorities in a domain in which they were increasingly relegated to the margins.

At the same time practical gardening was becoming an increasingly gendered activity, the garden itself was being framed as a gendered space. William Lawson's companion manuals, *A New Orchard and Garden* and *The Countrie Hovsewife's Garden* (1618) distinguish between the "country housewife's garden" and the

---

29   See also, for example, Hugh Plat, whose books emphasize aesthetics, much as Lawson and Markham do in their own manuals for housewives, interspersing decorative recipes throughout and dividing his book into the following sections: "The Art of Preserving," "Secrets in Distillation," "Cookerie and Huswiferie," "Sweete Powders, oyntments, beauties, etc.," and a Glossary that defines the different terms he uses. By publishing his recipes and preserving concoctions, Plat weighs into an increasingly competitive field in which male writers formally codified knowledge otherwise circulated more informally among men and women alike. Like the men who wrote gardening manuals throughout this period, Plat lays claim to an arena of common knowledge increasingly authorized as the (male) professional's. Plat's book, *The Garden of Eden* (Pt. 1, 1652; Pt.2, 1659), also lauded female dedicatees for their skill in gardening, though it is clear that such praise is possible because such skill does not compete directly with that of their male counterparts.

30   Thomas Marriott publishes a pamphlet of knot and maze designs. Although not solely for women, Marriott's designs would likely have been the basis for many women's garden designs. Markham's *English Housewife* describes the housewife's duties in particularly decorative terms, the food she makes for the family to be on display and to tempt the senses. William Lawson writes in *The Country Housewife's Garden* (1618) that women should use their "delight and direction" when designing their own flower gardens that incorporate knot and maze designs, also included in his text.

31   Cahn discusses the effects of professionalization on textile production in this period. Textiles, like gardening, became the domain of the professional in some ways, but it did not change the fact that women still pursued these activities within the private sphere of the house. See my discussion of women's gardening and embroidery as creative and powerful activities for women as they relate to Lady Mary Wroth's poetry in Chapter 4.

husband's orchard and garden—articulated for the first time as two separate garden spaces. Contained within the husband's orchard are garden plants that maximize both pleasure and profit: "And chiefly consider: that your Orchard, for the first twentie or thirtie yeares, will serve you for many Gardens, for Safron, Licoras, roots, and other Hearbes for profit, and Flowres for pleasure: so that no ground neede be wasted if the Gardiner be skillful and diligent" (25). Furthermore, the Orchard and cultivated grounds under the supervision of the owner are expansive, covering what would likely include significant portions of land, but even if not physically large, they would bear great ornaments and allow visitors to traverse the grounds they occupy: "Methinks hitherto we have but a bare Orchard, for fruit, and but halfe good, so long as it wants those comely Ornaments, that should give beauty to all our labours, and make much for the honest delight of the owner and his friends" (55). Such ornaments, as Lawson imagines them, include knots and borders, flower gardens, extensive walks, topiary shaped as men and beasts, mazes, a river, moats, vines, and warbling birds to enchant the senses of those fortunate enough to visit (57–59).

The housewife's garden, on the other hand, is smaller in scale and less lofty in purpose. In *The Countrie Hovsewife's Garden*, the companion book he writes for his female reader, Lawson maintains that the housewife's garden is in "no way comparable to the fruites of a rich orchard" and "may be done with small labour, the compasse of [her] Garden being nothing so great" (*Countrie Hovsewife's* 9, 1). Like Markham, Lawson insists that women should grow only "common hearbes," because women are not "skillfull Artists." Instead, Lawson writes, "Let her first grow cunning in this [his teachings], and their she may inlarge her Garden, as her skill and ability increaseth" (19, 17). He associates the relatively small size and "common" aspects of the housewife's garden with inherently lesser ability, even if she can improve her skill by taking to heart his gardening advice; and, by distinguishing her garden from men's orchards in this way, Lawson also suggests that women's labor is less valuable than men's in multiple ways. Whereas the professional gardener's skill contributed to the owner's potentially endless profit, as Lawson explains, the "paines in a Garden is not so well repayed at home, as in an Orchard," and the amateur housewife's garden "challenge[s] to it selfe a profite, and exquisite forme to the eyes" (9, 10). The housewife's garden produces a different kind of profit, multiplying beauty through "exquisite forme" rather than advancing the household's economic yield.

Lawson may subordinate the housewife's garden to the husband's more profitable and prestigious orchard, but her garden, like that of the housewife characterized in printed books throughout the period, nevertheless enacts a productive and creative function in the household. Like professional gardeners, the housewife uses her art to improve on nature even if she is not paid for her skill, and the "knots and squares" that adorn the garden space she cultivates derive from her creativity and imagination. Lawson includes the following instructions with ten patterns for the country housewife:

> But for speciall formes in squares, they are as many, as there are devices in Gardiners braines. Neyther is the witte and art of a skillful Gardiner in this point not to be recommended, that can worke more variety for breeding or more delightsome choice and of all those thinges…[but] the number of formes, mazes, and knots is so great, and men

are so diversely delighted, that I leave everie housewife to her selfe, especially seeing to set downe many had bin but to fill much paper, yet lest I deprive her of all delight and direction, let her view these few, choyce, new formes, and note this generally, that all plots are square, and all are bordred about with Fruit, Rasens, Teaberries, Roses, Thorne, Rosemarie, Bee-flowers, Hop, Sage, or such like. (2–3)

Whereas in *A New Orchard and Garden* Lawson distinguishes between the gardener's design role and the owner's managerial role, the housewife here takes on both roles at once. He attributes specialized skill to the professional gardener in both cases, but because the housewife's garden is less directly associated with the household's financial advancement, she retains a considerable degree of independent, creative decision-making. Her garden, Lawson reminds his women readers, ultimately depends on her "delight and direction."

At the same time, while Lawson's country housewife may have been instructed to keep her garden small, elite women both grew gardens and were commended for doing so. Lucy Harington, Countess of Bedford, was well-known for her gardens at Twicknam and Moor Park. Calling the gardens as Twicknam "true paradise," John Donne asks Harington if he might "some senseless piece of this place be" ("Twicknam Garden" 9, 16). And William Temple calls the gardens Harington had planted at Moor Park "the most beautiful and perfect, and altogether the sweetest place which [he] had ever seen in England or in foreign countries" (Qtd. in Lewalski, *Writing Women* 98). Elizabeth Shrewsbury (Bess of Hardwick), likewise, engaged in large-scale building and garden projects. Notorious for her self-aggrandizing architectural plans for Hardwick Hall, which feature her initials emblazoned in conspicuous iron parapets, Shrewsbury designed gardens that trumpeted her status as an early modern Englishwoman.

Gender and the Written Garden

While manuals like those discussed thus far reveal a gendering of gardening practice and the garden itself in early modern English history, the story they tell is necessarily skewed by the fact that our source material has been almost exclusively printed texts, all written by men. The developing "creation of a masculinized notion of authority [and authorship]" that helped make writing a gendered activity went hand in hand with a masculinized notion of gardening authority (Wall, *The Imprint of Gender* 282). Men who wrote practical manuals about husbandry and gardening were instrumental in setting the parameters for what would constitute the specialized knowledge and expertise relative gardening when they represented gardening practice and the gendered roles in the gardens they wrote about.[32] These men constructed themselves as authors as well as authorities and their readers as up-and-coming (even if still amateur)

---

32   To my knowledge, there are no manuals of this type in this period published by women. I discuss more at length in my first chapter, however, manuscript evidence of how women made and used gardens in this period. Until now, women's transmitted knowledge about plants has come mainly from work on such topics as midwifery and women's life writings.

gardeners. At the same time, their expertise could help those who used their advice to gain the skills, education, and practical experience necessary to augment their own status as gardeners in the future.[33] But what was at stake in codifying modes of masculinity through professional gardening and the act of writing about gardens? What happens if we look at alternative modes of representation and production too—specifically unprinted manuscripts by women? Collectively, these modes of production, both written but circulated in very different ways, produce a version of social and literary history that is otherwise circumscribed by printed sources alone. If, as the men who wrote manuals suggest, experience granted one the authority to write about gardening, then women whose writing about gardens is documented in manuscript collections were also authorities on the topic, even if that authority has been largely unexplored because scholars have turned only to printed sources to understand the place of women in the garden.[34] A gendering of the garden space may have been reified and codified in print when men put their "experience" to paper, but when we look at what was printed alongside manuscript writings by women, these two sources together reveal how the garden was gradually transformed into a gendered space not just on the landscape but in literary history as well.

Men who published gardening books used their experiential link to gardening to establish authority and lend credibility to their writing on the topic. Thomas Tusser includes an autobiographical account of his experiences as a husbandman in the "Life of Tusser," which opens the 1573 edition of *Five hundredth points of good husbandry* and was included in later editions as well.[35] Discouraged by his unsuccessful attempts to gain status at court, Tusser moves to the country to try his hand at husbandry, where he meets with insurmountable obstacles, including illness and problems with his lease. Ironically, Tusser turns his inability to subsist as a husbandman into his authority to write about household management and agricultural endeavor. William Lawson likewise cites his extensive experience gardening, likely acquired while serving as the vicar of Ormesby, as his authority too. According to Lawson, his friends implored him to make use of his gardening know-how by writing about it for the public's benefit: "When in many yeares by long experience I had furnished this my Northerne Orchard and Country Garden with needfull plants and usefull hearbes, I did impart the view thereof to my friends, who resorted to mee to conferre in matters of that nature, they did see it, and seeing it desired, and I must not deny novv the publishing of it (which then I allotted to my private delight) for the publicke profite of others" (Sig. A2). In *The English Husbandman,* Gervase Markham goes so

---

33   Wendy Wall develops her article, "Renaissance National Husbandry," largely around this theme. Wall's discussion of this topic focuses almost exclusively on Gervase Markham's texts. Other writers from the period analogize their texts to gardens, though, including Tusser and Fitzherbert, who punningly calls the pages of his texts "leaves" and the information contained within them "fruits" for the reader.

34   Though I am indebted to the work of Rebecca Bushnell on this topic, her recent book, *Green Desire*, does this too. While Bushnell devotes an entire chapter to "The Ladies Part" and asks, "where were women in the early modern garden?" (108), she only explores printed sources to find them, which necessarily leaves women in the position of represented objects of men's "green desire," not as active subjects who write their own story.

35   Especially those editions printed between 1573 and 1580.

far as to say that his experience as a husbandman qualifies him as a "Graduate in the vocation": "Besides, I am not altogether unseene in these mysteries I write of: for it is well knowne I followed the profession of Husbandman so longe my selfe, as well might make me worthy to be a Graduate in the Vocation" (2).

Like professional gardening, publishing books about gardening provided an opportunity to make money, even if what one might earn as a published writer would have been substantially less than the potential profits of a successful gardener. The marked increase in publications on the topic suggests the growing interest over the period in formalizing gardening discourse at the same time lines were being drawn between professional and amateur gardeners, and the relationship between different types of gardening and social status. Miss Blanche Henrey cites at least "nineteen new titles on botany and horticulture during the sixteenth century, one hundred or so new titles in the seventeenth century (of which over eighty came after 1650), and over six hundred during the eighteenth century."[36] Of all the writers I study in this chapter, Gervase Markham most clearly sought literary and social status through his publications, and he came closest to making a living wage as a writer in this genre ("Introduction," *The English Housewife* xi).[37] A shrewd businessman and prolific writer, Markham redirected his failed experience as a farmer into writing about husbandry and gardening, his relatively successful career as a writer largely predicated on exploiting loopholes in the contemporary copyright system. Because there was no copyright protection at the time, Markham would only receive payment for the first issue of each book; therefore, instead of reissuing his books under the same title, he published consecutive manuals under different titles, with considerably little variation in their content.[38] Markham was thorough yet specific in his subject matter, identifying himself as an authority on all topics of husbandry and farming, including kitchen and aesthetic gardens, horses and cattle, orchards, and bees. In 1764, essayist Canon Harte branded Markham with the not-so-illustrious title, "the first English writer who deserves to be called a hackney writer" (Qtd. In Fussell 24).

John Rea's *Flora* (1665) illustrates how know-how, writing, and reading in the context of gardening were further intertwined and gendered in printed books. In his

---

36 See Miss Blanche Henrey, *British Botanical and Horticultural Literature Before 1800,* vol. 1. Henrey's is perhaps the most comprehensive bibliography of published texts on gardening and is an excellent reference tool; it does not, however, make reference to or list any unpublished materials, which means that it does not represent women's knowledge about gardening. See also Harvey, who traces the chronology of the nursery business in England during this period, which grew in number along with professional gardening and the increase in numbers of published husbandry and gardening manuals.

37 Michael Best explains that "He was a younger son from a noble family in decline, and believed in the old, chivalrous virtues, particularly in the ideal of an orderly hierarchical society led by an aristocracy that was noble in action as well as in birth" (xi).

38 Michael Best details this history at length this history in his "Introduction" to *The English Housewife,* xiv. In fact, those at the Stationer's Register became so frustrated with Markham's circumventing of the system that they made him pledge to stop publishing works on the same topics under different titles: "Memorandum, that I Gervase Markham of London, gent., do promise hereafter never to write any more book or books to be printed of the diseases or cures of any cattle, as horse, ox, cow, sheep, swine, goats, etc." (Qtd. in Best, xiv.)

dedicatory material, Rea lauds his male patron, Lord Gerard, for his successes in his gardens at Bromley (which Rea himself designed), and likens the "Excellence" of Gerard's "Natural Inclinations" to his own. To his other male patron, Sir Thomas Hanmer, he writes similarly that Hanmer's "Noble Inclination" is characterized by excellent taste in flower cultivation. In his dedicatory material for Lady Gerard and Mistress Trevor Hanmer (later, wife to Sir John Warner), on the other hand, Rea focuses not on their experience but instead on their beauty, likening them to the flowers their husbands have planted: he invites Lady Gerard, for example, to look to the hyancinth, lilies, heliotrope, the violets and cowslips that "invite [her] Smelling"; and he compares the women with the flowers they might admire in his book, as he does when he tells Lady Gerard, "Thus your rich Beauty and rare Parts / Excel all Flow'rs, exceed all Arts." As he explains to Lady Hanmer, the real work of art on display, "we all conclude 'tis You." But the differences in the way Rea writes to each is also significant. When relating to his male patron, Rea writes in prose, an epistolary dedication that links experience to value through language similar to the manual that will follow. When addressing Lady Gerard, on the other hand, Rea writes in couplets, using arguably more simple language that calls to mind the doggerel verse found in Thomas Tusser's *Five hundredth points of good husbandry*, which Tusser's modern critic, G.E. Fussell argues served to accommodate the "sluggish brains of the rural community" (8). While we can reasonably assume that Rea did not intend to insult his female patrons with his verse form, the couplets he writes to them, combined with the notion that they, like the flowers in his book, are beauties for viewing pleasure, casts the ladies as dependent on him, and their husbands as the authorities. He is the artist, both poet and gardener, for whom the ladies serve as patron-flowers that his verse prunes and perfects.[39]

The gendered division between professional and amateur in practical gardening during this period resonates with a general division between artist and artisan, characteristic of writing among other endeavors. Such a division emphasized the difference between "work of the hands and work of the mind" and established art as that which "referred [to] any application of human skill and especially those skills by which human agency produced things, ideas, or wealth" (Halasz 50). Men who wrote manuals for public circulation fancied themselves, as Gervase Markham and William Lawson do in the aforementioned passages, "artists" as both gardeners and as writers. Their manuals offered advice for men who might become skilled, like they did, in the art of gardening, and, though none of these writers explicitly say as much, if their readers were to become artists in gardening, they too, could presumably also become artist-writers about gardening. Of course, such a suggestion ignores the fact, as was the case with Markham (and Tusser before him), that one could fail at husbandry or gardening in practical terms but still write about it. By contrast, the female gardeners of whom these men write, who have (as these male writers frame it) inherently less skill and remain amateurs in gardening, would never, by logical extension, be artists in gardening or skillful in writing about it either. Still, as Alexandra Halasz argues of the print marketplace, the amateur "artisan"

---

39   See Chapter 2 for further discussion of how this same impetus to see women as flowers manifests in Spenser's *The Faerie Queene* in the context of Belphoebe and Amoret.

nevertheless retains the ability to claim "a kind of mastery of the process" (117). In other words, just because men could become professional gardeners and writers for the marketplace, while women were disenfranchised from these activities, the amateur woman gardener influenced dominant cultural forces when she planted her gardens and recorded her gardening instructions in manuscripts; and, if she wrote about her garden in manuscript (or even planted her garden), she would still be an author(ity), even if not in print.

The history of printed books on gardening and husbandry in early modern England, therefore, only tells part of the story and reinforces the way that the divide between artist and artisan undervalued women's contribution to gardening practice. Manuscript accounts routinely show women readily identifying themselves as authorities, at times even by writing directions for gardening, much like the men whose books these women were presupposed to have read. In 1608, Mary Gee pens her own directions for planting what she claims will be "monstrous greate" radishes:

> Dig your ground 2 or 3 feete deepe so that the mould[es] may bee very soft [and] hollow then take a walking sticke as big as your finger put yt a foote downe into those soft mould[es] then put a radish seede into that deepe hole, cover yt not above one intch let the rest of the hole bee hollow that hollowness will make the radish grow monstrous greate.[40]

Gee represents herself as more than just an assembler of others' work; she is an authority (by experience) who advises on planting methods much as the men who published gardening manuals did. Margaret Cavendish, best known for her philosophical writings, also pens some directions on gardening: "To colour Roses bore holes wth an Aul under the knots and put colours in wth a feather. Cut the first stalks of beanes w[n] ripe, apply muck and others will sprout out. Elme tree chips set in ditches will become trees. To destroy Caterpil, besmear the bottom of the T[ree] hang on a bow a bagg of Ants, etc."[41] Cavendish's directions convey an intelligence not just about basic skills in gardening that women would have been encouraged to have, but they also show how she was knowledgeable about caring for trees, which was a domain exclusively reserved for men in printed books.[42]

Manuscripts also demonstrate how women were not, as printed manuals suggest, primarily relegated to decorative positions in the household but actively participated in a range of household management positions, including paying wages, ordering goods, and supervising the garden. Anne Archer's household accounts (early- through mid-seventeenth century) record the payments she made to her gardener and the woman who weeded her garden. She typically paid her (probably male) gardener between 3s–6s for his work, while she paid "Goody Gladyn" (a term for a wife, usually from a "farming or artisanal community" as well as for "Iris") between

---

40 *BL* MS Eg 2608, f.16.

41 *BL* Sloane 1950 f. 8b. See also ff. 8-8b for her observations on household management more broadly, especially those related to cattle and horses.

42 See, for example, books printed throughout the period on grafting and tree care and, especially, John Evelyn's *Sylva* (1664), perhaps the most comprehensive and cited work on trees from the period.

2s–7s for weeding and/or making hay, which makes their pay surprisingly almost comparable. While the accounts do not specify how frequently each received payment from Archer, it is possible that their income was roughly the same, suggesting a degree of parity among them in this case. As Archer's accounts testify, gentlewomen and women laborers alike contributed to the household economy in ways that took them both indoors and outdoors. Elizabeth Powell's "preseruing book," for instance, records "what of rosemary ys most principall."[43] Cisilia Haynes includes in her book recipes "From hon[ble] Mr[s] Dames to Mr[s] Kent" including one for "pickled lemons" from her garden.[44]

The division between print and manuscript culture, particularly as they respectively characterize what scholars now deem "public" versus "private" modes of production, is not quite so clear, though.[45] It is true that women did not publish gardening manuals during the period for public consumption, which might suggest that their knowledge remained relegated to private domains. However, women's manuscript writing complicates public/private demarcations, suggesting how, "What we tend to see is a 'private' mode that, by its very nature, is permeated by 'public' moments of readership, when the text is circulated and copied" (Ezell 38). The manuscripts I cite here, for instance, exist as part of collections, copied and circulated among men and women alike. Notes in the margins and on pages strewn throughout the collection suggest that the different women who owned these books cherished and practiced the remedies they contained and that these women added their own recipes for the next generation to use. While printed books may have increasingly marginalized women, as Bushnell argues in *Green Desire*, these manuscripts reveal elaborate networks of female alliances alive and well, as well as women using their plants to empower themselves, even if they remained relatively disempowered socially, politically, and economically in England at this time (111).[46] These manuscripts, as recent work shows, reveal that women did not necessarily assemble their thoughts in manuscript solely because of the prohibitions against women's writing, but rather, they used manuscript circulation as a viable means of agency.[47]

Medicinal and cookery recipe collections compiled by women, for example, attest to the way that women used garden plants to forge intergenerational connections. In one such collection we find a recipe for "Extracting oil from feathers" for which "Mrs. Jane Richards rec'd 20 guineas" and "An excelent drinke to cure a thisbola it is that my mother Allways yoused."[48] Representative of such collections, this entry exemplifies some of the myriad ways that women employed the medicinal uses of plants, more complexly and richly than men typically gave women credit for in printed books. First, Mrs. Jane Richards received payment for her recipe; second, she passes down that information from another female source, her mother,

---

43   *BL* MS Add 20057, f.12.

44   *BL* MS Add 34722, f. 45–46.

45   For further discussion of issues of public and private in early modern England, see Orlin, *Private Matters and Public Culture in Post-Reformation England*.

46   See Bushnell, "The Ladies Part."

47   See Justice, Tinker, and Suzuki.

48   *BL* MS Add 34722, f. 46, f. 12.

whom she credits for the effectiveness of the recipe; and finally, this entry is part of a collection of recipes exclusively by women, which circulates in written form women's shared knowledge and experience and represents an alliance among them. These manuscripts, as well as others like them, evidence the complex relationship between how discourses about roles in gardening propagated by published manuals and the actual experiences of women whose own practical gardening experience stood in tension with what those manuals represented.

In fact, collections such as these challenge the simple assertion that the garden was clearly the province of either men or women.[49] On the one hand, historians Crawford and Mendelson have called the garden "women's province" because of the "web of interconnections related women's responsibility for food preparation and medical care, the tending of both ornamental and kitchen gardens, and female expertise in the use of plants grown or gathered for foodstuffs and medicine. To these tasks some women added gardening of soft fruit and salads, and the production or use of flax for linen, straw for bedding, rushes for floor coverings, and herbs for cookery and housewifery" (224). A case in point, Elizabeth Powell's "preseruing booke" used rosemary to cure "watyr of all odyr for the cankyr and for all syknes."[50] Cultivating medicinal uses of rosemary, thyme, chamomile, and wormwood (among countless other herbs), women like Nurs Bowin, Elizabeth Powell, and Mrs. Clark appear in manuscripts as authorities on herbal treatments for men and women alike, and their skills helped establish networks of women whose knowledge warded off green sickness, the "cankyr," and the ague. And who could argue with cures recommended by mother herself, often promised by these collections?[51]

On the other hand, such manuscripts reveal that such work was not demarcated in everyday terms with respect to clear gender binaries. In the context of everyday activity, where the lines between public and private presentation of self become quite blurred indeed, men and women seem indiscriminately to be considered authorities on topics related to plants. Countless collections still exist, that is, in which men and women together compiled recipes, where both are indiscriminately identified as authorities on the topic. In a collection of medical recipes in both a man's and a woman's hand, for instance, we find recipes by men and women that used such plants as rue, wormwood, sage, chamomile, and rosemary, a remedy for the "ache" by Mr. Drew and one for kidney stones by Lady Herbert of Cowcam (perhaps Cooke-ham?) which involved radish roots, parsley, and saxifrage.[52] Such collections were neither purely "private" in the sense that they were reserved for individual use, since they

---

49   Mendelson and Crawford, for example, call the garden "women's province" (224).

50   *BL* MS Add 20057, f.12.

51   See *BL* Add 36308 (for a book of medicinal recipes assembled by Dorothy Wasbourn, including recipe by Mrs. Ward); *BL* Add 20057 (a manuscript collection titled, "Elizabeth Powell her preserving booke); and *BL* Add 34722 (a book given to Cisilia Haynes by Lady Anne Lovelace, including numerous recipes attributed to women. Sandra Sherman has recently argued that women in the eighteenth century formed these networks by publishing recipe books for women to use. These publications show how the networks I am suggesting existed earlier yet became more developed and public a century later. A parallel development is the publication of a gardening manual for women by Hannah Woolley in 1670.

52   *BL* MS Add 36308.

were clearly circulated among a cadre of people, nor were they "public" in so far as their circulation was limited. Moreover, these collections show that the way printed books privileged male authority reveals anxiety about the extent to which male authority was securely in place with respect to day-to-day gardening practice.

Female authorities on herbal medicine, such as Lady Grace Mildmay, also serve as examples that challenge the notion that male authority in gardening was the undisputed norm. As part of her regular medical practice, Mildmay "compiled a list of herbs and flowers and the parts of the body they treated" in much the same way John Gerard did in his *Herball* or Gervase Markham did in *The English Housewife* (Pollock 103). While not a professional physician or published writer, Mildmay clearly achieved status in herbal medicine; she kept her own herb garden that included exotic and rare herbs, such as cardus benedictus, dulcamara, and scordium, as well as some of the more common herbs, such as marjoram, sage, rosemary, and fennel, which Gervase Markham and William Lawson specifically cite as belonging to a "housewife's" garden (Pollock 127). In fact, professional (male) apothecaries in London sought out Mildmay's expertise and plant collection to aid them in their own practice. Mildmay records in her autobiography that she would consult the printed works by men "in the herbal and books of physic," and adapt them into "works of [her] own invention without sample of drawing or pattern before me, for carpet or cushion work and to draw flowers and fruits to their life with my plummett upon paper" (Pollock 35). Even as she was readily identified as a proper English gentlewoman, with its attendant modesty and humility she readily espoused for herself and for other women, Mildmay clearly established autonomous identity as an herbalist and amateur apothecary in a way that differentiated herself not only from other women, but also from noteworthy men as well.

Lady Margaret Hoby's *Diary* suggests that she too was regarded as an amateur authority on herbal medicine, which would have been part of her routine tasks in the household. While Lady Hoby twice remarks that she reads in the evening from "the arball [herbal]" (probably *The Herball* by John Gerard), she more often describes the salves that she prepares for others using knowledge she had passed down to her from informal sources as well as from books.[53] Hoby often remarks, for example, "I dressed the hand of one of our seruants that was verie sore Cutt," or that she "dressed a poore boyes legge that was hurt"; or, on another occasion, after she finished making candles for the household, she "gaue a poore woman of Caton saulue for hir arme."[54] Lady Hoby also gave the cuttings from her herb garden to a wife in Erley, so that

---

53   In her edition of Hoby's diary, Moody notes here that Hoby is referring to Gerard's *The herbal or generall historie of plantes*, which seems plausible, since his was the most extensive herbal at this time in English. However, I see no reason to assume, in the absence of more specific evidence, that she reads from Gerard. Hoby may indeed be reading from Dodoens, a Dutch herbalist and author of probably the most widely read herbal at this time and before apart from Gerard, or it might even be possible that Hoby reads from an unpublished source. After all, Hoby mentions numerous times that she reads from "Perkins" (the Puritan preacher William Perkins), from Foxe's *Book of Martyrs*, or from Bright's *Treatise on Melancholy*, which establishes that she does cite specific authors on other occasions.

54   See 58–59 (January 30 and February 1, 1600; and 112 (September 18, 1600). During the final week of January and the first few weeks of February, 1600 Hoby actually notes nearly

she could start an herb garden of her own.[55] Hoby's garden yielded the necessary ingredients for household provisions and served as the means by which Hoby make a space for herself as a healer. Her gardening skill also linked her to other women and to women's systems of exchange, as her plants circulated from her household's to another woman's and formed the basis for other gardens.

Later in the seventeenth century, Lady Mary Capel Somerset, the Duchess of Beaufort, a well-known plant collector and amateur botanist, made advances in the field and had her work printed, though her achievements too were obscured by her male counterparts who sought to establish the parameters of a New Science largely without women. Somerset was certainly admired for her gardens at Badminton, which displayed what was then perhaps the most extensive collection of exotic plants and flowers in England; but she was also an amateur botanist in her own right, traveling between 1699 and 1701 to Surinam to collect plants and insects with Maria Sibylla Merian, who was highly regarded for her own advancements in botany and entomology.[56] Somerset compiled her gardening observations with the intention of having them bound into a twelve-volume set. The manuscript collection in Somerset's hand that later became the printed set attests to her interest in the specific properties and nature of each plant at Badminton, as she meticulously records its genus and other qualities, including its adaptability to English growing conditions based on the information provided by such horticulturalists of her day as John Evelyn, who authored the great work of the time *Sylva* (1665).[57] At the same, her collection demonstrates that she had every intention of making her own mark in the world of botany. What would later become the twelve-volume herbarium included plant specimens from her gardens and handwritten comments from the Duchess that mapped out and otherwise revised the work of such respected authorities, leaving instead her own commentary, and often contradicting the established thinking of the time. She distinguishes the specific ways that plants grow in her garden, often elaborating on or deviating from the conventional wisdom from printed books, as she does with respect to the "Geranium Africanum," which, she writes, "grows very well, but the best way of raising is by cuttings it grows very well in the tubs in the windows" (f. 51v)[58]; or, in her description of "Thora Paeron. The plant and flower well, but mine has a great number of flowers" (f. 54v). [59] Somerset even lists plants

---

every day that, immediately following her morning prayers, "I dressed my patients," which attests to her daily involvement and reputation as a practicing healer.

55   April 27, 1601.

56   Merian was the first, male or female, to produce drawings of multiple species of plants on the same page. By placing multiple plant species on the same page, Merian's work helped establish plant 'families'. Her sketches also presented for the first time plant and insect species together, suggesting a more holistic approach to understanding the relationship between the two.

57   The twelve-folio herbarium, which Somerset was in the process of compiling throughout this manuscript series is discussed further in Chambers, "'Storys of Plants.'" Chambers maintains that it was likely not assembled formally into volumes until after her death in 1714.

58   BL Sloane 4070.

59   Ibid.

that "she can find no figures of in any of my books, they are therefore to be described as they grow now in Badminton," such as the "Bullybay tree," "Bonavist," or "Sugar Apple" (f. 73v).[60] Moreover, among her correspondence, we find a letter to Mr. Adams from Jacob Bobart (Somerset's gardener) that identifies another woman's book (presumably unpublished as well) highly regarded by those familiar with wild plants. In the letter, Bobart seeks advice from Adams with respect to the "immediate commands from Her owne hands" to find a man who knows wild plants; however, Bobart suggests Adams reference "Mrs. Ray's Catalogue" of wild plants, which he calls the best source to date on the topic.[61]

Women may not have published manuals of their own until the eighteenth century, but manuscripts like the ones I have discussed demonstrate that they not only grew plants, but they wrote about them too. It was not until the later eighteenth century that women wrote manuals of their own, and aesthetic gardening had evolved into a "womanly" activity, with men dissociating themselves from the flower gardening increasingly regarded as a "feminine" practice. In the early seventeenth century, however, what would later become a "feminine" practice was still in the process of coming into its own; women vied with men for status and authority to create aesthetic gardens, using the plants they grew as identifying markers of their newly-negotiated identities in this domain.

A study of gardening manuals published during the sixteenth and early seventeenth centuries in England reveals the complex relationship between these texts as a form of popular literature and the gendered practice of gardening during this period. These manuals engaged social and economic change affecting both the English landscape and the men and women who altered that landscape when they planted their gardens. As "how to" manuals for men and women to use, these texts were more than just literary representations, though; they were tools that made changing economic, social, and cultural practices possible. The transition from gardening for subsistence to gardening as an art form involved a reconfiguration of gendered social positions, both within the household and in English society. That is, the more men and women gardened as part of their everyday activity of running a household, the more each individual was valued for his or her contribution to the household economy; however, the more the status of gardening depended on its artistic associations, the more hotly contested the social positions associated with aesthetic gardening became.

Although broad indicators and co-producers of this social change, husbandry and gardening manuals reveal only part of the panorama of the English social history of this one hundred or so years. The more one examines other evidence of the everyday practices of gardening—the way men and women used the garden plants in herbal medicine and cooking, manuscript account books, recipes, and letters, and women's diaries, for example—the more obvious the complexities in the process of social negotiation that took place between men and women from a range of classes and social backgrounds. What the mass of evidence overwhelmingly shows is that gardening stood at the center of these active negotiations for gendered power

---

60 Ibid.
61 BL Sloane 3343 f. 142.

positions. In studying the published husbandry and gardening manuals alongside these manuscript writings, a fuller picture emerges that suggests that this social negotiation was in fact always in flux, a process of *renegotiation* much like that which took place in the garden itself.

Published manuals may have subordinated common knowledge circulated and authorized by women and other amateur practitioners to a hierarchically superior male authority, but separate manuals appear for women in the early seventeenth century that represent women's gardens as sites of their creative authority and relative independence. Tenuously balancing these different representations of gardens—as primarily creative sites for women and primarily productive and authoritative sites for men—manuals nevertheless reveal how these gendered uses coexist in tension with one another in the representational space of the garden. The poets I discuss in the remaining chapters, Edmund Spenser, Aemilia Lanyer, and Mary Wroth, draw on the tension inherent to gendered power relationships represented in the published manuals integral to gardening practice and garden spaces in early modern England. In shaping the gendered relationships relevant not just to gardening practice and actual gardens, but also those which extended into other domains of early modern English society, these manuals influenced how men and women poets might imagine the garden spaces they could create in their own writing, too.

Chapter 2

"Planting English" and Cultivating the Gentleman: Spenser's Gardens

When Edmund Spenser publishes the first three books of *The Faerie Queene* (1590; 1596) the art of gardening had become an established practice among an increasing number of men and women from the middling sort in England. As discussed in Chapter 1, printed manuals detailed gardens for profit and pleasure of special interest to many upwardly mobile men, who might use their available funds to accumulate still more wealth and prestige in a market economy they occupied in increasing numbers. Spenser's literary gardens draw on the way gardens for profit and pleasure were associated with male authority and status in England, and he applies this status and authority to the domain of Irish colonization, where \violent domination enacted by male English subjects was held in check by both a female sovereign and native Irish rebels. But Spenser's imagined gardens also had a more immediate material relation to real English gardens during the period. His participation in the Munster Plantation in Cork County, Ireland made him master of his own plot of land, supervising the gardens planted on it, and serving as an authority over what he and others called the "planting" of the New English settlers there. The Munster Plantation was predicated on a literal cultivating of the Irish landscape, followed by the importation of English men and women who would do the farming and who would replace the native Irish. As such, this plantation project proposed to eradicate what was Irish about the landscape and those who inhabited it. In this context, Spenser's literary gardens extend beyond actual gardens in England, as his poetic gardens are grafted onto the related practice of colonizing Ireland. They figure as both sites for actual planting (of people and land) across the sea and as spaces to imagine as the metaphorical English garden grown wild and in desperate need of English hands to cultivate it and make it productive.

The gardens in Spenser's *A View of the State of Ireland* (1633; 1596)[1] and the early books of *The Faerie Queene* (1590; 1596) represent his agenda for colonizing Ireland as a male-authorized endeavor to depict his vision of "fashioning a gentleman" in early modern England. This chapter focuses specifically on garden episodes from Spenser's Irish text and the first three books of *The Faerie Queene*, published together for the first time in 1590 when the Munster Plantation was still in its developmental stages. In so doing, I situate the early books of his epic poem in the

---

1 Even though Spenser's *View* was not printed for the first time until 1633, it was entered in the Stationer's Register in 1596 and was likely little changed between these dates, since Spenser died after his brief return to England in 1599.

center of a highly contentious and politically-charged debate about England's role in "civilizing" both the "wild Irish" and the landscape they inhabited.

My work here thus aims to call attention to the impact of Spenser's Irish experience on his literary vision in books previously not otherwise considered heavily influenced by it. Understanding the first three books of *The Faerie Queene* (1590 ed.) in the context of Irish colonial endeavor and English gardening therefore allows us to see two different versions of English-Irish relations represented in the same epic poem. Written during the early years of the Plantation process, the first three books offer a more optimistic assessment of English colonial enterprise in Ireland, while by the time the last three books were published the situation in Ireland had deteriorated for the English. Guyon's multiple temptations in garden spaces throughout Book 2, and his destruction of the Bower of Bliss in its final canto, act as a preparative for "reform" and "replantation" in the Garden of Adonis in Book 3. Such reform lays the groundwork for the perpetually fecund and productive Garden of Adonis in Book 3, a re-writing of the infertile, unproductive Bower of Bliss under Acrasia's authority in Book 2. The changes Spenser makes when he transforms the Bower of Bliss into the Garden of Adonis depict what we find in the *View* as the vision for civilizing and "planting" the actual landscape of Ireland. Destroying and replanting the garden can best be understood in light of Spenser's own adamant quest in his *View* for the Irish landscape either literally to be cleared of people (depopulated) or have its native inhabitants stripped of their cultural practices and be replaced with New English settlers and English cultural practices more befitting a "civilized" and "ordered" society.

Spenser's revision of the garden space in these episodes also reveals a critique of the way Elizabeth managed her colonial interests in Ireland. The female figures associated with these garden episodes in fact point to two alternatives for female rule: first, the destructive seductress whose gardens are fertile yet unproductive, such as Acrasia and Phaedra; and second, the chaste yet powerful woman whose power derives from the ordered garden, and she the "fruit" of the garden that ripens under auspices of the male knight or the poet's pen. Spenser imagines gardens, then, that specifically authorize the stripping away of female authority to restore order and replant them. His literary gardens reinforce the preeminence of male authority vis-à-vis a female sovereign over Irish subjects and over the Irish landscape the male colonizers sought to make "English."

Ireland-as-Garden in Spenser's *A View of the State of Ireland*

Irish colonization during the late sixteenth century was seen by English undertakers in Ireland as a noble struggle for land ownership/management and for a civilized society, a revamping of what they saw as a culturally and ecologically degenerate countryside.[2] New English attitudes about Irish colonization relate to geographer

---

2   "Undertakers" is an ironic term used for the men who "undertook" the management of Irish colonization; the term also documents the way that these men were responsible for the deaths of tens of thousands of native Irish men and women in the name of civilizing Ireland—they were, to be sure, undertakers of the most morbid sense, too.

Denis Cosgrove's notion of "landscape" as the union of land and social systems, a "discourse through which identifiable social groups historically have framed themselves and their relations with both the land and with other human groups" (xiv). The dialogue in *A View* centers on two figures, Irenaeus, whose views were representative of the prevailing sentiment among New English undertakers in Ireland, and Eudoxus, who reasons in much the same way as some of the policy-makers in England who were openly skeptical about England's potential for success in this colonizing endeavor. Much of Irenaeus's argument hinges on issues of land management, private property, and cultivation practices (or, rather, the lack of them among the native Irish). He contends that Ireland should be contained, ordered, and controlled by English law just as the English garden might be fortified by fences or hedges to protect its interior and create the illusion of "an idealized, controlled representation of nature" (Strong 14). As was true of enclosed English gardens, New English mastery over the Irish wildness (and the Irish wilderness) by enforcing English law is equated in the text with a "containing of the people" that also requires having "the land thus enclosed and well fenced" (Spenser, *View* 48, 122). In this way, Irenaeus repeatedly forges a conceptual link between containing the landscape and containing its native populations. Orderly cultivation, he reasons, goes hand in hand with civility and social order.

During the sixteenth century, England instituted with renewed vigor a process of colonizing Ireland begun in the twelfth century, one conceptualized as "planting" English men and women on Irish soil and typified by different plantation projects, the Munster Plantation chief among them. The successful quelling of the Desmond Rebellion, which took place while Spenser was Secretary to Lord Grey in Ireland in the early 1580s, freed up confiscated rebel lands for use in the plantation project.[3] Situated in the fertile countryside of Munster in south Ireland, the Munster Plantation epitomized the imagined possibilities for colonizing Ireland with New English settlers much as Lefebvre describes the representational spaces to be altered through the imagination. As Andrew MacCarthy-Morrogh writes, lands seized from the Desmond rebellion

> were to be divided into units of regular size and granted to suitable Englishmen, who in turn would undertake to inhabit with a stipulated number of English settlers...For a full seignory the undertaker had to settle ninety-one families including his own. The nature of tenancy was ordained: six freeholders, six farmers holding from the undertaker in fee farm, forty-two copyholders, and thirty-six base tenures and cottagers. So too the amount of land each class was to have: the freeholders 300 acres each, farmers 400 acres, copyholders 100 acres, the remainder fifty, twenty-five, or ten acres each, at the discretion of the undertaker. Lesser amounts in due proportion were demanded from those who undertook eight, six, or four thousand acres. (30–31)

---

3   To my knowledge, the most comprehensive study of the Munster Plantation is by MacCarthy-Morrogh. See also an extensive study by Canny, which covers more broadly the English colonial "reformation" of Ireland during this period. Another historical study concentrates on the heightened crisis of English colonial endeavor during the 1590s, an especially violent period. See also McGurk. And for broad coverage of this "conquest" in Renaissance literature, see Murphy.

Moreover, those initial settlers "planted" on the land thus distributed had to be English born. Only later might tenants (or second generation settlers) derive from the Old English who settled in Ireland from the twelfth century, who would have been able to trace their family lines to an English heritage, but who by the later sixteenth century posed a particular threat to the project of converting the inhabitants and landscape of Ireland to English customs and laws. The Plantation project was, therefore, a highly regimented and controlled process of eliminating all traces of what was deemed Irish by the New English settlers, transforming the landscape by enacting English planting methods, and populating it with English men and women. By the time Spenser became involved in the Plantation project, that is, "proper" land management was paramount to making Ireland civil.

Spenser was one of the chief recipients of land in the Munster Plantation, and thus had a personal investment in its success or failure. Although Spenser likely occupied the Kilcolman castle and its lands from the mid-1580s, he officially acquired it in May 1589, at which time he established a colony of six householders (with their families) on the 3,000 plus acres in his posession. In a land survey from 1586, Kilcolman castle was unflatteringly hailed as "a large castle, old, and dilapidated, which at the present time has no use except to shelter cattle in the night" (Qtd. in Maley, *Spenser Chronology* 43). However, Spenser characterized Kilcolman and its surrounding area in Munster as "a most riche and plentifull countrey, full of corn and cattell" (Qtd. in Judson 44); and when biographer Alexander Judson made a pilgrimage to the area in the early twentieth century keeping Spenser's experience of the estate in mind, he seemed to agree:

> Surely today the acres that once constituted Spenser's estate and the whole valley over which old father Mole presides impress one with their fertility and prosperity. They teem with life. Cattle and sheep are everywhere, the latter grazing even to the top of the highest mountains. Not one beast did I see during my stay but looked sleek and well-fed, even the horses of an itinerant show that were making their supper from roadside grass. (44, 47)

Characterized by fertility and abundance, Kilcolman (and the whole of the Munster Plantation lands in Cork County) was ideally suited for a key component of English colonization, cultivating unused land to make it productive and profitable.

However, like the characterization of English-Irish relations in the *View*, Spenser's personal involvement in colonization met with strong opposition. His possession of Kilcolman castle and lands precipitated a notoriously contested case in which Lord Roche (Irish) challenged Spenser's claim to the land by asserting that Kilcolman was not in fact part of the Desmond family lands but rather his own inherited property. Roche claims that Spenser, "falsely pretending title to certain castles and 16 ploughlands, hath taken possession thereof. Also, by threatening and menacing the Lord Roche's tenants, and by seizing their cattle, and beating Lord Roche's servants and bailiffs he has wasted 6 ploughlands of his Lordship's lands" (Qtd. in Maley, *Spenser Chronology* 52). Spenser and others responded to Roche's accusation with a bill in rebuttal that certified their own accusations against Roche, which included such claims as "He speaks ill of Her Majesty's government," that he slaughtered cattle belonging to tenants who were believed to have supported

Spenser, and that he "has forbidden his people to have any trade or conference with Mr. Spenser or Mr. Piers [another undertaker] or their Tenants" (Maley, *Spenser Chronology* 52). Roche lost the suit, and Spenser continued to occupy the lands at Kilcolman and to administer over 3,000 acres of the Munster Plantation.[4] Centered around issues of land-use, ownership, and nationalism, the dispute between Spenser and Roche typified the New English practice of taking possession of and occupying land; hardly a smooth enterprise, colonizing Ireland involved getting their hands dirty by either evicting or starving out tenants and landholders and seizing land for queen and country.[5]

Spenser stipulates his plan for the Munster Plantation under his administration by responding point by point to the official Articles governing the plantation process. Queen Elizabeth, who was notoriously skeptical about how best to pursue the colonizing process, and who was interested in protecting her investment in Ireland, assigned a commission to investigate the plantation's progress. In 1589, after nearly nine years of work on the plantation, Spenser explains his personal land management policy in a detailed list of seven points:

1.   To the first he saith that he hath undertaken the peopling of a seignory of 4,000 acres allotted to him by a particular from the undertakers, in which the castle and lands of Kilcolman and Rossack were appointed to him, the which want much of the said whole population of 4,000 acres.

2.   To the second he saith he hath not as yet passed his patent of the said lands, but so soon as Justice Smythes, who is only left now of the quorum, returns from England, the patent will be passed.

3.   To the third he saith that there wanteth his due proportion 1,000 acres as he supposed at the least.

4.   To the fourth, fifth, and sixth he knoweth of chargeable lands and chief-rents within the compass of his particular, but only four nobles upon Ballingarragh and 6/8 upon Ballinfoynigh.

5.   To the seventh and eighth he saith that as yet he hath not made any division of his lands to his tenants, for that his patent is not passed unto him nor his lands established.

6.   To the ninth, tenth and eleventh he saith that he hath hitherto but six households of English people upon his land for former causes.

7.   To the twelfth he saith that sundry honest persons in England have promised to come over to inhabit his land as soon as his patent is [passed]. (Qtd. in Maley, *Spenser Chronology* 50–51)

Reassuring his queen back home in England that her investment was progressing steadily toward successful completion, Spenser emphasizes the strides he had already made and promises future successes as well. However, Spenser's points reflect an anxiety on his part about how much he could quantify his successes after

---

4   See also Heffner for a detailed account of the dispute between Roche and Spenser as it related to the original landowner Andrew Reade. During the years between 1586 and 1589, Spenser leased Kilcolman from Reade, whom Heffner speculates left Spenser to occupy the land and castle in his absence in order to avoid legal suit with Roche.

5   MacCarthy-Morrogh cites Spenser's landholdings as 3,028 acres in County Cork (Table 1, 292).

nearly a decade of work toward colonizing and cultivating the Irish countryside. At best, he offers his queen the qualified reassurance that, after years of trying, he has six English tenant farmer families poised to work the Irish fields, and, should they fail, "sundry honest persons in England" were prepared to take their place. The only roadblock to success, he argues here, is the queen's willingness to grant a patent that would allow him to proceed with dividing the 4,000 acres among the tenants to be worked and turned into productive, arable farms.

Spenser's Irish text likewise emphasizes the conceptual relationship between cultivation and civility manifest in the twin tasks of planting land and planting New English settlers. Throughout the text, Spenser links the colonization process to the process of clearing a plot of land to plant a garden. Just as the early modern garden in England was seen as an ordering of a wild landscape, so too was the process of colonizing the "wild Irish" conceived as the reforming of the Old English in terms of "planting," pruning, and cultivation. At the same time, civility was mapped onto the actual landscape in the form of cultivated New English-owned land that might yield profits for both the private landowner and the English commonwealth (*View* 123). By linking the Irish to the land grown wild and describing the English government as being planted in Ireland as an English landowner might plant a garden, Ireland becomes the metaphorical equivalent of the part of England that needs to be placed back under control and tamed.[6]

The garden as a metaphor for this process exemplifies what Andrew Hadfield characterizes as "competing and intersecting identities" that surface in Spenser's writing time and again (*Spenser's Irish Experience* 4). Defining English subjecthood in a land across the sea threatened the identities of New English undertakers, such that, as Hadfield explains, they were "worried that unless they defined their own identity in an aggressive way it would disappear before their very eyes" (*Spenser's Irish Experience* 4). Hence, and in line with a common refrain in printed gardening books during this period in England, acquiring and cultivating Irish land becomes crucial for defining English subjecthood. The concept of "competing and intersecting identities" and the "aggressive" re-shaping of identity are perfectly encapsulated in gardening as a practice and evinced by printed manuals on the topic, as discussed in Chapter 1. Planting a garden, too, was a type of "aggressive" and destructive working of the soil, using the plow to turn and reveal the fertile layers of soil that cradle the gardener's seeds as they germinate and grow.[7] When weeds struggle to displace viable plants in the garden space, they enact a competition like that Hadfield describes as characteristic of Spenser's social identity. Likewise, practical gardening became a way for men and women to negotiate gendered identity in similarly "competing and intersecting" ways. Spenser's text thus captures the competitive elements of practical gardening and (re)creates a garden paradise that metaphorically services

---

6   "Even as they made disparaging remarks about it [Ireland]," Canny reminds us, "that part of Ireland which had been subject to English rule since the twelfth century was still part of the English polity and *recoverable* to the standards of civility obtained in England itself" (9).

7   See, for example, Hill's *The gardener's labyrinth* and *The profittable arte of gardening* and Lawson's *A New Orchard and Garden*.

the New English agenda for colonizing Ireland. His perfected garden becomes the site for perfected English cultural values.[8]

The garden as a metaphor for English colonization of Ireland was hardly unique to Spenser; it was a commonplace association among the New English undertakers in Ireland. Fellow colonizer, Lodowick Bryskett, employs the garden in just such metaphorical ways in his *Discourse*, which features Spenser as a main character and which was written while Spenser's *Faerie Queene* was still a work-in-progress,

> My Lord Grey hath plowed and harrowed the rough ground to his hand: but you know that
> he that soweth the seede, whereby we hope for harvest according to the goodnesse of that
> which is cast into the earth, and the seasonablenesse of times, deserveth no lesse praise
> then he that manureth the land. (Qtd. in Maley, *Salvaging Spenser* 64)

For Bryskett, as for so many English colonizers who served under Lord Grey and his administration, Ireland was the site of the figurative "planting" of English values. The English undertakers in Ireland, such as Sir Walter Ralegh, Barnaby Googe, and Edmund Spenser were among those who "plowed and harrowed the rough ground" and "soweth the seed" in preparation for the native Irish and Old English to receive New English cultural values, and they were as valuable to the colonizing process as those who, perhaps much later, bore witness to the "harvest." But colonizing Ireland also entailed literally planting unused pasture and "waste" land to cultivate fields of madder, woad, and other crops commonly planted back in England.[9] The New English prescribed plowing, harrowing, manuring, and sowing seeds on the otherwise uncultivated, untamed, Irish landscape as the means of imposing English civility and order in Ireland.[10]

---

8   MacCarthy-Morrogh cites the general agreement among New English to "Anglicize Munster" (20).

9   Spenser proposes farming as a remedy for dearth, arguing that planting corn, for example, will not only add to the local Irish economy and the commonwealth of England, but that corn is a good crop because it can be stored for future years when the harvest is not plentiful. In *A Brief Description of Ireland* (1589), Robert Payne lists the many crops potentially well-suited for the Irish climate and soil: "Their soyle for the most part is very fertil, and apte for Wheate, Rye, Barly, Peason, Beanes, Oates, Woade, Mather, Rape, Hoppes, Hempe, Flaxe, and all other graines and fruites that England any wise doth yeelde." (Qtd. in Hadfield, *Spenser's Irish Experience* 34–35). According to Gervase Markham's *The Countrey Farme,* these crops are, perhaps not just coincidentally, some of the most profitable one could plant. That the New English imagined planting in Ireland many of the same crops already planted in England further constructs Ireland as an extension of the English realm. Ireland, that is, is imagined as already like England, except that those who occupy it (the Old English and native Irish) have failed to develop what is "English" about it. Such assertions served to justify the colonization of Ireland by the New English and the large-scale reform policies, predicated jointly on changing cultivation and cultural practices.

10   Irenaeus repeatedly offers husbandry as the solution for Irish degeneracy. He not only suggests that uncultivated land is a mark of Irish barbarism, but he lists enclosure methods, tenancy, and specific crops that the New English should plant that would be most profitable to individual men and the English commonwealth.

In Spenser's *View,* "civilizing" Ireland requires "planting" New English because early failures at colonization resulted in the "displanting" of the original English settlers when the Irish

> Fled from his [King Henry's] power, into the deserts and mountaines, leaving the wyde country to the conqueror: who in their stead eftsoones placed English men, who possessed all their lands and did quite shut out the Irish, or the most part of them…Then the Irish who before they had banished into the mountaines, where they lived only upon white meates, as it is recorded, seeing now their lands so dispeopled, and weakened, came downe into all the plaines adjoyning, and thence expelling those few English that remained in them, and, growing greater, have brought under them many of the English, which were before their Lords. This was one of the occasions by which all those countreys, which lying neere unto any mountaines or Irish desarts, had been planted with English, were shortly displanted and lost. (22–23)

Irenaeus's concern is two-fold: first, even though the English previously gained control over the Irish and displaced them to less hospitable areas of the country, much like the American government did to Native American populations, the Irish managed to gain strength and reclaim what was taken from them as they "brought under" the once-powerful English; and second, the Irish could "displant" the English originally "planted" there, which meant that the Irish effected a rebellion that simultaneously reclaimed power over a people and over the land. When Irenaeus says, "Through wisdom it [Ireland] may be mastered and subdued," he identifies both the Irish people and the wild landscape as both in need of English mastery.

In turn, Irish barbarism is defined by, both before the original planting and after, inadequate cultivation practices or by a non-agricultural economy. Irenaeus argues that the Irish lords, for whom the head of the tribe is the "Lord of the soyle," are not effective landlords or land managers.[11] To the great misfortune of the land and their would-be English conquerors, he laments, the Irish are a migratory people who "keepe their cattle" and "live themselves the most part of the yeare in boolies, pasturing upon the mountaine, and waste wild places; and removing still to fresh land, as they have depastured the former" (36). Instead of cultivating the land, he insists, they waste it. "Moreover the people that thus live in those boolies," he adds, "grow thereby the more barbarous, and live more licentiously than they could in townes, using what manners they list, and practizing what mischiefes and villainies they will, either against the government there, by their combynations, or against private men" (55–56). Irenaeus equates the Irish who subsist on what he calls "wild waste land" and their migratory pasturing practices with their "barbarous" behavior in the towns. The migratory Irish, he contends, undermine the fecundity of the "fresh land" by depasturing it just as they wreak havoc on towns across the Irish countryside when they "practice what manners they list." Although the Irish had English law

---

11   This claim by Irenaeus is bitterly ironic, since disputes between landlords and tenants in England after the Reformation—with the advent of extensive private property practices—are well documented and hardly a rarity. In fact, Parliament often intervened, under the argumentational skill of Lord Burleigh and Francis Bacon, and imposed or discussed imposing restrictions on land use practices.

"planted among them at the first," what was "planted" in Ireland was more than the laws and customs of the home country—it was also the English themselves (101–2). In order for this same civility to be replanted in Ireland, then, Irish cultural and political traditions must give way to English ones, even as the English themselves must take over as occupants of the land. The "plant[ing]" of civil government means that Ireland, like an overgrown garden, must be stripped of its undesirable occupants and replanted.[12]

Civilizing the "barbarous nation" of the Irish envisioned in *A View*, then, required an equally barbaric replanting of the Irish landscape and reform of those who lived on it. Irenaeus trumpets the call for violent reform by declaring the English should seize both people and land "Even by the sword; for all these evills must first be cut away by a strong hand, before any good can bee planted, like as the corrupt braunches and unwholesome boughs are first to bee pruned, and the foule mosse cleansed and scraped away before the tree can bring forth any good fruite" (93). Elsewhere, New English reformers must similarly "cut away" "what was "corrupt" and "unwholesome" about the Irish landscape and its inhabitants. After Irenaeus informs him that the Lords hold titles to the land yet leave it unused, Eudoxus concludes, "without first cutting of this dangerous custome, it seemeth hard to plant any sound ordinance." Furthermore, they deemed it necessary for the English to seize the land, by force if necessary, so that they can "plant a peaceable government amongst them" (18–19). Irenaeus responds, "So as it is vaine to speake of planting lawes, and plotting pollicie, till they be altogether subdued" (21). This very principle typified Spenser's own stance toward governance in Ireland, and the male undertakers did in fact seize vast amounts of land and brutally murdered over 30,000 Irish men and women in the name of civility.

Once the Irish and Old English are "mastered" and "subdued," the best way to bring "civility" to Ireland, imagined in the *View*, is to implement an agrarian economy and through staunch controls over land distribution and land use:

> Though Ireland bee by nature counted a great soyle of pasture, yet had I rather have fewer cowes kept, and men better mannered, then to have such huge increase of cattle, and no increase of good conditions…[they] should keep a plough going; for otherwise all men would fall to pasturage, and none to husbandry, which is a great cause of this dearth now in England, and a cause of the usuall stealthes in Ireland: For looke into all countreyes that live in such sort by keeping of cattle, and you shall finde that they are both very barbarous and uncivill, and also greatly give to warre…And therefore since now wee purpose to draw the Irish, from desire of warre and tumults, to the love of peace and civility, it is expedient to abridge their great custome of hardening, and augment their trade of tillage and husbandrie. (150)

Civility here is typified by husbandry, industrious labor that reforms the land by means of a plow, and controlled agricultural practices to distract the Irish from their "barbarous" tendency to war. Irenaeus aligns the way the plow orders the soil beneath it into neat rows to receive seeds planted by the husband's diligent hands with the way that husbandry turns men's minds to an orderly occupation that makes

---

12   See 120–25 for Irenaeus's argument to this effect.

them more inclined to peace and civility than the migratory pasture practices of the native Irish or the other groups he deems disorderly and "uncivill."

"That sacred soil where all our perils grow": Dangerous Gardens, Book 2

Given the centrality of the garden metaphor in Spenser's Irish text it is not surprising to find it, too, in Spenser's *Faerie Queene*, since Spenser likely began composing his epic poem shortly after his arrival in Ireland, and he published its first three books at roughly the same time he began to write his Irish tract. While it may appear at first anachronistic to discuss Spenser's *View* (1633; 1596) as a context for the two episodes in Books 2 and 3 from the 1590 edition of *The Faerie Queene*, the prose work crystallizes his conception of Ireland as a garden-grown-wild that was most certainly present while he was composing his epic poem in the intervening years since his appointment in Ireland (1580–90). Fashioning, or cultivating, the gentleman is articulated in these first books of Spenser's epic poem relative the relationship between land and social status, religious reform, gendered authority, and the colonization project Spenser was so deeply and personally invested in from the 1580's onward. His experience in Ireland left visible traces in these early books as scholars have already insightfully noted it did in later ones.[13]

Guyon's destruction of the Bower of Bliss at the end of Book 2, prefigured in the earlier episodes with Phaedra (Canto 6) and Mammon (Canto 7), enacts a clearing of the unproductive garden under the female authority of Acrasia, which makes it possible later for a new, perpetually fecund garden-space that resembles the first Paradise to appear in the Garden of Adonis in Book 3. Other scholars have seen the Bower of Bliss and the Garden of Adonis as companion pieces in the poem, and in fact, Michael Leslie draws on the context of the gardens at Kenilworth where Elizabeth was entertained in 1575 by Robert Dudley to argue that Spenser's poetic gardens force the reader to make moral judgments akin to those that each book's knights must make.[14] Spenser's Bower of Bliss and Garden of Adonis resemble one another, Leslie argues, in general ways, but a careful reader would notice their subtle differences, especially the way the gardens in the Bower of Bliss resemble those of

---

13   See Fitzpatrick, whose "Spenser and Land" focuses on the figure of Malengin from Book V; Fitzpatrick elsewhere concentrates on the later books, looking at dangerous female sexuality in the context of anxiety about Irishness and Irish rebellion: "Pastoral Idylls and Lawless Rebels"; see also Cavanaugh, "'The fatal destiny of that land'." In another article, "Licentious Barbarism," Cavanaugh relates Spenser's prose work to the later books of his epic poem by analyzing references to specific geographic locations, such as Arlo Hill, and through characters who parallel historical figures, such as Pastorella, Artegall, and Radigund; and finally, see Bernhard Klein, "The Lie of the Land: English Surveyors, Irish Rebels, and *The Faerie Queene*." Klein looks at the fields of surveying and cartography in relationship to Book V of *The Faerie Queene*.

14   Leslie asserts the parallels between the way that spectators at the Kenilworth had to make subtle distinctions in the way different aspects of the garden design and statuary called to mind idealized classical forms or even, sometimes, bawdy jokes.

Italian gardens from Rome—a reference that may well have also called to mind for Spenser's mindful reader the Catholic Church.

While Leslie's reading calls attention to the specific ways these garden episodes resonate in the context of actual early modern gardens, his focus on *English* gardens (or even Italian ones as understood through the English imagination) as his only context for the relationship between, as he writes, "literary gardens" and "real gardens" ignores the fact that the real gardens Spenser would have been familiar with were as likely to be found on Irish soil as on English. Spenser may well have known about the Kenilworth entertainments and the gardens at Dudley's estate, but his more immediate, practical concerns involved the plantation project on the 3,000 plus acres of land he owned across the sea. Furthermore, seeing Spenser's companion garden episodes in an expressly English context, as Leslie does, suggests that Spenser might use them to reflect on the tributes to Elizabeth at Kenilworth and, thus, bears the implication that Spenser's gardens, too, expressly pay tribute to his queen. Reconsidering these episodes in relation to one another in an Irish context as I do here, however, suggests quite the opposite: that Spenser was in fact quite critical of his female monarch's authority over himself, the other male undertakers, and the colonizing project in Ireland. Gloriana is an absent-presence throughout the poem, and Faeryland always eludes the grasp of the questing knights, exemplifying the distancing of power and authority that Spenser effects throughout the poem but quite tangibly in the gardens of Books 2 and 3.[15]

Arguments about the interface between human labor, human art, and nature central to Cantos 6 and 7 of Book 2 ask a similar question to the one that begins Spenser's *View*: "But if that countrey of Ireland, whence you lately came, be of so goodly and commodious a soyl, as you report, I wonder that no course is taken for the turning thereof to good uses, and reducing that nation to better government and civility" (*View* 11). Contextualizing the civilizing process in terms of how best to develop the "goodly and commodious" soil exemplifies the link Spenser also makes throughout Book 2 between the twin practices of gardening and colonization. Phaedra's island, after all, is a "chosen plot of fertile land," and the Garden of Proserpina is a "gardin goodly garnished / With hearbs and fruits," but these gardens are neglected, and, like the Ireland Eudoxus describes, require the "turning thereof to good uses" (2.6.12, 2.7.51).

The ostensibly naturally fecund qualities of Phaedra's island garden in Canto 6, Book 2 similarly evoke the metaphorical Irish garden in *A View*:

> It was a chosen plot of fertile land,
> Emongst wide waues set, like a little nest,
> As if it had by Natures cunning hand,
> Bene choisely picked out from all the rest,
> And laid forth for ensample of the best. (2.6.12)

---

15 Hadfield writes that Spenser's Colin Clout figure exemplifies the "double" self-fashioning of identity in Spenser's *Faerie Queene*, and that Spenser displaces the figure of the queen by portraying himself as "no longer straightforwardly English, but a loyal servant of the queen in a land where her authority counted for little" (*Edmund Spenser's Irish Experience* 15). See Hadfield 1–12 for a broader discussion of Spenser's double identity as both Irish and English.

Significantly, though, this island (like Acrasia's later in Canto 12) merely conveys the *semblance* of perfection: qualifiers such as "as if" and "like" are evocative of this garden's deceptive allure. We find out that the "Trees, braunches, birds, and songs were framed fit" on that island "to allure fraile mind to carelesse ease" and serve to distract the knights who would visit it (2.6.13). Like this island, the county of Munster in Ireland is hailed as "the sweetest soyle of Ireland" in the *View*, "a most rich and plentifull countrey" that lured English men to convert to native Irish customs, and caused them to shed all traces of what defined them as "English."[16] Spenser's knight of Temperance plays out the same tempting encounter with the deceptive beauty of Ireland experienced by the English settlers.

Like the Ireland described in Spenser's *View*, the landscape featured in Canto 6 is lush and fertile, full of possibility; yet also like Ireland in the *View*, the beauty of this landscape preempts the knights' journey instead of spurring them on to further labors. Not long after the enticing description we learn from Phaedra that this garden space neither resembles human artifice nor requires human labor for its upkeep:

> Behold, o man, that toilesome paines doest take
> The flowres, the fields, and all that pleasant growes,
> How they themselues doe thine ensample make,
> Whiles nothing enuious nature them forth throwes
> Out of her fruitful lap...
> Yet no man for them taketh paines or care,
> Yet no man to them can his carefull paines compare. (2.6.15)

That the landscape in this garden grows up out of "ensample" rather than "toilsome paines" emphasizes how Phaedra's temptation rests in the appeal of this garden space to produce beauty without labor, a notion contrary to the purpose of both Spenser's knights and the Irish colonial project. Phaedra openly mocks the idea that human labor would render this garden more beautiful and persuades Cymochles that attempts to order the natural world are not only "fruitlesse labours" and "fruitlesse toile," but they result in men's enslavement. "Why then dost thou, o man, that of them all, / Art Lord, and eke of nature Soveraigne, / Wilfully make thy selfe a wretched thrall," she chides, and she insists that Cymochles "Refuse such fruitlesse toile, and pleasant pleasures chuse" (2.6.17). Her admonishment to the knight to choose pleasure over "toile" directly contradicts the values underpinning Spenser's poem, that "endlesse worke," not idleness, yields virtue. In so doing, this episode establishes that Guyon must vanquish not so much a specific entity as the idea that perfection (exemplified here by the Paradisal garden space) is possible without human labor.

---

16 Eudoxus asks, "Are not they that were once English, English still?" to which Irenaeus replies, "No, for some of them are degenerated and growne almost mere Irish, yea, and more malitious to the English then the Irish themselves" (55). By "English" Irenaeus clearly means English identity represented by the New English settlers, such that "English" does not refer so much to the group of people (Old English or New English) per se, but rather English identity characterized by an adherence to English cultural customs and English Law as opposed to Irish customs and law.

Developing knightly virtue, Spenser shows time and again in Book 2, involves resisting the idea that agricultural and horticultural labor makes men slaves. Like Cymochles, Guyon travels to the island garden enjoying Phaedra's enchantments as he traverses the sea. Unlike Cymochles, however, when Guyon sees the island he immediately realizes that she means to disempower him:

> But when as Guyon of that land had sight,
> He wist himself amisse, and angry said;
> Ah Dame, perdie ye haue not doen me right,
> Thus to mislead me, whiles I you obaid:
> Me litle needed from my right way to haue straid. (2.6.22)

Despite Guyon's early reservations he continues toward Phaedra's island paradise, and once on shore, Phaedra introduces him to the "gardins pleasures," which represent "Their natiue musicke by her skilfull art" (2.6.25). Earlier Phaedra plays her music for Cymochles, who succumbs to her wiles, a scene echoed by Phaedra's temptation of Guyon later, which reinforces the idea that the threat facing both knights is to linger in the garden to enjoy its pleasure and avoid human labor. Temptation is contextualized in this garden as a test of how active a gardener the knight is, and Cymochles fails where the Old English fail, whereas Guyon (like the hoped-for fate of the New English) succeeds admirably. The imperative for Guyon to resist this temptation and focus on the civilizing influence of human labor evokes that of the New English in Ireland, who likewise must focus on "tempering, and managing, this stubborne nation of the Irish to bring them from their delight of licentious barbarisme unto the love of goodnes and civilitie" (*View* 20–21). In this prefiguration of the garden Guyon will later encounter in Acrasia's bower, Guyon must eliminate the distracting and destructive potential of unproductive pleasure here as a pretext for his trial at the end of the book.

The Garden of Proserpina in Canto 7, like Phaedra's garden, has a seductive appeal; unlike Phaedra's island, however, the Garden of Proserpina requires perennial labor, garden work that finally yields nothing. Human labor in this garden abused nature and disrupted the natural "meane" instead of developing the inherent beauty found there:

> The antique world, in his first flowring youth,
> Found no defect in his Creatours grace,
> But with glad thankes, and unreproued truth,
> The gifts of soueraigne bountie did embrace:
> Like Angels life was then mens happy cace;
> But later ages pride, like corn-fed steed,
> Abusd her plenty, and fat swolne encreace
> To all licentious lust, and gan exceed
> The measure of her meane, and naturall first need. (2.7.16)

The "meane" that characterizes temperance, which Guyon develops throughout this book, is contextualized here as maintaining a balance, or "meane," in nature. The "antique world" Guyon describes embraces the "gifts of soueraigne bountie" while the "later ages" "abusd" these gifts and fostered excess and "encreace." To frame this discussion as a question of how best to use nature's resources relates Guyon's temptation to the threat posed by the native Irish and Old English-turned-Irish, who are, likewise, accused of abusing the "gifts of nature by continuing a migratory lifestyle that, as Irenaeus argues in the *View*, brings "lewdness," gambling, and theft. (78).

Mammon's assault on Guyon's sensibilities (and senses) in this garden centers around a seduction similar to the one Irenaeus claims in the *View* lured the Old English from their English customs to Irish ones. Philotime, whom we are told "was not that same her owne natiue hew, / But wrought by art and counterfetted shew," tries to seduce Guyon, and her father Mammon proposes a marriage between the two that would give Guyon dominion over the Garden of Proserpina (2.7.45, 50). Philotime typifies counterfeiting artifice, and such a proposition of marriage aligns her with the recurrent anxiety in the *View* about the allure of native Irish culture and the degeneration of Old English when they intermarry with the native Irish. Like the near-irresistible charm of Philotime's beauty and song, and like the artificial appeal of Mammon's cave, where most objects are made of gold, the fear expressed in the *View* is that the Irish may lure the English with "lascivious layes, and loose jiggs, by which in short space their mindes were so mollified and abated, that they forgot their former fiercenesse, and became most tender and effeminate" (*View* 73). Guyon's swoon at the hands of Philotime's seductive song suggests that fear of such effeminization is very much at the heart of these gardens, too.

If Phaedra's garden depicts the consequences of believing that nature can be civilized without human labor, the Garden of Proserpina endangers Guyon's quest for the virtue of Temperance by depicting how gratification could be possible without intense work. This garden of perpetual death, not fertility, threatens Guyon's quest by luring him to linger there rather than continue. Spenser foregrounds the inherent danger Guyon faces in this episode, when the narrator interjects,

> All which he did, to doe him deadly fall
> In frayle intemperance through sinfull bayt;
> To which if he inclined had at all,
> That dreadfull feend, which did behind him wayt,
> Would him haue rent in thousand peeces strayt:
> But he [Guyon] was warie wise in all his way,
> And well perceiued his deceiptfull sleight,
> Ne suffred lust his safetie to betray;
> So goodly did beguile the Guyler of the pray. (2.7.64)

The Garden of Proserpina is designed to lure Guyon to the same fate as others who dwell there—to cause him to fall victim to immediate gratification without sustained labor. He faces the potential eradication of his identity as the knight of temperance much as the English "planted" in Ireland in Spenser's *View* face cultural eradication, a loss of "English" identity. At stake if Guyon succumbs is violent dismemberment, a fate that he in turn enacts on the landscape when he destroys Acrasia's Bower at the end of Book 2. The gardens in Cantos 6 and 7 successively offer different threats to the knightly pursuit of temperance in the context of the relationship between nature and human labor—and labor in the context of gardens here, as it is in the printed gardening manuals, means applying human art to improve the inherent imperfections of nature.

Similarly, in Acrasia's Bower later in Canto 12, we find "A place pickt out by choice of best aliue, / That natures worke by art can imitate" (2.12.42). The Bower's excessive artifice competes with nature; it does not build on the inherent value of the natural landscape or improve it any more than Phaedra's garden or the Garden of Proserpina. In fact, in Acrasia's bower, nature and art seek to "undermine" each other, such that, even though it appears to be "the most daintie Paradise on ground,"

> The art, which all that wrought, appeared in no place.
> One would have thought (so cunningly, the rude,
> And scorned parts were mingled with the fine,)
> That nature had for wantonesse ensude
> Art, and that Art at nature did repine;
> So striuing each th'other to undermine,
> Each did the others worke more beautifie; (2.12.59)

The way art and nature strive to outdo and "undermine" each other in this garden rests expressly counter to the goal of English gardening, which was to build on the naturally-occurring fertility of the landscape and, as William Lawson writes in *A New Orchard and Garden*, use aesthetics to order the "provident and skillful Collectrix of the faults of nature" (A3). Here, artifice obfuscates the boundaries between art and nature, revealing that this garden is in fact a mock Paradise. Like English formal gardens in this period, this garden contains a fountain in its center, which lends a self-consciously artificial element to the garden space. Fountains employed human workmanship obviously not part of the natural landscape but that represented a heightened example of how human art could supplement nature's qualities; but what makes this fountain characteristic of the excesses of Acrasia's garden is the fact that it is "over-wrought." This fountain, for example, is surrounded in ivy that appears natural, or "trew" to its "natiue hew" yet is covered in gold (2.12.61, 60).

Like so many formal gardens in England in the late sixteenth century, this garden is surrounded by a fence, as described in numerous printed manuals from the period; however, it deviates in significant ways from the ideal imagined in gardening books. Quite unlike the ideal enclosed garden, which would have used hedges and walls to offer protection from the outside, the fence in Acrasia's garden space is "weake and thin," allowing everything to pass through it, and it is formed "Rather for pleasure, then for battery or fight" (2.12.43). Acrasia's bower presents a deception for the eye and the senses by evoking many of the same qualities familiar to English garden admirers yet taking them to an altogether new degree of excess. Her bower may resemble the lush, private spaces found in English gardens, but closer scrutiny reveals that they simply mimic the real thing, a distinction, Spenser asserts, a virtuous knight with a noble cause not only should, but must be able to discern.

In sharp contrast with Acrasia's garden space in the Bower of Bliss, Spenser's *View* repeatedly endorses cultivating the natural fertility of the landscape through (English) human labor as the means to and sign of "planting" civility in Ireland. The "reasonable man," as argued in the *View*, would "by such good meanes bee drawne to build himself some handsome habitation thereon, to ditch and inclose his ground, to manure and husband it as good farmours use" (*View* 83). And Irenaeus likewise elsewhere directly relates landscape improvement to cultural refinement: it "chiefly redoundeth to the good of the common-wealth, to have the land thus inclosed, and well fenced," which deters thieves, rebels, and outlaws and diminishes the "savage condition" of its inhabitants (84). The garden in Acrasia's bower, whose fence merely pretends to enclose, stands at odds with the actually-enclosed landscape required for succeeding in the parallel tasks of civilizing the landscape and its inhabitants. Guyon's quest, like that of the New English in the *View*, is to decipher the difference between productive artifice and its deceptive mirror image, which leads to excess, desire, and lust. Temperate and virtuous use of art improves on nature's inherent qualities rather than surpasses them. Excessive artifice, the only laborious element in these gardens, may make the space appear as a formal aesthetic garden, but its appearance is deceiving and is at the heart of Guyon's temptation to dismiss temperate virtue.

The best corrective for bad land management, in Spenser's *Faerie Queene* as it is in the *View*, is to clear the uncultivated and waste landscape using whatever means necessary so that it can again be put to productive uses. Similarly, Guyon's violent reclamation of Acrasia's over-cultivated yet unproductive garden space parallels the violence Irenaeus argues will restore English Law and English customs in Ireland. Once inside "The sacred soile, where all our perils grow" (2.12.37), Guyon and the Palmer discover

> A large and spacious plaine, on euery side
> Strowed with pleasauns, whose faire grassy ground
> Mantled with greene, and goodly beautifide
> With all the ornaments of Floraes pride,
> Wherewith her mother Art, as halfe in scorne
> Of niggard Nature, like a pompous bride
> Did decke her, and too lauishly adorne… (2.12.50)

The "sacred soile" where Guyon and the Palmer land is dangerous because it may appear "goodly beautifide" but its ornamentation is deceptive, "too lauishly adorne[d]," and it derives from a "scorne" of nature instead of laborious improvement of it. Here, Guyon must resist the deceptive beauty of intemperate artifice much as he has done in Cantos 6 and 7. That this artifice is framed as a garden, as it is in Cantos 6 and 7, situates temperate artifice and labor in the context of the aesthetic cultivation practices that typified early modern gardening and in the context of the metaphorical Ireland-as-garden in Spenser's prose treatise.

Situating the Bower of Bliss (and later the Garden of Adonis) alongside Spenser's metaphorical gardens in his Irish text helps explain Guyon's destruction of the unproductive garden in Book 2, Canto 12 in the context of Book 2's Virtue of Temperance, a much discussed topic among scholars for some time. Using Spenser's Irish experience as a context for reading this episode offers an alternative to a conventional interpretation of Spenser's definition of temperance, exemplified by Lauren Silberman's assertion that "While Guyon has sworn to defeat Acrasia, the enemy of Temperance, the intemperate violence with which he destroys the Bower of Bliss and fulfills his quest seems aesthetically disturbing because it appears excessive for the triumph of Temperance it purports to express" (9). William Melaney similarly qualifies the nature of Spenser's Virtue of Temperance in Book 2, as he suggests that Temperance is not, as some have argued, to be interpreted as a "measured control of reason and will" but instead a "certain order in the realm of desire" (116).[17] Spenser's *View* suggests that civilizing Ireland is possible only through violent means of reform; such an orientation to violence, Spenser repeatedly insists, is not to be taken as excessive but as the necessary means to remove intransigent and dangerous elements that impede the colonizing process. Guyon's actions are not, therefore, intemperate, but rather epitomize temperance as defined by the necessary use of violence to impose order. Recontextualizing temperance vis-à-vis the English agenda to colonize Ireland thus helps explain how the destruction of the Bower of Bliss by the male knight might enact exactly what Queen Elizabeth hesitated to authorize in Ireland herself—indefatigable reform by the sword. In fact, it was Elizabeth's reluctance to authorize such unmerciful violence that led to accusations that England's lack of success in Ireland stemmed directly from Elizabeth's policies being too soft.

Given this context, Guyon's destruction of the entire garden space at the end of the Canto directly links his violence with Spenser's call to use violence as the means to prepare Ireland for the "planting" of English men and women and English civility. That Guyon leaves Acrasia in chains yet destroys her bower suggests that land acquisition is specifically critical the civilizing process:

> But all those pleasant bowres and Pallace braue,
> Guyon broke downe, with rigour pittilesse;
> Ne ought their goodly workmanship might saue
> Them from the tempest of his wrathfulnesse,
> But that their blisse he turn'd to balefulnesse:
> Their groues he feld, their gardins did deface,
> Their arbers spoyle, their Cabinets suppresse,
> Their banket houses burne, their buildings race,
> And of the fairest late, now made the fowlest place. (2.12.83)

Whereas Guyon's "wrathfulnesse" might suggest an intemperate response, his violence is commensurate with the excesses of the space and is fully in line with the violence proposed in the *View* vital to turning Ireland from "savage" to "civil." Guyon's complete devastation of all indications of workmanship and artifice in this space is a *necessary* component to the development of his virtuous Temperance, and it recalls how Spenser's *View* advocates "reformation" in Ireland "Even by the sword" (93). In fact, Guyon's destruction of the Bower of Bliss mimics the scorched earth policy in Ireland, which entailed burning fields and villages to forcibly depopulate areas that would later be reclaimed by New English settlers, the land redistributed and cultivated by English men and women. That Spenser personally engaged in such

---

17 To make this distinction, Melaney contrasts the Platonic versus Aristotelian notions of Temperance; Spenser, he argues, suggests a definition of Temperance more in line with Aristotle's views.

policies suggests that his depiction of Guyon's "rigor pitilesse" falls in line with what was considered the ready path to civility.

Guyon thus enacts what Irenaeus proposes in the *View* as the means by which civilization might return to the Irish landscape. Civilization depends on both a change in the landscape and a change in the men turned to beasts when they submitted to their excessive desire and made Acrasia authority over them and their manhood. Verdant, who rests in Acrasia's lap at the beginning of the episode, is captured but ultimately released before Guyon destroys the bower, to receive "counsell sage" and repent for losing his "nobilitie" under Acrasia's seductive charms. In this context, Verdant stands in for the Old English in Ireland who had, as Spenser writes in the *View* become "meere Irish," reduced to degenerate and savage sub-humans; and, as other scholars have noted, Grill represents the Old English in Ireland who refuse to reform.[18] Guyon calls Grill the "beastly man, / That hath so soone forgot the excellence / Of his creation" (2.12.87). When Guyon destroys the garden and releases the men-turned-beasts, he prepares the landscape for its rejuvenation in Book 3 as the Garden of Adonis. Given this context for understanding Canto 12, Guyon must destroy the Bower, just as a gardener must plow under the soil if he is to plant his seeds and make the landscape productive, and just as the New English were convinced they must use violence to squelch signs of dissent or rebellion.

"In that Gardin planted bee againe": The Garden of Adonis, Book 3

The Garden of Adonis in Book 3 functions as a revised garden space made possible by the violent reclamation of the Bower of Bliss at the end of Book 2, and it exemplifies the conditions for and material signs of cultivating a gentleman so central to Spenser's Irish text and epic poem. It is, we learn, "So faire a place, as Nature can deuize" and "the first seminarie / Of all things, that are borne to liue and die, / According to their kindes" (3.6.29,30). Like the Garden of Eden, all things originate in this garden, where order according to "kindes" prevails in much the same way as it was "spoken by th'Almightie Lord" in the beginning (3.6.34). In the Garden of Adonis, just as gardening manuals suggested should be true of ideal English gardens, Spenser goes back to the beginning, to the Edenic garden created by God as the paragon of God's perfection on earth, and the foundation for what he will plant in the garden created and legislated by his own poetic authority, a garden unlike the uncultivated Irish land or Book 2's dangerous gardens.

If in Acrasia's garden, pleasure, excess, and artifice stunt growth and mobility, rendering the knights who linger there immobile and animalistic, in the Garden of

---

18   Cavanaugh, for example, claims in "Licentious Barbarism" that Grill represents the Old English who turn from their English identity (271). Freerick similarly relates Verdant and Mordant to those who have substituted their Englishness for Irishness, arguing that "Mordant and Verdant are linked by their failure in submitting to Acrasia and in thereby severing themselves from honorable genealogies, "erasing" both themselves and their offspring. In the text's characteristic punning, that is, they have 'raced' their 'races'."

Adonis one discovers the source of life, perpetual movement, and eternal mutability.[19] The "thousand thousand naked babes" that come and go from the gates originate in this garden, receive bodies, and are sent out into the world, where they dwell until they die and return to the garden to be purified of their "fleshly corruption" and "mortall paine." Genius, who mans the gate, sends them

> forth to liue in mortall state,
> Till they againe returne backe by the hinder gate.
> After that they againe returned beene,
> They in that Gardin planted bee againe;
> And grow afresh, as they had neuer seene
> Fleshly corruption, nor mortall paine. (3.6.32–33)

Like the "naked babes" who are "planted" in this Garden, Spenser's *View* holds that once Irish customs are "rooted out," the New English may be "sowed and sprinckled" there (144). The fleshly excess key to Acrasia's seductive power, and central to the garden space where she is sovereign, is revised in the Garden of Adonis, where the "mortall state" is shed and where the babes "grow afresh." The Garden of Adonis resembles the Paradise created by God, and its gates are monitored by Genius; spontaneous, asexual reproduction renders bodily form, so that the "corruption" of the fleshly maternal body, and a female source of generation, might be bipassed entirely.

While this garden closely resembles Acrasia's Bower in form and structure, it serves a radically different symbolic purpose. Like Acrasia's bower, this garden is located on fertile soil:

> It sited was in fruitfull soyle of old,
> And girt in with two walles on either side;
> The one of yron, the other of bright gold,
> That none might thorough breake, nor ouer-stride:
> And double gates it had, which opened wide,
> By which both in and out men moten pas. (3.6.31)

Whereas Acrasia's bower was established on fertile land, its fence "weake and thin," and its walls neither prevented "unruly beastes" from entering nor prevented "entred guests" from exiting, the Garden of Adonis has a fortified wall that none may "breake." As opposed to just containing the pleasurable contents as we see in the Bower of Bliss, the perimeter of this garden is defensive, structurally sound, and it modulates the flow in and out of the garden.

The Garden of Adonis is characterized by perpetual re-creation and flow, which proves a stark contrast to the stagnation typified in Acrasia's garden space. From this perfected garden, all beings come and go, "like a wheel around they runne from old to new":

---

19   See Spenser's *The Cantos of Mutabilitie* (1609), in which he develops this theme further.

Daily they grow, and daily forth are sent
Into the world, it to replenish more;
Yet is the stock not lessened, nor spent,
But still remaines in euerlasting store,
As it at first created was of yore. (3.6.33, 36)

Not only do all things originate in and return to this garden ad infinitum, but what is contained in the Garden of Adonis perpetuates in "euerlasting store." Flux and productive change characterize this garden space, but only in the context of this garden as a perfected model of what was "first created." The only mortal being we see in the Garden of Adonis is Adonis himself, whom, we are told, "All be he subiect to mortalitie, / Yet is eterne in mutabilitie, / And by succession made perpetuall" (3.6.47). Mutability and immortality are interchangeable terms in the Garden of Adonis, as mutability here reaffirms eternal, immutable perfection.[20]

While the Garden of Adonis is a "ioyous Paradize" and may resemble the garden at the end of Book 2, it differs radically from the earlier gardens of excess, pleasure, and artifice in that it is represented as a natural Paradise, defying the need for human labor in the first place. Deep within the recesses of this garden, "There was a pleasant arbour, not by art, / But of the trees owne inclination made" (3.6.44). We find hyacinths, eglantine, and narcissus, "To whom sweet Poets verse hath giuen endlesse date" (3.6.44). And at the same time, "Infinite shapes of creatures there are bred, / And uncouth formes, which none yet euer knew, / And euery sort is in a sundry bed / Set by it selfe, and ranckt in comely rew" (3.6.35). In this garden, moreover, where the trees shape themselves into arbors, and the "uncouth formes" organize themselves into beds:

Ne needs there Gardiner to set, or sow,
To plant or prune; for of their owne accord
All things, as they created were, doe grow,
…Ne doe they need with water of the ford,
Or of the clouds to moysten their roots dry;
For in themselues eternall moisture they imply. (3.6.34)

Within the Garden of Adonis, plants spontaneously emerge, a self-regenerative ecosystem that perpetually reproduces Paradisal conditions without the help of a gardener. If the Garden of Adonis is a revision of the Bower of Bliss, then Guyon's labor of violence at the end of Book 2 eliminates the excesses in the gardens in that book and restores the "fruitful soyle" that lies beneath the Garden of Adonis, which in turn means that the fertile conditions of this garden no longer need to be mediated by human endeavor. The Garden of Adonis does not require a gardener because Guyon's labor at the end of Book 2 has already restored paradise—and, if labor perfects what is imperfect because of a postlapsarian state, then here such a purpose is moot because this garden resembles instead the unfallen landscape first created by God and is, therefore, always-already perfect.

---

20   This notion appears elsewhere in Spenser's writing, as it does, for example, in *The Cantos of Mutabilitie*, which show that "mutability," or change, over time, actually produces a kind of stability or timelessness.

The parallels between the Garden of Adonis and Ireland-as-garden in the *View* seem to break down at this point, then. In Spenser's *View*, industry is not only applauded but is essential to civility, whereas in the Garden of Adonis labor appears to be unnecessary. Whereas Spenser's Garden of Adonis is an ideal garden plot, Ireland-as-garden in the *View* takes into account the practical limitations of a fallen world and a fallen landscape. In the *View*, husbandry is one of the primary indicators of civility and a deterrent of idleness and barbarism:

> The first thing therefore that wee are to draw these new tythed men into, ought to be husbandry. First, because it is the most easie to be learned, needing onely the labour of the body. Next, because it is most generall and most needful; then because it is the most naturall; and lastly, because it is most enemy to warre, and most hateth unquietnes … for husbandry being the nurse of thrift, and the daughter of industrie and labour, detesteth all that may worke her scathe, and destroy the travaile of her hands, whose hope is all her lives comfort unto the plough. (149)

New English settlers are to "keep a plough going … to the love of peace and civility," and they promise great profits and social order to those who farm the fertile land (150). Labor and industry are, therefore, essential parts of Spenser's vision for Ireland-as-garden, while in the Garden of Adonis they are unnecessary components of order. The Garden of Adonis depicts the garden's inherent perfection, a state possible for a poet's imaginings even if not manifest on the actual landscape where the poet imagines.

These differences seem especially apt when one considers the inescapable differences between Spenser's twin roles as Irish colonizer and as poet. In the Garden of Adonis, Spenser can imagine and create a perfect garden space of his own making unhindered by the actual constraints of a fallen landscape. What Spenser critiques in the gardens of Book 2, and what his revision implies, then, is the notion that art only imitates nature, that art does not improve it, which recalls the poet-gardener connections discussed in Chapter 1, such as we find in John Rea's *Flora*. Here, Spenser-as-poet creates a model of the perfect conditions represented in Paradise. That early modern gardens sought to recreate these conditions in a fallen world would have been a familiar notion to Spenser. Even more immediately relevant is the link he makes between replanting Ireland and recreating the idealized conditions present in Ireland before the degeneration of the landscape and the English who were originally planted on it.

Just as Guyon's labor restores paradise and makes possible the Garden of Adonis, so too does poetry make it possible to create a perfected garden, while colonization can best be conceived of in terms of maximizing, not perfecting, the landscape's potential. In the dedicatory sonnets to both the Earl of Ormond and Lord Grey, two companions in Irish colonization, Spenser equates his composition of *The Faerie Queene* to an act of cultivation, its textual form to "fruit" grown on the landscape where they both sought to cultivate the Irish. Spenser urges Lord Grey to receive his "Rude rymes, the which a rustick Muse did weaue / In savadge soyle, far from Parnasso mount," and in the sonnet to Ormond he identifies his poem as "wilde fruit" of a "saluage soyl" and proclaims his "fruit of barren field" a restorative that the

Earl could relate to because he, too, lived in Ireland and was complicit in the same colonizing endeavor as the poet himself:

> Receiue most noble Lord a simple taste
> Of the wilde fruit, which saluage soyl hath bred,
> Which being though long wars left almost waste,
> With brutish barbarisme is ouerspredd:
> And in so faire a land, as may be redd,
> Not one Parnassus, nor one Helicone
> Left for sweet Muses to be harboured,
> But where thy selfe hast thy braue mansione;
> There in deede dwel faire Graces many one …
> Such therefore, as that wasted soyl doth yield,
> Receiue dear Lord in worth, the fruit of barren field.[21]

As Spenser reminds his patrons, his purpose is to create "fruit" out of the waste and barren landscape, a change that resonated in Guyon's destruction of the Bower of Bliss to create the productive and fertile Garden of Adonis. Reading the Garden of Adonis as a revision of the Bower of Bliss thus links Spenser's project of cultivating Ireland-as-garden and his own poem as bringing the "fruit" that comes from the "saluage soil" by virtue of the competent land management of the poet/colonizer.

Growing Distance: Spenser and Elizabeth

That excesses and mismanagement of the garden space are violently reclaimed and later reimagined as the perpetually reproductive garden space under the male poet/ Irish colonizer's control resonates with the directives in so many gardening manuals from the period that imagined men as the real authorities in the garden. Spenser's description of the Garden of Adonis seems to negate the importance of human labor and artifice, but its constitutive elements mimic the most formal, aesthetic qualities of early modern English gardens which conferred artistic status upon their creators. While the Bower of Bliss rests under the female sorceress's dominion, the Garden of Adonis exists at least in part because of the male knight's violent suppression of her authority and obliteration of the garden space she presided over; once seized by the male knight, this garden ultimately re-emerges as uniquely under the control not of one of the poem's virtuous characters, but rather of the poet himself, who alone uses his art to re-create the dimensions of the garden space.

As such, Spenser's revision of the garden space in these episodes also points to a critique of Elizabeth's authority over her (male) English subjects in her employ in Ireland. While scholars have already suggested the allegorical relationship between Acrasia and Mary, Queen of Scots, the garden spaces in Book 2 also point to a

---

21 See the dedicatory sonnet to Lord Grey: "To the Most Renowmed and Valiant Lord, the Lord Grey of Wilton, Knight of the Noble Order of the Garter, &c." (29); see also "To the Right Honourable the Earle of Ormond and Ossory" (28).

Fig. 3   Plate XII, John Derricke, *The Image of Irelande* (1581)

critique of Elizabeth as female monarch in authority over a *male* colonizing project.[22] To contextualize this debate, let us turn to two competing versions of colonization, both present in a woodcut from John Derricke's *The Image of Irelande* that attests to the contested authority over Irish rule (Fig 3).[23]

Derricke's depiction of these two versions of the same Lord Deputy, one subject to his queen and one who makes the Irish his subjects, suggests that Sidney was regarded as more than just a representative of his queen; he was also a substitute for Elizabeth. The woodcut pictures Henry Sidney, then Lord Deputy of Ireland, in seated rule over the supplicant Irish men who kneel at his feet. Pictured here (and in the other plates from Derricke's text) at the height of his power after putting down the rebellion headed by Turlogh Lynagh O'Neale, Sidney is not so much as proxy for his monarch back home, but very-nearly as sovereign himself. However, the caption below the woodcut emphasizes his potentially contestatory role as both loyal subject and queen's representative:

> Who promiste then by pledge of life, of vertue of his hand,
> For euer to her noble grace, a subject true to stand,
> And to defend in each respect, her honour and her name,
> Agaynst all those that durst deface the glory of the same.

---

22   See Hadfield, *Edmund Spenser's Irish Experience* 13–50 for a broad contextualization of the crisis of the 1590s and the conflict between Elizabeth and the male undertakers over authority in Ireland.

23   Hadfield likewise suggests that this depiction of Sidney reflects what we might interpret as an "alternative," not just representative authority in Ireland (14).

Which things, with other accions moe, redound vnto the fame
Of good Syr Henry Sydney, Knight, so called by his name.
Loe where he sittes in honours seate, most comely to be seene,
As worthy for to represent the person of a Queene.[24]

In the upper left corner followed by his knights an alternative Henry Sidney is pictured. As ambassador of England, Sidney kneels to receive the penitent rebels, while below, we witness Henry Sidney, clothed in finery as he "sittes in honours seate," poised upon what might pass as a throne, which represents him as a surrogate monarch in the absence of the queen across the sea. Sidney's position in the woodcut is so ambiguous that it leads Andrew Hadfield to ask, "Was Sidney standing for the absent power of the crown, a manifestation of its necessary displacement? Or was he seeking to usurp the authority of English prerogative based at Westminster by claiming greater legal power for the office of a vice-royalty in Ireland?" (Hadfield and Maley, *Representing Ireland* 14).

Derricke's *The Image of Irelande* casts Sidney as hero, much as Spenser's *Faerie Queene* portrays the valiant knight at its narrative center, not the queen herself. Like Derricke's Sidney, Spenser's knights pursue virtue on behalf of their absent Fairy Queen. As the woodcut bears witness, their noble deeds confer an authority that stands on its own. The representation of Sidney receiving the Irish karne at his feet like a king at court dominates the space of the woodcut, placing the Sidney-as-ambassador image in the distant background. Similarly, Spenser repeatedly reminds the reader of the significance of the Fairy Queen to the knightly quest (and often refers directly to Elizabeth) in the Proems, but the several stanzas devoted to his sovereign are easily shadowed by the arguably more interesting challenges faced by Red Crosse, Guyon, and others. It is *their* pursuit of fame and virtue, one might argue, that Spenser's epic poem finally celebrates, not Elizabeth's.

That Spenser's reorientation of authority takes place in the gardens in Books 2 and 3 is conceivably possible in direct relation to the historical context of gendered gardening practice and garden spaces in early modern England. Such revisionist garden episodes play out cultural anxieties about how, on the one hand, Elizabeth defied convention by being a woman in power and, as Louis Montrose argues, Elizabethan texts "illuminate the interplay between sexual politics in the Elizabethan family and sexual politics in the Elizabethan monarchy, for the woman to whom *all* Elizabethan men were vulnerable was Queen Elizabeth herself"; and, on the other, as Maureen Quilligan shows, Elizabeth's female rulership was a "shock to the patriarchal system" that needed to be recuperated by the ideological function of masculinizing court literature.[25] Seeing gardening practice linked to the way Spenser imagines the efficacy of gardens in his writing gives us a point of entry into the territory where claims for gendered authority collide when ideology meets with material practice. By the late sixteenth century, when Spenser writes *The Faerie Queene*, gardening for profit as well as pleasure (and professional status) was increasingly marked as men's endeavor, which conferred economic and social authority on the men in charge of

---

24   See Plate XII of John Derricke, *The Image of Irelande*.

25   Montrose, "Shaping Fantasies" (77); Quilligan, "The Comedy of Female Authority in *The Faerie Queene*" (163).

such gardens. At the same time, women's gardening was developing as a separate domain, which coincided with developing codes of domesticity, and both had similar aims: to encourage women to withdraw from the public sphere of the marketplace (and thus the spaces of economic exchange) to the private spaces of the house and use their skills for decoration. Spenser positions his revision of authority, therefore, squarely in the center of a material context in which a similar negotiation of authority is at the heart of changes to the early modern landscape and domestic sphere.

However, the revisionist gardens in *The Faerie Queene* also play out very specific, material complaints about Elizabeth's Irish policy, suggested in more subtle ways in Derricke's woodcuts, but in more overt ways in other published writings. Richard Beacon, who served in Ireland in the later sixteenth century during the height of the plantation campaign, implicates Elizabeth in the English failure up to that point to "reform" Ireland and accuses her of being too lenient in her administration of it. In *Solon his Follie* (1594), Beacon implores his queen to bestow his "Majesties accustomed clemency," an ironic plea for Elizabeth's sympathy toward *him*, since he readily proposes excessive force, not clemency, as necessary to reforming the Irish.[26] Barnaby Rich, who also served in Ireland during this period, writes that through "overmuch clemency" Elizabeth had "defeated her selfe."[27] Such criticism may well have been in response to Elizabeth's effective pardoning of key rebels in 1581 ("By the Queene") and, later, all Irish who desired to be known as English subjects, as she states in a proclamation of 1587: "For so is her Princely mind disposed, to make no difference for respect of Persons or Countrey, against Justice, esteeming the Noblemen and good Subjects of that Land, as deare in degree of subjection, as any borne in England, making no difference betwixt the one and the other" ("By the Queene"). In 1607, King James revokes the amnesty bestowed on the Earles of Tyrone and Tyrconnell (two of the key Irish rebels mentioned in her earlier proclamations) by Elizabeth and by himself earlier in his reign and calls them "monsters in nature." And, in 1626, E.C.S. publishes a text that looks back on Elizabeth's Irish policy between 1584 and 1588 with contempt. In the long dedication "To the Reader," E.C.S. rails against Elizabeth's ineffective approach of pardoning and taking pity

---

26 See "The Epistle Dedicatorie" to Elizabeth in Beacon (4). In this tract, Beacon proposes a tiered system of reform, which involves first attempting to persuade a "declined" country to reform, and later, if such persuasions fail, using necessary violence to force compliance and reform. I would argue that, while Beacon offers peaceful negotiation as an alternative, he seems to have little faith that negotiations would actually work to enact reform on a large scale. This attitude prevailed in his actual experience in Ireland, during which time he openly advocated, along with Spenser and others, violence as the means to subdue the Irish and impose English rule. See 61–64 and 66–71, where Beacon describes "cutting up all mischiefes by the rootes" and argues, "For not thoroughly conquering our enemy, neither by sworde, neither yet by our bountie and liberalitie, we may not long holde them, either as subjects or friends" (67, 71).

27 Qtd. in Highley (71). Highley characterizes New English criticism about Elizabeth's foreign policy in Ireland as "widespread" and writes, "Disaffection with Elizabeth's handling of Irish policy, especially with her sensitivity to Old English opinion and her reluctance to prosecute large-scale war, was widespread among the cadre of New Englishmen who took up posts in Ireland from mid-century" (70).

on the Irish and advocates more violence still as the only means by which the Irish might be subdued. Text after text published both during and after Elizabeth's reign reflect deep skepticism about Elizabeth's ability to quell rebellion in Ireland and offer instead violence as the only way to reform, a path that they argue Elizabeth herself was unwilling to take.

Spenser's use of gardens in Book 3 reiterates this skepticism over Elizabeth's Irish policy and further confirms what Louis Montrose argues of Spenser's work in general and points to a rather arrogant claim, that *he* confers status and notoriety to Elizabeth and to England, not the other way around.[28] In the stanzas that precede the description of the Garden of Adonis, Belphoebe (who Spenser writes in the Proem of Book 3 is a shadow of Elizabeth) and her twin Amoret are "fruitfull seades" that spring from the "saluage forests" and "wild woods." Conceived without fleshly pleasure, delivered without pain, these twins are separated at birth; Diana takes Belphoebe, who is characterized by her "fresh-flowring Maidenhead," to be raised with the Nymphs, and Venus takes Amoret to be raised in the Garden of Adonis until, we are told, "she to perfect ripenesse grew" (3.6.28, 52). Although presumably taken to the same "wastefull woods" where Venus finds Diana early in the Canto, Belphoebe "was trayned vp from time to time, / In all chaste vertue, and true bounti-hed / Till to her dew perfection she was ripened" (3.6.3). Just as Spenser isolates his role as creator of the "fruits" in the gardens he writes, he here seems to suggest that he might isolate Elizabeth as one of the "fruitfull seades" of his making.[29] As a mirror of Elizabeth, Belphoebe is seized by the poet's capable hand to be "trayned up," "ripened," and then released.

Spenser's account of the conception and birth of Belphoebe and her twin Amoret is strategically linked with his description of the Garden of Adonis later in the same canto as if to suggest that they derive mutually from Spenser's poetic impulse. But his creative prowess in the context of his relationship to Elizabeth vis-à-vis the English colonial project in Ireland positions him as master over her, the Irish landscape, and its inhabitants. Using actual gardens and the colonizing project in Ireland as a context for understanding these episodes in *The Faerie Queene*, then, not only helps situate Spenser's realignment of authority relative gardening practice (where a similar realignment was taking place), but also helps explain how Spenser might, as both Mary Villeponteax and Maureen Quilligan conclude, represent Elizabeth's "femaleness" as idealized and her "political sovereignty" as less than certain.[30] As in the Garden of Adonis, Belphoebe and Amoret are conceived out of chaste reproduction, "enwombed" in Amphisa's "chaste body" and are progeny conceived outside of "fleshly slime" (3.6. 3). Spenser's "mirrors" of Elizabeth are the flowers that come into being and "ripen" in the garden space over which he stands sovereign as poet and over which, if the Garden of Adonis resembles the

---

28   See Montrose, "Eliza."

29   Villeponteaux calls Belphoebe a "literary 'mask of youth' through which the poet implicitly criticizes his queen" (209). Throughout the essay, Villeponteaux situates Spenser's critique of Belphoebe and Britomart in the context of the unnatural female ruler, Radigund of Book V.

30   See Villeponteaux (209) and Quilligan, "Female Authority" (163).

perfected Irish landscape "ripe" for colonization, the other male undertakers like him also stand in authority rather than as subjects. Because Spenser was in Ireland, not in England, when he imagined these gardens, he could create distance between this conceptual versus actual realignment of authority. After all, Elizabeth's authority was fundamentally splintered in Ireland; she may have been its official sovereign, but Spenser and the other male undertakers acted on a daily basis as its immediate authorities. She may have been the figurehead of the Irish garden, but they directed its planting. In depicting Belphoebe and Amoret as flowers subject to ripening in this garden space, Spenser not only positions himself and the other male undertakers as no longer in need of a queen to rule over them or their Irish subjects, but, like the female dedicatees of John Rea's *Flora* discussed in Chapter 1, he even more boldly depicts her as coming into being in the same way the garden does: through the masterful stroke of his pen.

Spenser's revision of the garden in fact places creative authority in the hands of men. Whereas scholars like Lauren Silberman and Maureen Quilligan interpret the Garden of Adonis as a "privileged site of feminine production," I would argue instead, as Katherine Eggert does, that the gendered authority in this space is far more ambiguously constructed.[31] Spenser makes it clear that in the Garden of Adonis Venus may luxuriate in her "joyous Paradise" enjoying the company of her lover, but she did not create it; she is neither its author nor does she have authority over its constituent parts. In fact, Venus and Adonis are both subjects in this garden, much like Adam and Eve were the first subjects under God in the Garden of Eden. In so constructing them, Spenser inserts himself into the position originally occupied by God, thereby realigning his own role as "Author"/sovereign/ creator, with implications, to be sure, for his role vis-à-vis his own ostensible sovereign, Elizabeth. This restored garden space, having eliminated the dangerous female authority of the garden spaces in Book 2, resembles the restored landscape Spenser readily imagines is possible in Ireland under the aegis of the male undertakers and governors there.

Considering the garden episodes in the early books of Spenser's *Faerie Queene* in light of the New English agenda for "reforming" Ireland sheds light on how Spenser imagined making space for (masculinized) Englishness to prevail in Ireland and for himself as poet and participant in Irish colonization. Spenser represented garden spaces in a way that liberated him to some degree from the traditional shackles of the courtly relationship between male subject and female sovereign. While scholars readily point out the Irish context of a more pessimistic Book 5, the gardens in the early books, published during the still-hopeful period of the Munster Plantation,

---

31 See Quilligan, *Milton's Spenser*, especially 191–94 and Silberman, "Singing Unsung Heroines." Eggert argues that, beginning with the Garden of Adonis, "*The Faerie Queene* starts to expose its own feminized poetics as eminently unsatisfying...From the midpoint of Book 3 in the Garden of Adonis this feminine center will not hold; rather the narrative embarks upon a sea of digressions that, like the sea at whose edge the habitually pursued Florimell makes yet another near escape (3.7.27), offers no assurance of fruitful outcome" (32–33). While Eggert contextualizes her reading of this scene in terms of narrative strategy and the gendered use of language, her conclusions concur with my own—that the "fruitful outcome" in these episodes are possible only by way of proper cultivation by a male authority, whether that authority is a male New English undertaker in Ireland or the male poet.

reveal optimism about the potential for colonizing Ireland that all but disappears later. By the time the final three books were published in 1596, the Munster Plantation was threatened by imminent rebellions by the Irish, one of which resulted in the sacking and burning of Spenser's own castle Kilcolman in 1598, which would, no doubt, have clouded his depiction of the imperative to colonize the barbaric Irish.

That the garden is a model in the early books, not in the later ones, for this colonization through cultivation practices and the revamping of Irish customs reflects the hopefulness and idealism early in the process that became increasingly jaded and cynical later. Spenser's garden spaces in Books 2 and 3 depict the civilizing forces imposed on an Irish landscape through its cultivation by New English settlers. From 1584–1590, when a majority of these lands were distributed and when the plantation process was still ripe with potential (even if that potential had yet to ripen), Spenser most likely composed Books 1–3 of his epic poem. During this time, he was most active in the early "planting" of the Irish countryside with gardens and arable fields resembling those in England, with the New English men and women who would help cultivate the landscape and propagate the virtues of English cultural values. His epic poem, *The Faerie Queene*, offers a literary enactment of this "planting" whereby Guyon takes on the role of New English colonizer/gardener and clears the land of people and plants that impede the cultivation (and civilization) process, thus readying the landscape for the ideal gardens to grow.

In short, Spenser helped develop another England on an island across the sea at the same time he helped define Englishness through the knightly virtues of Temperance and Chastity. As an undertaker and administrator in this English colony, Spenser was a co-creator of this other England, and the garden scenes in the early books of his *Faerie Queene* most certainly position him as creator in the garden where he restores life and productivity to a barren landscape. To do so, Spenser stakes a claim for himself as an independent authority over his female monarch while he simultaneously sings her praises. Elizabeth may be Gloriana, or the teleological endpoint of each knightly quest. But Elizabeth is also a divided image: she is Belphobe and Amoret, the twin "seedes" that Spenser "grows" in the Garden of Adonis; her negative attributes are mirrored in Phaedra, Philotime, and Acrasia, whose seductive allure stalls the knightly journey toward reform and who must be confronted and captured before order can be restored. What Guyon destroys, Spenser recreates, claiming a position for himself and for the men with whom he served in Ireland separate from his sovereign and unique to themselves. The gardens in Books 2 and 3, that is, like the Ireland-as-garden throughout Spenser's *View* serve "both to let you see what it now is, and also what it may bee by good care and amendment" (*View* 160).

Chapter 3

Inheritance, Land, and the Garden Space for Women in Aemilia Lanyer's *Salve Deus Rex Judaeorum* ("Hail, God, King of The Jews")

By the early seventeenth century, when Aemilia Lanyer published *Salve Deus Rex Judaeorum* (1611) the garden had become an increasingly *gendered* space, one in which men and women vied for positions of authority. Not long after Lanyer's publication, for example, William Lawson's companion manuals appeared, *A New Orchard and Garden* and *The Countrie Hovsewife's Garden* (1618), which rendered more distinct boundaries than before between gardens for men and gardens for women. Men may have competed for status and economic returns as gardening experts and landholders, as we see in Spenser's case, but women vied for status that stemmed from the decorative uses they made of land, rather than from land ownership itself. On the one hand, women were increasingly encouraged to plant flower gardens, which mobilized positive associations of women as creative agents; on the other, the land on which women planted their gardens was more often than not the legal property of their husbands, fathers, or brothers, which reinforced notions of women's dependence on men. As William Lawson assures his housewife with a green thumb, her garden will be the result of her "delight and direction," but if that housewife is married, which Lawson's manual presumes she is, the garden she plants would be on her husband's legal property, not her own. Aemilia Lanyer's poetry draws on the idea that women might make gardens of their own and represents the garden as an ideal space for women to recoup the actual, material losses they experience when disenfranchised from property and land ownership; at the same time, her text suggests that this recuperation is an imagined ideal more than it is a material reality.

Lanyer publishes *Salve Deus* as a book with three distinct parts: first, eleven dedicatory poems, all to women; second, a long religious poem that depicts the Passion of Christ and which includes passages that interrupt the narrative in which she addresses directly to Margaret Clifford (her primary dedicatee of the book); and finally, what is perhaps the first country house poem in English (and certainly the first by a woman), which takes place at the Cooke-ham estate. Although the three parts of Lanyer's book appear to address disjunct subject matter, they are in fact linked thematically in terms of issues of land ownership. In the dedicatory material, she represents women as similarly and wrongly alienated from the property that belongs to them. Then, in her long poem on Christ's Passion, Lanyer revises conventional discourse about the Fall and Christ's death and resurrection, a discourse that underwrote men's claims of superiority and prohibited women (especially married) from owning land and property in early modern England. Women in early modern England had limited access to land ownership, but, in Lanyer's poem, Christ offers the promise of their inheriting "lands" in heaven. Finally, in her country house poem, "The Description of Cooke-ham," Lanyer represents the garden space where she and two other women find community with each other at the Cooke-ham estate.

Land is the common material sign of women's alienation, but the garden in Lanyer's book serves as the pivotal site for women to reclaim it, even if such reclamation is ultimately untenable in the most practical, everyday terms. The Garden of Gethsemane in the "Salve Deus" is the place both "blest" and "curst," Lanyer writes, since it is there that Christ ratifies the messianic prophecy that brings salvation, yet also where he is betrayed by one of his disciples and issued to his death. In Lanyer's country house poem, "To Cooke-ham," the garden is also a place both blessed and cursed. Lanyer's Cooke-ham garden is a recreation of the Edenic garden, an as-yet unblemished manifestation of God's prelapsarian perfection on earth that predates the social injunctions against women's land ownership and their subjection to men. Yet the Cooke-ham garden simultaneously represents their dispossession and exile. If the Garden of Gethsemane offers Lanyer's female readers the promise of salvation and inheriting the kingdom of heaven later, the Cooke-ham garden offers them the hope of enjoying the circumstances of Edenic perfection in the present, perpetually re-experienced in Lanyer's poetry and in the memory of the women who lived there with her. Lanyer's garden spaces call attention to women's unjustifiable subjection to men on earth; yet they also serve as an alternative spaces that women might call their own. Moreover, while scholars tend to regard the three parts of Lanyer's *Salve Deus* as separate pieces, conjoined in publication more than in theme, I show here how the three parts form a unified garden space of Lanyer's making.

"Yea in his kingdome onely rests my lands": Earthly Disinheritance in the Dedicatory Poems

Aemilia Lanyer's dedicatory material serves as the staging ground to establish how women of different classes similarly experience the inability legally to own land. She foregrounds women whose "Virtue" supersedes their earthly merits, such as fame and beauty, and who hold a more significant claim, or "title," to the kingdom and "lands" in heaven. While Lanyer represents the women in her dedicatory material as having been prohibited in one way or another from owning land or made subject to their husbands, Lanyer confers upon them a spiritual authority, such that their exemplary virtue makes them worthy of a different husband, Christ, who will restore their inheritance and reward them with "lands" in heaven.

That Lanyer addresses her book to women whose rights, especially those related to land ownership and inheritance, were most likely compromised in England during this period bears directly on the argument found later in the "Salve Deus" and her country house poem. Isolating land as both the problem and, later, the resolution, lends the series of poems a thematic unity and binds the women together, even though the English social system, governed by men, sought to keep them apart. Nearly one-third of the women Lanyer addresses are "Dowagers," or widows, and she appeals to most of her patrons in terms of their own personal, material losses of land or other property; the rest of the women in her dedicatory poems are wives, and Lanyer similarly appeals to their material losses from their status as a feme covert.[1]

Englishwomen like those to whom Lanyer writes found themselves vulnerable to evolving English legal codes that governed inheritance portions for widows and daughters. In theory, wives retained as their "jointure," or estate portion left to them by their husbands, the property they brought with them into marriage. In practice, however, this was not always the case. In fact, Amy Louise Erickson estimates that wives retained rights to their pre-marriage property as little as ten percent of the time; women from lower classes were more likely to retain what they brought with them when they married, while women of the merchant and gentry classes or the aristocracy were less likely to do so because of the greater value and dynastic interests in distributing the lands in other ways.[2] English law did not always honor the expectation that widows be able to keep their premarital property either. Ecclesiastical law dictated that when a husband died one-third of the total estate went to his widow and one-third to any surviving children. Although women's property legally became their husbands' upon marriage, ecclesiastical law presented women with the option of regaining some property they may have brought with them into the marriage. Under common law (which increasingly took precedence in the English legal system) a husband had more flexibility in distributing his estate, and widows and daughters were more likely to receive little or no inheritance. Only widowed and single women might own freehold land, and the economic and social position of widows was made complicated by difficulties in acquiring the land they were legally (or would have been legally) entitled to and their unmarried status (Laurence 229).[3] Under common law, widows had still more tenuous legal claim to property than they would have under ecclesiastical law.[4]

---

1   The spelling of this term is often disputed, so I have chosen to use Erickson's spelling. In *The Law's Resolution of Women's Rights* (1632), T.E. uses the same spelling. "Feme Covert" refers to the legal status of women's property rights once they married. As "hidden women," their wealth and property legally became half their husbands'. At the same time, even though husbands had legal claim to half of their wives' property, there was nothing to keep husbands from accessing its entirety without their wives' consent.

2   See Erickson, especially Chapter 6, "The nature of marriage settlements" (102–13), Chapter 8, "Marriage settlements in probate documents" (129–51), and Chapter 9, "Widows of men who made wills" (156–73).

3   See also Amussen, 91–98, and Mendelson and Crawford, 176–84. See also Erickson, 156–202, for a detailed account of the legal and social conditions for widows.

4   See Erickson 5–6 for further descriptions of this type of law and others relevant to property transmission and distribution. See also T.E., *The Law's Resolution of Women's Rights*, one of the first legal manuals published in England that covers this topic. This text is excerpted in Joan Klein, 27–61. Though not published until 1632, the information contained in it was based on legal statutes from as early as 1597–98.

The discriminatory nature of English jurisprudence necessitated that women enter into marriage with caution. Early modern legal writer T.E. writes *The Law's Resolution of Women's Rights* (1632) with the express interest in informing women how to protect their property once married. While his would have been considered a relatively liberal text, he nevertheless reiterates many of the dominant attitudes about the husband-wife relationship that undergirded restrictive English codes:

> But the prerogative of the husband is best discerned in his dominion over all extern things in which the wife by combination divestesth herself of propriety in some sort and casteth it upon her governor, for here practice everywhere agrees with the theoric of law, and forcing necessity submits women to the affection thereof. Whatsoever the husband had before coverture [a married woman's legal status] either in goods or lands, it is absolutely his own; the wife hath therein no seisin at all. If any thing when he is married be given him, he taketh it by himself distinctly to himself. If a man have right and title to enter into lands, and the tenant enfeoffe the baron and feme, the wife taketh nothing. The very goods which a man giveth to his wife are still his own: her chain, her bracelets, her apparel, are all the good-man's goods...For thus it is, if before marriage the woman were possessed of horses, neat, sheep, corn, wool, money, plate, and jewels, all manner of moveable substance is presently by conjunction the husband's, to sell, keep, or bequeath if he die. And though he bequesth them not, yet are they the husband's executor's and not the wife's. (46–47)

Once married, a woman could have her property exploited or squandered by her husband, and she had no legal recourse to reclaim or protect it; once widowed, a woman might find herself in possession of more freedom to do as she would choose, as T.E. elsewhere reassures widows, "now you be free in liberty, and free...at your own law," but she might not find herself with the land and property that should legally have been hers (29). English legal codes seemingly protected women's interests in the property they held before their marriage, but their husbands could effectively decide how they wanted to distribute all their property that had since become jointly owned as part of the marriage contract, and wives had little clear legal recourse to reclaim it.

Aemilia Lanyer and many of her dedicatees found themselves in this very position—as daughters and widows unable to lay claim to their family inheritance or as women whose husbands squandered the wealth their wives brought with them into marriage.[5] When Lanyer's father died, she inherited one hundred pounds, which she would (and did) inherit when she turned twenty or married; along with her sister and mother, she also inherited "the rentes yssued and proffitte of [her father's] three messuages or Tenements with their appurtenances situate and rentes yssued...and also use and occupation of the said three Tenements." (Woods, Introduction, xvii and n.3, xvi). Before Lanyer married, she was mistress to Henry Cary, Lord Hunsdon (Elizabeth I's Lord Chamberlain) and circulated among the courtly circles of influence and wealth. When she became pregnant (in all likelihood with Cary's child), she was married to Alphonso Lanyer, a court musician, and she

---

5   See Woods, Introduction, *The Poems of Aemilia Lanyer*. See also Woods's full-length study of Aemilia Lanyer, *Lanyer: A Renaissance Woman Poet*.

no longer enjoyed such a privileged lifestyle. Although she entered into marriage with a respectable inheritance, most of Lanyer's fortune vanished as a result of her husband's overspending. Once married, after all, her husband became the joint legal holder of her estate. Alphonso Lanyer did secure a grain and hay patent while they were married, which would have provided some security for Lanyer and her children after his death, but when Alphonso died in 1613, the patent became subject to legal battles between Lanyer and Alphonso's relatives that stretched over the next twenty years (Woods xxvii). Therefore, having come into the marriage with considerable wealth for a middle-class woman, and having prospects for increasing it later, Lanyer grew older with barely enough money in her pockets to feed herself.

Lanyer's primary dedicatees, Margaret and Anne Clifford, likewise, each suffered from their husbands' overspending and the law's preference for male relatives. Partners in an arranged marriage, Margaret and George Clifford were estranged from one another much of the time, and George had the reputation for being neither a good husband nor a good father. Nevertheless, historical records indicate that Margaret and Anne stood dutifully at his deathbed when his illness "brought with it some serious and compunctious feelings for his past domestic errors, and with them an entire reconciliation with those whom his previous indifference had estranged" (Wiffen 94).[6] When Margaret married George Clifford he possessed more land and wealth than any other member of the Clifford family at the time; when he died, he had the most modest fortune in his family. Despite the apparent deathbed reconciliation, George's will dictated that his estates would go to his brother, and that Anne would receive £15,000 compensation. It appears that Margaret, his widow, received little or nothing in the will, even though she should have been legally entitled to at least her "widow's portion," or one-third of the estate.

Anne and Margaret formally challenged the will in the English courts for over thirty years, their dispute based on Anne's claims to inheritance under inheritance laws that had governed the distribution of Clifford lands since the reign of Edward II. These laws promised the estates to any surviving children, male or female, and should have taken precedence over Clifford's will. At one point, Anne Clifford sought Queen Anne's intervention in the suit, but to no avail. King James declared that the estates remain in George's brother's name and that Anne Clifford would receive £20,000 in installments, to be paid once she agreed in writing that she had no rightful, legal claim over the land and property she had been seeking. Anne Clifford repeatedly refused to relinquish her suit, even when pressured by her husband to take the money, and even after he cut off her allowance.[7] In the end, Anne did receive her inheritance, but not because the courts favored her suit; Anne inherited her land by default after her uncle and cousin died, leaving her the only surviving Clifford heir.

Throughout her dedicatory material, Lanyer represents how many of her dedicatees have experienced similar losses, and she offers reassurance of their

---

6   See Woods, *Lanyer*, 28–32 for more details about Lanyer's relationship with Margaret and Anne Clifford and their attempts to reclaim their inheritance after the death of George Clifford in 1605. See also Lewalski, "Imagining."

7   See Lewalski, "Claiming," especially 125–30.

compensation in spiritual terms.[8] Many had been alienated or cast out of the spaces they might identify as their own, yet, in the poem, all are represented as sharing the same promise to inherit lands in heaven because of their exemplary virtue. In her dedication to Lady Susan Bertie, Lanyer consoles Susan and extols the fortitude her mother demonstrated while in exile during Mary Tudor's reign. Catherine, Duchess of Suffolk, fled England along with her daughter Susan to avoid religious persecution and, according to Lanyer, deserves to be commended because she "From Romes ridiculous prier and tyranny, / That mighty Monarchs kept in awful feare; / Leaving here her lands, her state, dignitie; / ...When with Christ Jesus she did meane to goe" (25–27, 29). Lanyer commends Catherine's self-imposed exile, when she left her "lands" and "estate" in England for religious reasons, a decision that constitutes virtue that Christ rewards with "lands" in heaven.

Lanyer's dedicatory poem to Catherine and her daughter Susan emphasizes how they lost and unsuccessfully fought to regain their inheritance, which makes them exemplary models of women displaced from their home and property.[9] Catherine (Willoughby) Bertie saw her first husband's estates all go to his two sons, leaving her widow of an extinct dukedom. When Susan Bertie's husband died, his earldom went to his younger brother. Since the couple had no children, Bertie's second husband may have reestablished her ties with money and the court, but, after fifteen years of marriage, he died and left her with only "three score and ten pound a year" (Barroll 33). Lanyer proposes that her book of poems will restore a sense of home to Susan, and Lanyer and Susan become figured as together energizing the place, the landscape itself, where virtue is visible: "You the Sunnes virtue, I that faire greene grasse / That flourish fresh by your cleere virtues taught" and, "Onely your noble Virtues do incite / My Pen, they are the ground I write upon" (9–10, 45–46). Using the theme of displacement or exile, Lanyer promises that she will restore Susan to her land; Lanyer becomes "the grasse" and, alternatively, Susan's patronage gives Lanyer the material security and inspiration to write, and becomes the "ground" out of which her poetic lines grow.

In the poems to Margaret, Countesse Dowager of Cumberland and her daughter, Anne Clifford, Lanyer similarly casts her patrons' virtuous suffering and redemptive potential in terms of materiality and "place." In this poem, Lanyer prioritizes the "health of the soule," which she calls the "pearle of all perfection," the "rich diamond of devotion," and the "perfect gold growing in the veines" of all virtuous women (10–12). As Amy Louise Erickson points out, however, secular wealth was defined by inheritance, and constituted "the most important component of wealth" for men or women, "whether that inheritance consisted of a landed estate, of a single cottage

---

8   The exceptions to this would be Queen Anne, Princess Elizabeth, and Arabella Stuart. The dedicatory poems to these women, however, focus on reorienting material, secular wealth to a more primary (and hierarchically preferable) spiritual wealth in heaven. Even if the three women mentioned here did not actually experience dispossession, they were subject to their husbands, a position that Lanyer proceeds to argue in "Salve Deus" is unnatural, too.

9   See Barroll, who refutes Lanyer's claim to have spent time with Lady Susan, Countess Dowager of Kent and goes to great lengths to argue that Lanyer constructs such a story of her involvement with the Countess as the means to appeal for patronage. Barroll also provides an account of the inheritance woes of Susan and her mother on 31–33.

and garden, or even of a cow, a kettle, a brass pan and a bed" (2). Therefore, when Lanyer focuses on the key material loss Margaret experienced, she supplies her with hope by re-contextualizing wealth and reward in spiritual instead of secular terms. This hope potentially applies to other women as well, since they too, experience this same kind of loss, according to the book, and Lanyer's re-contextualization also frames wealth in terms that casts Margaret as just one woman among many who has seen her wealth compromised by a legal system that favored men.

Lanyer further develops the same theme of material dispossession in the dedicatory poem to Anne Clifford. Here again, Lanyer re-places the property and land taken unjustifiably from these women with "the fittest place" in Anne's mind: "To you I dedicate this worke of Grace, / This frame of Glory which I have erected, / For your faire mind I hold the fittest place, / Where virtue should be settled and protected" (1–4). These lines assert a similitude between "this worke" (Lanyer's poem), which she "erects" as one might a house, and the "place" where "virtue" is "settled" and "protected." Lanyer frames her work as the edifice she erects to replace their displaced lands and estate. As was true in her poem to Susan Bertie, Lanyer contextualizes her hopeful message to her female patrons as restoring the "place" where their true virtue carries value.

In the context of Anne Clifford's actual struggle to repossess the land and property she lost when her father died, the theme of material dispossession in Lanyer's poem to Anne would have had a special resonance. Anne's personal account of her wrongful disinheritance suggests how women might be legally entitled to land and still dispossessed:

> Presently after the death of my father, I being left his sole daughter and heir, my dear mother, our of her affectionate care for my good, caused me to choose her my guardian, and then in my name began to sue out a livery in the Court of Wards for my right to all my father's lands, by way of prevention to the livery which my uncle of Cumberland intended to sue out in my name, without either my consent or my mother's, which caused great suits of law to arise between her and my uncle, which in effect continued, for one cause or other, during her life, in which she shewed a most brave spirit, and never yielded to any opposition whatsoever. In which business King James began to shew himself extremely against my mother and me; in which course he still pursued, though his wife Queen Anne was ever inclining to our part, and very gracious and favourable unto us...So about the 9th of June, in 1607, (to shew how much he was bent against my blessed mother and myself), he gave the reversion of all those lands in Westmoreland and Craven out of the crown, by patent to my uncle Francis, and to his heirs for ever...the grant of which to my uncle was done merely to defeat me. (Wiffen 95–96)

Anne and Margaret's struggles to inherit what George Clifford's will promised begins six years before Lanyer likely composed her *Salve Deus* (1611), including these dedicatory poems to Margaret and the other women and the country house poem that follows. Anne's account of the legal difficulties pits the women (with Queen Anne behind them) against King James, who, as Anne puts it, "shew[ed] himself extremely" against them. To remind Margaret, then, that her real treasure is in heaven deflects attention from and alleviates the stress associated with such legal matters as it simultaneously unites Lanyer, Margaret, and Anne—for all three (and, by extension, other women, too), wealth, land, and goods become things that they are entitled to but do not receive.

Authority to replace these losses, Lanyer argues in the letter to Anne, is not conferred by social rank but by God. Lanyer appropriates this divinely-ordained authority to question the class system that stratifies women (as well as men), when she says, "God makes both even, the Cottage and the Throne" and,

> Titles of honour which the world bestowes,
> To none but to the virtuous doth belong;
> As beauteous bowres where true worth should repose,
> And where his [God's] dwellings should be built most strong...
> All sprang but from one woman and one man,
> Then how doth Gentry come to rise and fall?
> Or who is he that very rightly can
> Distinguish of his birth, or tell at all,
> In what meane state his Ancestors have bin,
> Before some one of worth and honour did win? (19, 25–28, 35–40)

Lanyer reorients earthly authority, this time by calling into question conventional social hierarchies. What constitutes a "meane state" or high birth, Lanyer argues, (and quite pointedly to Anne, who had indeed seen her estate become more "meane" because of her legal problems) is arbitrarily determined; that women in early modern England, such as Margaret, Anne, and Lanyer herself, had possessions and "dwellings" revoked and handed over to men is contrary, Lanyer's poem seems to be suggesting here, to God's purpose. To do so contradicts the dominant discourse about women's "naturally" inferior status and necessary dependence on men, which underwrites the same English laws the poem here shows to be arbitrary and contrary to God's will.[10] By showing how social hierarchies involve arbitrary distinctions, Lanyer reframes not just the relationship between men and women, but also the relationship among all women. Unlike Milton's Eden, where gender hierarchy is present upon Adam and Eve's creation, hierarchies develop as a result of a fallen world in Lanyer's book. In fact, Lanyer boldly rewrites the literary tradition: hardly the inherently sinful or rebellious women so familiar to early modern readers, as descendants of Eve, all virtuous women in Lanyer's book deserve "titles of honour" and "beauteous bowres" on earth that reflect her revisionist take on the gendered power relationships in the divinely-inspired, and prelapsarian, condition.

In the material addressed to her "virtuous" (female) readers, Lanyer applies the model of shared affliction and hope to all women: all *women*, according to Lanyer,

---

10   See Brathwaite, who calls women "weak in sex and condition" and argues repeatedly that women are more predisposed to passion, less to reason than men. See also "The Form of Solemnization of Holy Matrimony" from *The Book of Common Prayer* (1559) and "A Homily on the State of Matrimony" from *The Second Tome of Homilies* (1563), both in Joan Klein. In both descriptions of the relationship between a husband and wife, these texts exhort women to remain subordinate to their husbands because of their natural condition as men's subjects. These writings are based in part on the teachings of the Apostle Paul in Ephesians, where he writes, "Let women be subject to their husbands, as to the Lord; for the husband is the head of the woman, as Christ is head of the Church" (Eph. 5:22–23).

have endured similar tests and will subsequently gain fame in heaven by persevering in such adversity by virtue of their "sexe." Lanyer writes that she pens her volume of poetry not simply for her wealthy women patrons, but "for the generall use of all virtuous Ladies and Gentlewomen of this kingdome; and in commendation of some particular persons of our owne sexe, such as for the most part, are so well knowne to my selfe, and others, that I dare undertake Fame dares not to call any better. And this I have done, to make knowne to the world, that all women deserve not to be blamed..." (5–12). The poem, "To all vertuous Ladies in generall" further insists that the argument of Lanyer's book applies not simply to noblewomen but also, and equally, to all women who are virtuous despite, and even because of, their displacement or their inability to secure land or property.

The dedicatory poem to Mary Sidney hails her as an exemplary woman, much like the other dedicatees, but Sidney uniquely models a woman whose poetry, like Lanyer's, represents an ideal space where nature and art exemplify this lost perfection in "perfit" and "equall sov'raigntie." In a move that Suzanne Woods argues "centers the figure of the divinely ordained woman poet," Lanyer traces Sidney's steps through "Edalyan Groves," where the Muses reside ("Vocation and Authority" 91):

> That sacred Spring where Art and Nature striv'd
> Which should remaine as Sov'raigne of the place;
> Whose ancient quarrell being new reviv'd,
> Added fresh Beauty, gave farre greater Grace...
> To which as umpires now these Ladies go,
> Judging with pleasure their delightfull case;
> Whose ravisht sences made them quickly know,
> Twould be offensive either to displace.
> And therefore will'd they should for ever dwell,
> In perfit unity by this matchless Spring:
> Since 'twas impossible either should excell,
> Or her faire fellow in subjection bring. (81–92)

In this vision, women's writing "ravishes" the senses of its women readers and inspires the conditions where "matchless Spring" captures an eternally fecund landscape that holds nature and art perpetually balanced by the Ladies' desire not to judge either as "Sov'raigne" but instead to hold both in equal sway. In the context of nature, Lanyer rejects the preeminence of hierarchies that subject one woman to another (or to men). Lanyer's dream vision celebrates the woman poet, female community, and the ideal "place" in the poem that calls to mind not just a fictional location for women to celebrate Sidney's abilities as a writer, but perhaps also an actual place where women could have sat together and read Mary Sidney's verse translation of the Psalms (Woods 90). Lanyer's commendation of Sidney thus emphasizes female community but in a specific locale where women would together enact the poetry and songs penned by another woman.

Lanyer frames her own writing as creating a space for female community, much as she commends Mary Sidney for doing earlier. As such, Lanyer acts as intermediary for her "virtuous" female readers "To be transfigur'd with our loving Lord," made possible by their attending the feast that coincides with Christ's Passion detailed in the central section of the *Salve Deus*.[11] As was true in Sidney's poetic locus amoenus, the poet invites "all vertuous ladies in generall" to "bring your Serpents to the fields of rest, / Where he doth stay that purchast all your loves.../ There you shall find him in those pleasant groves / Of sweet Elyzium, by the Well of Life, / Whose cristal springs do purge from wordly strife" ("To all virtuous ladies in generall" 58–59, 61–63). Whereas Lanyer's dedicatees are alienated from land ownership on earth, the "fields," "Groves," and "flowers" of her "Booke" transport women to an alternative space beyond "dull and sensuall earth" where they will "overcome all thoughts that would defile / The earthly circuit of your soules fair lands" (38–39). Lanyer's poetry itself takes on the cadences of a garden space, created by a woman for other women and re-placing their displaced position in secular, social spheres. Women's transfiguration, that is, amounts to a deliverance from their dispossession on earth and the rightful inheritance of their "soules fair lands" in heaven. Framing her dedicatory material as an invitation for disenfranchised women to use her book to facilitate just such deliverance serves to challenge in the most practical terms the laws governing property and land ownership and imagine an alternative space for women, typified by the Cooke-ham garden in her country house poem (the third part of the book).

Spiritual Inheritance in "Salve Deus"

In the religious poem that constitutes the longest part of the book, "Salve Deus," Lanyer reorients women's position relative earthly husbands (and men in general) to a different husband, Christ, an alternative husband who readily identifies with the women because he, too, is displaced. The Garden of Gethsemane episode in the "Salve Deus" serves as the starting point for Lanyer to propose alternatives for women's salvation that draw on the key themes of Christ-as-Husband and questions of rightful inheritance. In the Garden, Christ is at his most vulnerable, most human, and is most like the women whom Lanyer features in her poem: the daughters of Jerusalem, who weep at Christ's feet much as he weeps in the Garden; the Virgin Mary, who identifies with Christ as a lover, a husband, and a son at the crucifixion; and Eve, whose own expulsion from the Garden of Eden is reinterpreted by Pilate's wife. The Garden episode also situates Christ's sacrifice as reparation for Adam's, not Eve's, fall from grace. Christ's arrest in the Garden, crucifixion, and resurrection restores women not from sin, but from men's sin of displacing them, and such restoration entails their receiving lands and a kingdom in heaven at the same time it restores Christ to the divine status from which he was displaced while in human form on earth.

Whereas early modern English men strip women of their rightful inheritance, Christ as "Bridegroome" makes it possible for women to "possesse the land": "Who

---

11   McBride argues for the power of Lanyer's "eucharistic meal" in which Lanyer is the "priestly celebrant" and where "she [Lanyer] rather than a titled patron, is host—both provider of the feast and, in her identification with Christ, and his consecrated body" (61). See Guibbory 191–211, in which she also argues for Lanyer's position as priest or spiritual intermediary.

sees *this* Bridegroome, never can be sad / ...All those that fear him, shall possesse the Land" (77, 86, my emphasis). Lanyer realigns the marriage relationship so that only Christ, not earthly husbands, has authority over women.[12] Lanyer assures Margaret Clifford that Christ is the "Husband of [her] soule," which transfers the spiritual authority from Margaret's husband to Christ; in fact, Christ's death makes possible the Countess's and all women's salvation, not oppression, and they inherit everything in his "kingdom," not just as "Dowager" but as "Co-heire":

> And dying made her Dowager of all;
> Nay more, Co-heire of that eternall blisse
> That Angels lost, and We by *Adam's* fall;
> Meere Cast-awaies, rais'd by a *Judas* kiss,
> Christ's bloody sweat, the Vinegar, and Gall,
> The Speare, Sponge, Nailes, his buffeting with Fists,
> His bitter Passion, Agony, and Death,
> Did gaine us Heavn when He did loose his breath. (257–64)

Compliant with New Testament doctrine, the poem demonstrates how Christ's death raises women's status to "Co-heire" and grants them the inheritance of the entire kingdom of Heaven. Significantly in this poem, though, only women, not all human descendants, receive such a promise, which orients the recuperation of land and property, too, strictly with respect to Lanyer's female patrons and readers. As opposed to the feme covert status that applied to early modern women, and which was justified by conventional interpretations of Eve's culpability in the Fall, men are the source of betrayal and disobedience here. It is "Adam's fall," and "Judas kiss," that make men undeserving the rewards granted to women by Christ in this poem, while women are inherently entitled to legal, social, and material equality.

In contrast with Adam's unsuccessful stint as the first man and first husband, Christ is the ideal husband: the ultimate lover as well as "Lord" and women's perfect complement.[13] Only the women in Lanyer's poem and her virtuous readers can enter into this relationship, since they alone are faithful and worthy. Prior to the crucifixion, the men in Lanyer's poem betray him, though they pledge undying faithfulness; moreover, their infidelity is coupled by their ignorance and inability to perceive Christ's true nature: "Nor can their wisdoms any way discover, / Who he should be that proov'd so true a Lover" (671–72). The women, however, remain faithful to Christ their ideal lover, the "Bridegroome" that is described more like a traditional beloved than the male lover and in terms that echo the Song of Songs:

---

12 In *Christian Economy* (1609), Puritan William Perkins writes, "Now the duties of the wife are principally two. The first is to submit herself to her husband and to acknowledge and reverence him as her head in all things...The second duty is to be obedient unto her husband in all things, that is, wholly to depend on him both in judgment and will. For look as the church yields obedience to Christ her head and yields herself to be commanded, governed, and directed by him. So ought the woman to the man" (Joan Klein 172–73).

13 Guibbory calls Christ here the only "true Lover," the "only husband a woman needs" as she argues that Lanyer places Christ in this position while "Lanyer's reading of the Song of Songs ultimately points to a rejection of earthly marriage" (202–3).

This is that Bridegroome that appears so faire,
So sweet, so lovely in his Spouses sight,
That unto Snowe we may his face compare,
His cheekes like skarlet, and his eyes so bright
As purest Doves that in the rivers are,
Washed with milke, to give the more delight;
His head is likened to the finest gold,
His curled lockes so beauteous to behold. (1305–1312)

As Bridegroome, Christ is thoroughly masculine, yet he also possesses feminine qualities. This description blurs gendered boundaries, in that the male husband Christ is "sweet," "faire," and "lovely." Such a description distinguishes Christ from all other male characters in the poem and shows him to be like the women alone.

Reconceptualizing marriage with Christ as Bridegroome recontextualizes the religious justifications for men's dominion over women, their claim to land on earth. The poem thus reconfigures the relationship between husbands and wives, and between Christ and humankind, in a way that potentially destabilizes women's positions as subject to their husbands on earth. Figures such as Pilate's wife serve to contest the logic used by men to argue that women are inferior: "Pilate's wife inverts the culture/nature and reason/passion dichotomies to explicit female advantage," argues Janel Mueller, and "she spells out to Pilate the implications she [Pilate's wife] sees relative her assessment of the Crucifixion and the Fall as having for gender relations in the social and political spheres" (122–23).[14] Lanyer's argument therefore calls into question key moments in Christian history like this one that later served to justify women's socially, economically, and politically subordinate position to men. The implication for women in early modern England is that the contemporary English models are inadequate and oppressive to women, that they in fact contradict the ideal heavenly model instituted first by God and reinstituted here by Christ.

In the ways "Eve's Apologie" directly contradicts arguments for women's subjection to men, especially husbands, it resonates with such early modern treatises as *The Law's Resolution of Women's Rights*. Despite the general tendency in this treatise to sympathize with women who find themselves trapped in bad marriages, the author, T.E., argues that even though Adam and Eve are exiled from Eden together,

> Eve, because she had helped to seduce her husband, hath inflicted on herself an especial bane. *In sorrow shalt thou bring forth thy children, thy desires shall be subject to thy husband and he shall rule over thee.* See here the reason of that which I touched before, that women have no voice in parliament. They make no laws, they consent to none, they abrogate none. All of them are understood either married or to be married and their desires are subject to their husband. I know no remedy, though some women can shift it well enough. The common law here shaketh hand with divinity. (Klein, *Daughters,* 32–33)

---

14   Mueller sees this reconfiguration as applicable especially to Pilate's wife, through whose mouth come not only arguments about why Pilate should exercise compassion and have mercy with Christ, but also Eve's Apologie, in which the story of the Fall is retold through from a distinctly revisionist perspective.

By contrast, "Eve's Apologie" presents a counterargument that appropriates the same logic that underwrites early modern legal discourse in England, yet to a different end; men are in fact culpable for the Fall, not women. Eve's love for Adam, her simplicity, and her "undiscerning Ignorance" drove her to take the fruit, while it was Adam's inadequate governance over that which he ruled that caused Adam to fall, an indiscretion according to the poem that makes him (and by extension all men) responsible for the Fall and for their exile from Eden.

In particular, "Eve's Apologie" characterizes the material signs of women's unjust suffering as dispossession from property and land:

> For he was Lord and King of all the earth,
> Before poore Eve had either life or breath.
> Who being fram'd by Gods eternall hand,
> The perfect'st man that ever breath'd on earth;
> Ands from God's mouth receiv'd that strait command,
> The breach whereof he knew was present death:
> Yea having powre to rule both Sea and Land,
> Yet with one Apple wonne to loose that breath
> Which God had breathed in his beauteous face,
> Bringing us all in danger and disgrace. (778, 785–92)

The specific ways that Lanyer characterizes Adam's superiority over Eve before the Fall—dominion over "Sea and Land" and "King" over all of the earth—are similar to the ways women's unjustified oppression are apparent elsewhere. Within the poem, though, Christ, not Adam, rules over land and sea after the Fall, which divests Adam and all of his male descendents of their dominion over earthly realms. By implication, on Lanyer's postlapsarian earth, claims by men to property and land, as well as rulership over such domains, are not only unjustified but unnatural, unholy.[15] Just as Adam's authority is couched in material terms before the Fall as over "Sea and Land," and Adam and Eve's expulsion from Eden cast them from a concrete locality, so it follows that Eve's exoneration should carry with it material consequences too.

Christ's suffering stemmed from his rejection of outward signs of his majesty, but his humility, like that of Lanyer's female dedicatees', further evinced his rightful authority over all worldly things: "All might, all majestie, all love, all lawe / Remaines in him that keepes all worlds in awe" and, Christ, "Who being Monarcke of heav'n, earth, and seas, / Indur'd all wrongs, yet no man did displease" (1647–48, 1711–12). For Lanyer's women, though, the things of the world denied them are real, material objects—property, land, and wealth. Like Christ, the women in Lanyer's poem and her female readers can cling steadfast to the reassurance that their dispossession need only be temporary. Often deprived of material security, Lanyer's women still

---

15 T.E. also argues in *The Law's Resolution of Women's Rights* that a widow, "when she hath lost her husband, her head is cut off, her intellectual part is gone, the very faculties of her soul are (I will not say) clean taken away, but they are all benumbed, dimmed, and dazzled, so that she cannot think or remember when to take rest or recreation for her weak body" (Joan Klein 50).

have constancy and faith that align them with Christ himself, a "Monarcke" and "King" whose death "purchast them a place in Heav'n for ever" (1679). Ultimately, Lanyer's "Salve Deus" emphasizes heavenly concerns and virtue, yet asserts Christ as monarch and rightful ruler in earthly as well as heavenly terms. The connections between Christ and women, and the logical arguments in the poem that undermine male authority, might promise women lands in heaven, yet Lanyer makes it clear that women nevertheless deserve the lands they are stripped of on earth. Women's suffering on earth is as unjust as Christ's; like him, they should rule, and men should not.

Christ is described in ways that also associate him with nature, which links him to the garden here and suggests how women's connection with Christ might be likened to their connection with the Cooke-ham garden in the country house poem too. Lanyer writes that

> His lips like skarlet threeds, yet much more sweet
> Than is the sweetest hony dropping dew,
> Or hony combes, where all the Bees doe smeet;
> Yea is he constant, and his words are true,
> His cheekes are beds of spices, flowers sweet;
> His lips, like Lillies, dropping downe pure mirrhe,
> Whose love, before all worlds we doe preferre. (1313–20)

Lanyer strategically evokes a traditional description of the female beloved, though applied here to Christ, to foreground the fallacies in contemporary attitudes that insist women's connection to nature makes them inferior to men. Using this logic, that is, Christ would also be inferior because he, too, is described in these terms. However, in Lanyer's poem Christ is both delicate and powerful, associated with the "Lillies" and the "flowers sweet" *and* ruler over land and sea. Traditional descriptions of the female beloved, and notions that women are changeable like nature, which typically function as justifications for this subjection, instead become the foundational link between Christ and the women, making the women by implication simultaneously both delicate and powerful too.

Lanyer similarly associates women in her poem with flowers and nature, which further emphasizes their link to Christ. Christ as "Lord, Lover, and their King" comes to the Daughters of Jerusalem, who recognized him as the "Jessie floure and bud," and the "fautlesse fruit" (1021, 1025). Christ is described in traditionally feminine, natural terms, much like the Daughters themselves in the same section: "whose teares powr'd forth apace / On Flora's bankes, like shewers of Aprils raine" to move Christ even though their tears prove fruitless with other "Princes" on earth (973–74). Lanyer represents such an affinity between Christ, the Daughters of Jerusalem, and Nature in a way that empowers the women even as it signals their vulnerability. Articulating parallels between these women (and, given the logic of the poem, all women), Christ, and Nature, this scene suggests that suffering and subjection characteristic of a fallen world is only temporary, and Christ's death restores the world to a perfection manifest in Heaven in the future and perpetually.

Lanyer represents the Garden of Gethsemane as a space both "blessed" and full of "grief," where Christ's innocent sacrifice fulfills the messianic prophecy:

Now went our Lord unto that holy place,
Sweet Gethsemaine hallowed by his presence,
That blessed Garden, which did now embrace
His holy corps, yet could make no defence
Against those Vipers, objects of disgrace,
Which sought that pure eternall Love to quench…
Beeing sorrowfull, and overcharg'd with griefe,
He told it them, yet look'd for no relief. (361–66, 375–76)

The Garden as the "holy place" where Christ is most vulnerable forges an intimate connection between this garden and the location where the Daughters of Jerusalem also weep for Jesus during his trial. Characterizing this garden space has proven difficult for scholars today, though. Janel Mueller calls it a "liminal" space, neither public nor private, which is fully in line with contemporary garden designs and writing about gardens, as we saw in Chapter 1. While early modern gardens could indeed be both a place of private refuge and contemplation and a public setting for group gatherings and theatrical performance, the Garden of Gethsemane is significant in temporal as well as spatial ways (Mueller 10). It is in this garden that Christ initiates the chain of events that bring about his death and suffering in the poem's present, and salvation in the future. The garden thus bridges an ambiguously defined span of both time and space.

But the Garden of Gethsemane also highlights Christ's corporeality, which, combined with the nature imagery throughout the poem, links him to the earth itself. In this "holy place," that is, dwells Christ's "holy corps," and in this garden Christ delivers a solitary prayer to God that produces "pretious sweat" that "came trickling *to the ground* / Like drops of blood they sences to confound" (407–8, my emphasis). In this garden, Christ separates his desires from those of the Father God, thereby isolating his humanity, the product of which Lanyer frames as a "Kingdom" on heaven and earth:

Sweet Lambe of God, his deare beloved Sonne,
By this great purchase, what to thee remaines?
Of Heaven and Earth thou hast a Kingdom wonne,
Thy Glory being equall with they Gaines,
In ratifying Gods promise on the Earth,
Made many hundred yeares before thy birth. (411–16)

Christ's sacrifice is a "purchase" of the "kingdom" he was displaced from in Heaven and alienated from on earth. It is in this garden that Christ redeems what was lost in the original garden, Eden. At the same time, Christ's sacrifice, initiated here in the Garden, may prompt redemption, but reclamation of the heavenly kingdom takes place in Heaven in the future, not on earth in the present. The fruits of this garden are to be harvested later rather than enjoyed right away.

Women Inherit the Earth in "The Description of Cooke-ham"

Whereas in the Garden of Gethsemane Christ makes possible women's attainment of the kingdom of heaven, the Cooke-ham garden represents the idealized, alternative space based in women's experience and one that they might occupy in the future. Another Eden, the garden space in Cooke-ham is paradoxically part of the women's contemporary experience as it simultaneously stands outside the bounds of institutions that sanction men's unjustifiable subjection of women. While Adam had dominion over earth and sea in God's Eden, only women inhabit and have equal dominion over Lanyer's Edenic garden space in Cooke-ham; the postlapsarian effects only appear once men intrude. Lanyer depicts how, in the absence of men, Margaret and Anne Clifford and Lanyer herself enjoy autonomy and power in perfect relation to the landscape they occupy. Outside the garden, social imperatives, especially marriage, compromise their idealized community, severing the de-hierarchized alliances the women form in the garden and initiating the decay of the natural world they inhabit. The ideal space of the Cooke-ham garden exists in tension with the actual, hierarchized world outside of that space. While in Cooke-ham together, the women enjoy the pleasures of Eden itself—equality with each other and mobility and freedom in the garden space; male presence brings another Fall, instituting the same social roles and hierarchies in relation to men and each other that Lanyer argues throughout the *Salve Deus* are contrary to God's intentions.

Gardens were commonly viewed in the period as reconstructions of Eden, though Lanyer frames the garden here as a restored paradise specifically under the auspices of women as its artists and inhabitants. The frontispiece to John Parkinson's *Paradisi in sole paradisus terrestris* (1629) pictures the plants of Eden as some of the popular varieties found in England by the early seventeenth century, thus identifying the original garden created by God with contemporary secular English gardens. And Francis Bacon writes in his essay, "Of Gardens" that "God Almightie first Planted a Garden. And indeed, it is the Purest of Humane pleasures. It is the Greatest Refreshment to the Spirits of Man; Without which, Buildings and Pallaces are but Grosse Handy-works" (266). At the same time, however, the "art" of gardening was seen as "a prouident and skillfull Colelctrix of the faults of nature in her particular workes, apprehended by the sences," such "faults" evident, for example, "when good ground naturally brings forth thistles, trees stand too thicke, or too thin, or disorderly, or (without dressing) put forth unprofitable suckers and such like. All which, and a thousand more, art reformeth" (Lawson, *A New Orchard and Garden* A3). The "art" of gardening thus corrects the "faults" of nature that stemmed from the Fall and restores the first Garden "Planted," as Bacon puts it, by God.[16] Whereas the Garden of Gethsemane serves as the space where Christ initiates this restoration in the heavenly realm and for the future, in Lanyer's Cooke-ham garden space the restorative potential rests solely in the hands of women and it exists in the here and now.

Likewise, by emphasizing the garden space that surrounds the house, the poem draws readers' attention not to the architectural spaces like those created by men and

---

16   See Bacon, "Of Gardens" (1625).

that often helped define men and masculine identity in early modern England, but instead to the outside landscapes often associated with women and the garden spaces women designed.[17] By the time Lanyer wrote her country house poem, women had shown themselves to be influential in aesthetic gardening. Lucy Harington, Countess of Bedford, was well-known for designing large-scale gardens that garnered admiration from those who visited them; and Bess of Hardwick, who defied gender stereotypes about architecture when she designed an architectural masterpiece *and* extensive gardens that testified to her unrelenting quest to define herself as an example of an early modern woman who could stand on her own in a social milieu dominated by men.[18]

The Cooke-ham garden, like the way so many English formal gardens in the period were imagined, derives its beauty finally from a balance between productivity and pleasure. Philomela's song, the other birds that sing, the wind that blows through the hills, are all present for this purpose, according to the poem, "That Pleasure in that place might more abound" (42). While pleasure and productivity are typically conjoined in the context of male-oriented gardening in printed books, pleasure and productivity are linked here specifically to female generativity and nurture through reproductivity and birth imagery in connection with the Countess herself: "The swelling Bankes deliver'd all their pride, / When such a Phoenix once they had espide" (43–44).[19] The presence of the Countess inspires creative activity described here as a specifically female act of creation. The "swelling Bankes" that "deliver'd" suggest pregnancy and childbirth, issuing forth from the body of women through means available only to women.[20] The Cooke-ham garden, then, once established by the creative power of God is reinvigorated by a female source and mimics the natural reproductive authority of the women who dwell there together.

The "Place" itself derives from a communal, dynamic relationship between elements of nature and the women who reside there:

The Walkes put on their summer Liveries,
And all things else did hold like similies:
The Trees with leaves, with fruits, with flowers clad,
Embrac'd each other, seeming to be glad,
Turning themselves to beauteous Canopies,
To shade the bright Sunne from your brighter eies. (21–26)

---

17 See Erickson, who argues that the alignment of "good" women with indoor/private and "bad" women with outside/public contradicted in many cases actual practice, since many women bought and sold goods in the market place, and broadsides and ballads.

18 See Chapter 1, which details how gardening made it possible for men and women of multiple backgrounds to fashion spaces for themselves socially.

19 In her note for this line, Woods concludes that the Phoenix here refers to the Countess. I would argue instead that the Phoenix might instead refer to the late Queen Elizabeth, whom Lanyer esteems in the dedicatory poem to Queen Anne and who is earlier referred to a Phoenix in "To the Lady Elizabeth's Grace" (4). The Phoenix is also a traditional reference to Elizabeth, so to find it here is certainly not surprising. Lanyer also calls the Queen of Sheba a Phoenix in 1689. That Lanyer does not limit this assignation only to one woman further conflates all women into one indistinguishable group, since the term applies equally to many.

20 See Naomi J. Miller, "(M)Other Tongues," in which she makes an extensive and compelling argument for the significance of mothers and daughters in Lanyer's poem.

At this point in the poem, and until much later when the ladies prepare to leave Cooke-ham and are separated, the natural surroundings are linked to its female residents. The embrace and pleasure nature provides for the Countess (and the women) is not one of deference but of cooperation and community.[21] While scholars have argued that Cooke-ham operates as a hierarchy, albeit one that includes only women, Lanyer does not simply insert herself into a pre-ordained hierarchical garden but instead shows that all reside together equally within this space.[22]

"The Description of Cooke-ham" may imagine the potential for women to align themselves in positive and powerful ways with the landscape, but it also recalls the actual experiences of Margaret and Anne Clifford and Aemilia Lanyer when they spent time together at Cooke-ham. Although the date of their visit is not certain, the three women were likely there some time between George's death in 1605 and Anne's marriage in 1609.[23] The Cooke-ham estate functioned as a country retreat for Anne and Margaret, a secluded place where they could escape the demands of the court and family. Importantly, Cooke-ham was not one of the Clifford estates; it belonged to Margaret's brother, William Russell of Thornbaugh, from whom Margaret rented it. Cooke-ham, therefore, was a location where the women could find community together beyond the reach of men, but from which they were inherently displaced, since Cooke-ham did not belong to them either.

Such displacement is re-placed in the poem by the perfect complementarity between the women and the landscape. In the poem's Cooke-ham garden, the intersecting representation of women, nature, and God grant the women authority in much the same way that their fidelity and communion with Christ in "Salve Deus" grants them authority both in heaven and, as the argument suggests, on earth. Here in "Cooke-ham" the same joint heavenly/earthly authority is theirs:

---

21   What appears to be equality in the community Ben Jonson establishes at the Penshurst estate is in fact a clearly articulated hierarchical structure that Jonson inserts himself (and no others) into. Whereas he writes, "Where comes no guest but is allowed to eat / Without his fear and of thy lord's own meat" to suggest that all come equally to the Lord's table at Penshurst, the focus is actually on Jonson himself as recipient of the Lord's goods: "Where the same beer and bread and self-same wine / That is his lordship's shall be also mine" (61–64).

22   See Beilin, Lewalski, *Writing Women,* and Schleiner. More recent work comes to a similar conclusion about class differences between Lanyer's patrons and herself. Woods, for example, writes that Lanyer turns hierarchies "upside down" as she claims the authority for women to write. This authority, Woods claims, derives from the status of her female patrons, which means that the hierarchies Lanyer turns "upside down," then, are gender hierarchies, not social or class hierarchies ("Vocation" 83–98). McBride argues, on the other hand, that the spiritual realm takes precedence over the secular realm, which places Lanyer in a position perhaps higher than the female patrons she solicits in her dedicatory material (60–82).

23   Lewalski places their visit between 1604 and 1609, arguing that it most likely took place when Margaret was estranged from her husband, but she witholds the possibility that it took place shortly after his death (*Writing Women* 216). Based on Lanyer's emphasis in the dedicatory poems to Anne and Margaret, however, I am suggesting that the visit may well have taken place after George's death, during a period when Margaret and Anne quite possibly used the Cooke-ham estate as a refuge from their inheritance troubles.

Where beeing seated, you might plainely see,
Hills, vales, and woods, as if on bended knee
They had appeared, your honour to salute,
Or to preferre some strange unlook'd for sute:
All interlac'd with brookes and christall springs,
A prospect fit to please the eyes of Kings:
And thirteene shires appear'd all in your sight,
Europe could not affoard much more delight.
What was there then but gave you all content,
While you the time in meditation spent,
Of their Creators powre, which there you saw,
In all his Creatures held a perfit Law. (67–78)

While early modern formal gardens were often described in terms of human dominance over nature, the hierarchical subdivision of monarch and subject applies to the land outside of Cooke-ham, not inside of it. Beyond the borders of Cooke-ham, the Countess has almost empirical domination over all that she sees, but inside, reciprocity and mutuality preside.

As long as the women remain within the garden, any "difference" among them is subordinated by their shared pleasures. It is only when the poem shifts to describe Anne's state as "espous'd," for example, that the language shifts to past tense descriptions of what used to be: "And that sweet Lady sprung from Cliffords race, / To noble Dorset now espous'd.../ In whose faire breast true virtue then was hous'd" (93–94, 96). Once Anne marries, that is, the community of women breaks down, and the characteristic complementarity in the Cooke-ham garden before Anne's marriage resembles geographic and social isolation:

And yet it grieves me that I cannot be
Neere unto her, whose virtues did agree
With those faire ornaments of outward beauty,
Which did enforce from all both love and dutie. (99–102)

To be "neere unto" Anne, in close proximity within the garden, elides the hierarchical social divisions that separate the women in early modern England, but such closeness and equality exists only in the ideal garden space at the estate. It is radically reconfigured as Anne's marital status changes, which initiates their departure from the garden.

Therefore, Anne's marriage initiates a second Fall, one that affects the female community *and* the Edenic landscape, but in this case it is not Adam and Eve who are thrust out of Paradise but mother, daughter, and female friend. As happens in the Biblical Fall, the garden landscape itself deteriorates, a tangible deterioration coupled with the first instance of "difference" among the women. Such difference is not, however, as Ann Baynes Coiro has argued, at the fore *throughout* the poem depicting "the fated order of a society where some are privileged and some are low" (372). Rather, the "fated order" Coiro describes indeed emerges in "To Cooke-ham," but only outside of the immediate context of the Cooke-ham garden space. The poem aligns social difference with geographic distance, arguing "Where our great friends we cannot dayly see, / So great a difference is there in degree" (105–6); and the Cooke-ham garden itself physically deteriorates only "At their departure" (129). To emphasize the importance of geography in this way also shows how the Edenic departure is linked not just to Anne's marriage, but also to their disinheritance and displacement. The intrusion of social imperatives and restrictions to women's independence, in particular marriage and property ownership, manifests "difference" among the women, a state of being that is temporarily held at bay during their stay at Cooke-ham and lamented by Lanyer elsewhere in the book.

Although expelled from this other Eden, women can temporarily restore the garden and be united in mind and memory where they no longer experience unity in body or space. In the early lines of the poem, Lanyer calls on Margaret Clifford to think on the "pleasures past" and "worldly Joyes" they shared at Cooke-ham, yet she admits that what the memory hails are only "dimme shadows of celestiall pleasures" (13–15). Twice in the remaining lines of the poem Lanyer calls upon Memory to restore that space by recreating what has been lost, even if Memory, according to the poem, can only partially efface the difference generated by their departure. "Noble Memory" can "preserve their love continually," and earlier Lanyer says, "Therefore sweet Memorie doe thou retaine / Those pleasures past, which will not turne againe" (155–56, 117–18). This appeal to the memory as having re-creative potential in the garden also applies to the poet's re-creative abilities through memory of that past experience that allowed her to participate in the community: "Remember beauteous Dorsets former sports / So farre from beeing toucht by ill reports; / Wherein my selfe did alwaies beare a part" (119–24). To "remember" in this passage is also to "beare in mind," to make over again in the mind the "recreations" they shared. Even the term "recreations" suggests its double meaning as both the pastimes the women shared and their ability to re-create them by remembering.

More tangible than the powers of memory to evoke "celestiall pleasures" the women shared at Cooke-ham, though, is Lanyer's poetic recreation of the Edenic conditions in the garden space they occupied. The poem may have been inspired by the Countess as Lanyer claims, "I have perform'd her noble hest" (207), yet Lanyer boldly argues that, while at Cooke-ham, "The Muses gave their full consent, / *I should have the power* the virtuous to content" (4–5, my emphasis). Margaret's behest may prompt the act of writing, but the power to recreate the garden at Cooke-ham stems from the muses themselves and applies directly to Lanyer. Lanyer thus makes the argument that women's writing is a re-generative and re-creative process, much as she argued that Margaret's presence in the garden as "Mistris" of the "Place" maintained the perpetually reproductive characteristics of the natural setting in the Cooke-ham garden where she walked. Lanyer re-creates the Cooke-ham garden by re-creating it through the vehicle of the poem, which makes Lanyer the "Mistris" of the poetic garden space under her authorial control much as Margaret was "Mistris" in Cooke-ham.

Women occupy and claim creative authority over the garden at Cooke-ham, the earthly manifestation of the "heavenly kingdom" that Lanyer claims in *Salve Deus* belongs only to them, not to men. The garden works as an ideal setting for this argument because women readily used gardens during the period as spaces to define themselves, even if architectural structures and land were most often the legal property of their husbands.[24] For example, Gervase Markham even suggests that women's use of garden plants in food preparation puts the social prestige of the entire household, including her husband, at stake (*English Housewife* 154). When viewed within the context of the entire set of poems, then, Lanyer's "The Description of Cooke-ham" becomes the alternative space occupied, inspired, and created jointly by God and women, and Lanyer's purpose as poet is both to describe the setting of such inspiration and to re-create it, claiming the power to do so for God and women alone.

Not only do the memory and writing preserve that past experience in the present, but this recreated garden space is rendered permanent by the materiality of the poem. While the poet bids farewell to the Cooke-ham estate and the garden space that held the ideal female community, she simultaneously claims the poem's potential to preserve the sanctity of the garden space outside the bounds of time. The poem materializes the garden that is otherwise found only in the mind's ether; in the poem, the garden space still exits:

This last farewell to Cooke-ham here I give,
When I am dead thy name in this may live,
Wherein I have perform'd her noble hest,
Whose virtues lodge in my unworthy breast,
And ever shall, so long as life remaines,
Tying my heart to her by those rich chaines. (205–10)

Repeatedly throughout this and the other poems in the book, Lanyer draws attention to the work in front of the reader as her own creative work. Much like Spenser does in his epic poem, as I discuss at length in Chapter 2, in "To All Vertuous Ladies in Generall" Lanyer calls her book the "fruits" and "floures" inspired by the virtue of her female patrons, which extends the actual experience of three women in Cooke-ham to all women. Lanyer, Margaret, and Anne can recreate their time at Cooke-ham through memory and reading, but all "virtuous" women can participate in the space for women claimed by this poem when they read it as well. It is in this context that the poem itself becomes a garden space, too. While God may get the credit in the poem's context for creating the natural surroundings where the women first dwell at the Cooke-ham estate, the first Eden, Lanyer seizes the power over this space, this second Eden, for women and for herself as woman poet. She makes an alternative garden that belongs to the women who read it, made from the authority of the woman poet who imagined it, and derived from the experience of the women who remember it.

---

24 Ben Jonson's own country house poem, "To Penshurst," reproduces the developing dominant notions of women as hostesses in the houses their husbands own, relegated to interior domestic spaces:

And what praise was heaped
On thy good lady then! Who therein reaped
The just reward of her high huswifery;
To have her linen, plate, and all things nigh,
When she was far; and not a room but dressed,
As if it had expected such a guest! (83–88)

"Cooke-ham" is, after all, memorialized in its most inaugural moments by its re-creation through poetry, memory, and reading.

Just as actual early modern garden spaces allowed for a renegotiation of class and gendered relationships during this period, so too does Lanyer's book represent the garden space as an ideal site for such renegotiation for Lanyer and women like her. Focusing on material ways that she and other women were linked, Lanyer imagines the garden as a space where they might renegotiate the social relationships that in other contexts they found limiting or constraining. While women might find themselves subject to class markers in other social contexts, that is, they were all united by their shared subjection to men; and, while their claims to property and land might have been limited by their legal subjection to husbands, fathers, and brothers, women could use their gardens to form networks with other women and find pleasure in planting together.

But Lanyer's poetry also offers a conceptual alternative for women that stems from their actual everyday experience. Lanyer dedicates her book to women whose families owned property in early modern England and who planted and/or designed gardens of one kind or another, which means that the women who read Lanyer's *Salve Deus* could readily identify with the way women might work in and create gardens yet still not own the ground beneath; and Lanyer points out the ways that women could also readily identify with Christ's suffering and the way that female community yields to the demands of marriage. In the Garden of Gethsemane, Christ makes it possible for women to inherit "lands" in heaven, though their suffering (and Christ's) continues on earth. Yet the Cooke-ham garden is a locus amoenus that offers women the experience of unhindered community with each other, even if that community always lies perpetually in tension with the imperative that women marry. Lanyer's gardens foreground the ways that the spaces women occupy are both "blest" and "curst," offering the potential for women to be creative, active subjects, even as they remain inevitably dependant on men who own the land. The gardens in Lanyer's *Salve Deus* show how women might not become permanent dominant members of the representational spaces they occupy or make, since they ultimately belong to men, but these gardens nevertheless serves as *alternative* representational spaces that can temporarily satisfy.

Chapter 4

"In this strang labourinth how shall I turne?": Needlework, Gardens, And Writing In Mary Wroth's *Pamphilia To Amphilanthus* [1]

As we have seen of Aemilia Lanyer's poetry, so too does Mary Wroth's *Pamphilia to Amphilanthus* (1621) provide a window into how women writers might draw conceptual power from some of the ways that women had made advances in the domain of gardening. Rather than focusing on the way gardens signify a potential recuperation of women's dispossession and material loss, though, as Lanyer's poetry does, Wroth's sonnet sequence develops a different theme found in women's gardening (and foundational to the argument of the *Salve Deus*). Wroth's sequence situates gardening as one among other domains to which women had access during the period and uses the relative mobility women had in them to forge mobility in another that was in general off-limits to them: writing. Like gardening, needlework (another spatial practice) was associated with creativity, agency, and feminine identity; at the same time, writing original material was routinely held at cross-purposes with the development of feminine identity endorsed by male writers, philosophers, politicians, and religious authorities alike.

The gendering of the garden space during the late-sixteenth and early-seventeenth centuries demarcated a domain where women might exercise creative decision-making, as William Lawson emphasizes in his book to the country housewife, but these advances brought with them real costs for women, too, including the loss of economic power and the increased pressure for women to withdraw to private, domestic spaces. As I show in Chapter 1, women might make a name for themselves and their households through their decorative gardening and use of garden plants, and women were frequently recognized for their gardening skill in books that hailed some of the finest gardens in England as stemming from the ingenuity and labor of a woman. At the same time, such recognition often involved trade-offs for women;

---

1   A version of this chapter first appeared in *Tulsa Studies in Women's Literature* 24 (1) Spring, 2005: 35–55. I am grateful to Professor Lori Newcomb and her graduate seminar (Spring 1999), in which this chapter originated as a seminar paper. The thoughtful comments of other students in the class as well as Professor Newcomb's excellent insights helped the argument develop in its seminal stages.

women may have made extraordinary gardens (or oversaw their planting and design), but they did so in amateur capacities, and their labor, be it intellectual or physical, became part of an evolving definition of feminine activity that devalued women's accomplishments and further entrenched their positions in diminutive relation to men's.

Exemplifying the way that needlework, gardening, and writing were clearly demarcated in specifically gendered ways, Robert Burton writes in *Anatomy of Melancholy*:

> Now for women instead of laborious studies, they have curious Needle-workes, Cut-workes, spinning, bone-lace, and many pretty devises of their owne making, to adorne their houses, Cushions, Carpets, Chaires, Stooles, confections, conserves, distillations, etc., which they shew to strangers…This they have to busie themselves about, household offices, etc., neate gardens full of exotick, versicoloure, diversely varied, sweet smelling flowers, and plants, in all kindes, which they are most ambitious to get, curious to preserve and keepe, proud to possesse, and much many times to bragge of. (95)

By contrasting the "laborious studies" that occupy men's time and the "pretty devises" of women's making, Burton underscores the gendered boundaries between the different activities acceptable for men and women in early modern England. The needlework and gardening he describes (both "art" forms) would have reinforced notions of chaste and feminine behavior, yet, he explains, the different ways that women could appropriately "busie" themselves instilled in them a sense of pride and accomplishment. Women used what they made to "adorne their houses," and the "Cushions, Chairs, [and] Stooles" they embroidered accounted for some of the few property items that they could readily call their own. As the above quote demonstrates, women could indisputably make spaces for themselves as both creative agents and feminine subjects at the same time in these two artistic domains. While gardening and needlework offered creative outlets for women, published writing was one of the "laborious studies" that was only available to them under certain controlled circumstances. Although women were encouraged to work with their needles and plant gardens, they were actively discouraged from writing (and especially publishing) original poetry. Women could publish translations of others' work or write religious material, but to publish original secular compositions would likely compromise their reputations and leave them vulnerable to such labels as "whore" and, in Mary Wroth's case, "hermaphrodite."[2]

Wroth's sequence appropriates the material contexts of needlework and gardening, in which women had already actively (and successfully) negotiated positions for themselves, to make space for women in another domain, published writing. Her sonnet sequence foregrounds images of needlework and gardening and relates them to images of writing, thus blurring the gendered boundaries Burton clings to so adamantly. Evoking all three domains at once, the labyrinth image in particular featured in the Crown of Sonnets midway through the sequence figures the gender negotiation that is so prominent elsewhere in Wroth's *Pamphilia to Amphilanthus*. It suggests the actual labyrinth spaces found in so many elite early modern gardens,

---

2   See "Lady Mary Wroth to Sir Edward Denny" February 27, 1621 (Roberts, *Poems* 240).

Fig. 4   Garden knot pattern *The Countrie Hovsewife's Garden* (1623)

where gardeners literally shaped the landscape into mazes, while the labyrinth was also a popular design for women to work into their canvas with their needles. As such, it is both an idealized space experienced through the imagination and a model of the actual early modern garden spaces made by both men and women. The sonnet sequence exploits the involvement women already had in needlework and gardening to make space for them as writers, too, insisting that all of the domains equally fall within the range of appropriate feminine behavior and are mutually acceptable forms of women's creative self-expression. Women might, that is, create "neate gardens," "pretty devises" with their needles, and effectively master the products of "laborious study" all at the same time, even if engaging in these activities also meant that women were conforming to restrictive ideologies of domesticity.

Nature's Art: Books, Bands, and Curious Knots

Myriad examples of everyday practice illustrate the interrelationship between gardens and embroidery. For example, the same men often designed patterns for both needlework and gardens, as we see in the case of Thomas Trevelyon. In his *Miscellany* (1608), for instance, Trevelyon includes both a series of needlework patterns for women and a section devoted to garden designs (Beck 23).[3] In *Embroidered Gardens* Thomasina Beck cites two primary connections between these two art forms: first,

---

3   Beck reproduces a painting by Gervasius Fabricius (1613) of four women embroidering beside a formal garden with knots and a fountain at its center. In the painting, the women craft flowers with needle and thread that resemble actual ones in a vase near them, which Beck suggests might serve as a basis for their designs on canvas.

garden scenes often served as the backdrop in embroidery, and second, actual garden plants served as patterns for embroidered clothing (Fig 4).[4]

John Gerard also metaphorically analogizes the two in the dedication of his *The herball* (1597) to Lord Burghley (who nearly bankrupted himself when he built his gardens at Theobalds): "For if delight may provoke men's labour, what greater delight is there than to behold the earth apparelled with plants, as with a robe of imbroidered works, set with orient pearles and garnished with great diversitie of rare and costly jewels" (Qtd. in Beck 6).

In *Maison Rustique, or the Countrie Farme* (1616; translation of book in original French by Charles Estienne), Gervase Markham describes the knot designs for gardeners as like "divers coloured ribands," which suggests that, while the specific media were different, gardens and needlework produced similar aesthetic effects for those who used and admired them. The embroidered clothing worn by residents and visitors resembled the artfully-fashioned garden, thus creating a visual and material link between the two types of art. Such conceptual overlap between the two suggests how deeply their relationship infiltrated early modern ideology. For Wroth's sequence to reproduce this ideological connection reveals how the relationship between them might not just be at the level of the taken for granted, though, but also how it might be appropriated for use by women as well as men.

When Mary Wroth publishes *Pamphilia to Amphilanthus* (1621),[5] the first sonnet sequence in English by a woman, needlework and aesthetic gardening had become key identifying markers not just for elite women but, increasingly, for women of the merchant and gentry classes, too. Susan Frye's "Sewing Connections" elucidates how elite women, such as Katherine Parr, Mary Queen of Scots, and Queen Elizabeth ably crafted elaborate needlework designs that attested to their prestige and education; and the gardening achievements of elite women are, as we have seen, well documented.[6] By the early seventeenth century, though, women from the merchant class and gentry began to pursue status in both artistic domains in greater numbers, as Susan Frye explains, "women who had access to a print shop and money for thread could browse among a variety of prints and have a desired picture drawn on cloth" (Frye, "Sewing Connections" 166). William Lawson's *A Countrie Hovsewife's Garden* (1617) sought a new audience of women gardening enthusiasts, rural country housewives, who had new sources of expendable income and who might have enough leisure time and resources to plant flower gardens as well as the lettuce, peas, and beans that their families would eat. Without overstating, it is reasonable to conclude that both elite and non-elite women alike, that is, may well have wielded a needle or gotten their hands dirty. Even though women of different social rank might not have identified in

---

4   See Beck for further discussion of these interconnections.

5   All references to Wroth's *Pamphilia to Amphilanthus* come from Roberts's edition of the poems. I will refer to the sonnets by the numbering Roberts uses, which orders them from pages 1–103. Wroth's *Pamphilia to Amphilanthus* was originally appended to the 1621 edition of her longer prose romance, *The Countess of Mountgomeries Urania*.

6   See Frye, "Sewing Connections." See also Bushnell, 52–63 and 108–31; and Strong, 120 and 145–47.

the same way with needlework and gardening, both were practices that they might have identified with.

Using gardening and needlework imagery in this way evokes the freedom found in needlework and gardening, even if these practices, as we saw in Chapter 1, were constructed as subjecting women to men's authority. On the one hand, male writers saw needlework as an expressive alternative to women's writing that specifically reflected a woman's virtue, as Thomas Salter does in *The Mirrhor of Modestie* (1579). Salter equates needlework with female comeliness and an "honest reputation" and directly contrasts it with the shame and dishonor brought on a woman who wrote. "How far more convenient the Distaffe, and Spindle, Needle and Thimble were for them [women] with good and honest reputation," Salter writes, "then the skil of well using a penne or wrighting a loftie vearce with disfame and dishonour" (Salter, qtd. in Trill 47). In other words, Salter argues that the art that women of "honest reputation" make, needlework, is a more honorable and "convenient" alternative to that which would bring them "dishonour," writing poetry.

In a popular instructional needlework manual for women, *The needle's excellency* (1634), John Taylor similarly articulates this double-bind, explaining that sewing was intended to keep women quiet, yet it was also an outlet for them to develop creativity and autonomy:

And for my countries quiet, I should like,
That woman-kinde should use no other Pike,
It will increase their peace, enlarge their store,
To use their tongues less, and their needles more.
The Needles sharpness, profit yields, and pleasure
But sharpness of the tongue bites out of measure.

Taylor contrasts the "sharpness" of women's tongues, which "bite" and serve as weapons much as the warlike Pike, with the "sharpness" of the needle, which brings peace and quiet to England. In so doing, Taylor would seem to strip women of their authority as well as their voice, yet he later describes needlework as a creative activity, calling women's "Practice and Invention" "free": "For here they may make choyce of which is which, / And skip from worke to worke, from stitch to stitch, / Until in time delightfull practice shall / (With profit) make them perfect in all" (131–34). By associating women's "invention" with the "workes" and "stitches" that give them pleasure and a sense of accomplishment, Taylor ascribes agency and "choyce" to women's work. Therefore, even though Taylor constructs women's needlework in opposition to writing and speaking, it is still an outlet for self-expression and mark of a woman's identity.

William Lawson's *The Countrie Hovsewife's Garden* (1617) frames women's gardening, as Taylor does, as an adherence to the "formes" already established which women could choose or adapt, such as those evidenced by the male-designed and managed orchard:

Let that which is sayd in the Orchards form suffice for a [lady's] garden in generall…let her view these few, choyce, new formes, and note this generally, that all plots are square, and all are bordered about with Fruit, Rasens, Teaberries, Roses, Thorn, Rosemarie, Bee-flowers, Hop, Sage, or such like. (2–3)

At the same time, this adherence to form is coupled with Lawson's insistence that women's gardening derives from their individual tastes, too: "Yet I leave everie housewife to her selfe, lest I deprive her of [her] delight and direction" (Lawson 3).

Wroth's sequence represents overlapping needlework, gardening, and writing images to represent creative female characters who engage in all three and, therefore, negotiate positions for women in them all. By emphasizing the overlapping territory between needlework and gardening, though, the sequence also reinforces the way that these practices intersected in practical ways as well as discursively throughout the period. In so doing, the sequence foregrounds the positive aspects of women's roles as gardeners and needleworkers in order to represent positive and legitimate roles for women as poets of original texts. At the same time, these images also reflect on the double-bind facing early modern women who wanted to engage in these three practices. These domains might serve as creative outlets, yet they reinforced dominant ideological notions of these practices as exemplifying dominant codes of feminine behavior so often restrictive to women.

The first song of the sequence features a shepherdess who brings together embroidery, gardening, and writing using modes of textile *and* textual production and drawing on her symbiotic relationship with the natural world as her resource. First, we are told, she converts nature into her book:

> The barck my booke shall bee
> Wher dayly I will wright
> This tale of haples mee
> True slave to fortunes spight (7, 33–36).

The clothes the shepherdess wears reflect both the endeavors of needlework and gardening, as they are "imbroder'd all" with "Gyrlands" of flowers. And she says she will "weare" the willow as a testimony of her grief and "dress" herself with the "branches" of the tree under which she wearily rests (7, 29–30, 23, 25–26), the same tree, as we see here, she also converts into a book. The various elements of her dress and her environment collectively help her tell her story. The story the shepherdess tells, though, attests to the double-bind she experiences: on the one hand, the shepherdess can indeed utilize the tools of nature and art to tell her story, and the story she tells testifies to her constancy and purity; on the other, the garlands and branches she wears provide her only company in an otherwise solitary existence, and the book she writes will be read only after her death, subject to others' reception and response.

At the same time, the shepherdess scene also works as a metaphor for the inherent double-bind position common to early modern women who, in participating in these artistic domains found themselves also conforming to normative feminine behavior. The "booke" the shepherdess writes reveals her to be "slave" to as well as master of the material she writes, since her story describes how she is "kil'd" with "cruell care"; to write this story allows her to tell her tale and shows she "constant lov'd," yet at the same time it proves her "end." The shepherdess is "slave" to fortune and destroyed by the fact that her desire was never realized, her constancy never recognized. Pamphilia articulates a similar double-bind when she says, "I seeke for some smale ease by lines, which brought / Increase the paine; griefe is not cured by art" (9, 3–4). While the shepherdess finds only "small ease" in her lines, "art" and writing bring her only minimal satisfaction. Still, the plight of both female characters, whose ability to express themselves in their "lines" and their "booke[s]" is limited by the frameworks they have available to them for writing, works as a metaphor for the women in early modern England who find themselves caught in the same double-bind. For the shepherdess, Pamphilia, and women (including Wroth herself) who wanted to publish their poetry, their "lines" provide "smale ease" as they allow women to express themselves yet mark them as unruly and unchaste.

The double-bind characteristic of the shepherdess scene is elsewhere encapsulated in Wroth's frequent and striking use of the word "bands," a word choice that had specific relevance to an argument about women's viability in multiple artistic domains. The OED cites the word "bands" as strips of material, bound or sewn together as well as the shackles that enslave, or bind.[7] But the word "band" had special significance to needlework, as women embroidered strips of material and sewed them together to create band samplers. Band samplers were used as teaching devices for young girls, who began by copying others' patterns to learn the stitches they would adapt into their own designs as they grew older.[8] Girls (and women) would embroider strips of material (bands) and sew them together to complete a sampler of their work. Younger girls would start with relatively simple patterns, and as they grew, their designs became increasingly more difficult and complex. To make a band sampler, though, a girl (or woman) also made herself subject to patterns designed by others; and men authored the pattern books these girls used. At the same time, her teacher may well have been another woman, who shared successful patterns that she learned from her mother or another woman. While band samplers certainly gave women something to feel proud of, they nevertheless reinforced dominant notions of proper feminine behavior, as suggested in the manuals by Taylor and Salter discussed earlier, since the ostensible purpose of practicing samplers was that these girls would keep their hands and minds busy and conform to patriarchal norms.

---

7   Mid-sixteenth to mid-seventeenth century usage of this word included a strip of fabric used to bind clothing or as decoration on clothing. "Band" samplers, while not specifically mentioned in the OED definition, were common in needlework in this period. The OED also cites "bands" as a decorative identificatory mark, which also makes it relevant to Wroth's usage here in the context of the freedom and bondage associated with needlework for women.

8   In *Samplers*, Carol Humphrey provides a visual and textual account of sampler production across a range of historical periods. See especially 1–23 for an Introduction to needlework samplers and a specific account of samplers from this period. As Humphrey notes, the most typical sampler design were comprised of "neatly worked bands of repeated patterns on a long narrow strip of linen" (16). See also Cavallo, 27–37, for a more detailed account of the needlework techniques used by women in this period. He describes needlework techniques, saying, "English work dating from about 1550–1700 is cohesive not only in its artistic character but in its technical aspects" (53). In Chapter 3, Cavallo also explains further "Mainstreams" of needlework in Western culture.

Using the multiply-signifying word "bands" encapsulates the creative freedom found in needlework as well as the subjection to male authority that women reaffirmed when engaging in diligent needlework. In *The Subversive Stitch* Roszika Parker analyzes the seemingly invisible yet critically productive role women played in the household economy as needleworkers. That is, women's embroidery was both aesthetic and inherently practical: "[Embroidery] ensured that women spent long hours at home, retired in private," writes Parker, "yet it made a public statement about the household's position and economic standing" (64). We also know that women used their needlework as part of a female "economic network" in which "textiles were almost as fluid as money as a medium of exchange" (Mendelson and Crawford 222–23).[9] As such a "medium of exchange," women's embroidery was a kind of currency by which women could trade for other goods; women appropriated the aesthetic value placed on needlework and transformed it into social and cultural capital they could then use to negotiate their social positions.

The word "bands" therefore signifies in multiple ways. When Pamphilia declares on page 10, "Yett firme love holds my sences in such band / As since despis'ed, I with sorrow marry," her use of "band" suggests her enslavement to love itself (10, 11–12). However, she later uses it in a different way, saying that "Folly would needs make mee a lover bee / When I did litle thinke of loving thought / Or ever to bee ty'de; while shee told me / That none can live, but to these bands are brought" (72, 1–4). In this second case, Pamphilia's "bands" chracterize both her enslavement and her promise of liberation. The "bands" to which she refers forever keep her "ty'de," but at the same time, without them, she proclaims, "none can live." In this way, Pamphilia's relationship to these "bands" is similar to that of the women who produced band samplers in this period. Women made imaginative works with their needles that would be displayed in the home or exchanged as a gift, even if such works reinforced definitions of femininity and virtue often declared restrictive and confining.

Women needleworkers were also part of a community that engaged them in productive and creative ways in the household and across households with other women, exemplified by women's sewing circles.[10] An anthology edited by Susan Frye and Karen Robertson, for example, looks at the alliances between women who made textiles in the household, who functioned as artists and agents, and who exchanged their needlework as gifts.[11] Frye writes in her essay, "Sewing Connections," "these needleworkers did not confront their society's equation of needlework with chaste labor so much as they accepted it and made it their own" (166). Women's needles transformed into "pens" on the canvas and functioned as "minute, stabbing swords,

---

9   Mendelson and Crawford likewise assert that women, by working with their needles in such private spaces, "might also exercise spatial and cultural dominance in spheres which were under men's nominal authority" (205).

10   See Frye and Robertson as one such recent and groundbreaking example of scholarship that cites women's groups as loci of power.

11   See Frye, "Sewing Connections," in which Frye argues that Elizabeth I utilized agency and political power prior to assuming the throne by making gifts of embroidery to be exchanged in the court. These gifts showed Elizabeth to be capable and educated and in exchanging them, she established for herself a position in the court.

as women worked patterns and narratives into their lives that conveyed their sense of themselves in the world" (166). Wroth's sequence serves as such a "narrative" in both the literal and the metaphysical sense that unites needlework and gardening as modes for women's self-expression with the more stigmatized mode of authorship deemed unsuitable for women. The needlework and gardening images serve in Wroth's poetry as examples of "narratives" women created as part of their artistic practice that were aligned with appropriate feminine behavior; therefore, when Wroth uses parallel examples of women creating texts, these "narratives" become appropriate chaste and feminine behavior too.

This context of needlework as inherently linked to both women's power and their powerlessness is thus inherent to Wroth's word choices and images. Pamphilia's "bands" attest to her constancy at the same time they cannot ultimately liberate her:

> Soe in part, we shall nott part
> Though wee absent bee;
> Time, nor place, nor greatest smart
> Shall my bands make free
> Ty'de I ame, yett thinke itt gaine;
> In such knotts I feele no paine. (28, 13–18).

Pamphilia's struggle to create "bands" and "knotts" evokes the situation of women whose needlework testified to their individual creative impulses, yet in so doing complied with dominant ideologies of feminine behavior.[12] Likewise, Wroth's choice of "bands" and "knotts" as metaphors call attention to her own divided position as a woman who is both subject to restrictive definitions of femininity and a subject who actively challenges those restrictions by publishing original, secular texts.

The "knotts" that Pamphilia describes in the above passage also evoke a very specific image of early modern formal gardens.[13] This particular word choice draws on the link between garden knot designs, women's embroidered knots, and women's writing. Commonly found in early modern garden structures, knots consisted of hedge material (such as boxwood) or herbs (such as thyme or rosemary) shaped into artfully knotted, interlocking patterns that framed other plants or flowers (See Fig 4 earlier in this chapter). But, as we see in William Lawson's *The Countrie Hovsewife's Garden* (1618), for example, women's garden knot patterns involved a combination of others' patterns and their own original designs. In this way, the "knots" (like the "bands") Pamphilia describes, like the Shepherdess's book and her embroidered clothes, call to mind the multiple meanings of not just imitating others' forms, but also of creating something new. Wroth's choice of "knotts," then, links

---

12 As is true of the term "bands," the term "knotts" is not used by Shakespeare in his *Sonnets*, and Sidney only uses the word once, but with different implications: "Come sleep, O sleep, the certain knot of peace" (*Astrophil and Stella* 39, 1).

13 We do not, for example, find this same word choice in other sonneteers who refer to gardens. Both Sidney and Shakespeare use the word "garden" to suggest domination and cultivation, usually of the female body. Shakespeare uses husbandry imagery to persuade the young man in Sonnet 3, for example, that he should "till" the woman's "womb" and plant his "seed" so that the young man can gain immortality by reproducing children.

both types of art Wroth identifies as already available for women—needlework and gardening. When Pamphilia says, "Ty'de I am, yett thinke itt gaine," in reference to the "bands" and "knotts," she foregrounds yet again the double-bind so characteristic of her situation and relevant to Wroth's own as a woman writer. To appropriate these particular artistic designs associates the creative authority of women who worked with their needle with those who fashioned intricate garden patterns on the landscape, while it simultaneously reveals that such creative freedom resides within different artistic domains over which men claim primary authority.

The gardens at the Penshurst estate where Wroth grew up were in fact central to family life there. Wroth's father, Robert Sidney, surrounded himself with gardens on the estates where he lived, and the grounds at Penshurst reflected his passion for Italian garden design.[14] In 1590, when Robert Sidney took possession of the Penshurst estate, he embarked on expensive and large-scale renovations, including having the south courtyard planted in an Italian garden design, complete with parterres, knots, and terraces. Although we do not have estate plans that detail changes to the gardens, a letter from Thomas Goldyng (Penshurst estate agent) to Robert Sidney dated May 8, 1608 describes what must have been a striking scene that included multiple gardens that stretched a considerable distance:

> He [the painter] hath sett him selfe on worke (all the tyme I was in London) in colloring all the dores about the gardens and that gallery, that is to say the garden dore going to the churche, the doble dore going out of the open place into the neither gallerye, and all the rest of the dores from thence into the privie garden and waldrop: the dore going up the stayers owt of the open place up into the upper gallery: the dore going out of the privie garden up to Glocester's Lodging: and the dore going into the privie garden out of the house. There is yett nothing done of the painter tmy Ladyes banqueting house. (*HMCD* [May 1607] 3: 374)

While the letter focuses on the painter's work in and around the garden area, we still get a good sense of the garden's expanse and variety. Penshurst included a "privie garden," an open garden area, a garden adjoining the church, and perhaps another surrounding Lady Sidney's banqueting house (as would have been common during the period). Like many formal aristocratic gardens, the gardens at Penshurst were designed as an extension of the house, and as Roy Strong argues, an extension of the owner's identity. Mary Wroth readily ties her identity to her Sidney family heritage as evidenced by the title page of the *Urania* and, even though she married in 1604, before this letter was written, she resided in the house during the period of construction and frequently visited later, which ties her Sidney family identity to this period of construction and the gardens and estate the family enjoyed for years to come.[15]

---

14   When in Flushing (and before taking possession of Penshurst) in 1590, Robert Sidney and his wife had a house with a garden that combined the formal garden design with a park area "cultivated to give a charming illusion of wilderness beauty" (Hay 173).

15   An ironic turn in this chapter of Sidney family history, the Penshurst estate and gardens may have signified the splendor and affluence of a prestigious aristocratic family, but the ongoing renovations nearly bankrupted Robert Sidney. His correspondence with his wife,

Among the architectural changes to the estate during the 1590s while Wroth lived in the house included the addition of a long gallery at the west end of the house and a series of state rooms, including the Solar Room, the Queen Elizabeth Room, and the Tapestry Room, which stand adjacent to one another and all overlook the gardens in the south courtyard (Hay 186) (see Fig. 5). The building project not only involved simultaneous construction of the gardens and rooms which either displayed embroidered tapestries or served as the place where women might embroider, but Wroth may well have associated it with a source of female authority. Robert Sidney spent much time away from home, and he left this project in the hands of his capable wife, reassuring her in a letter later, "I need not send to know how my buildings goe forward…for I ame sure you are so good a housewife you may be trusted with them" (*HMCD* [May 1594] 2: 153). Therefore, these renovations to Penshurst in the most practical sense highlight the material relationship between women's authority, writing, gardens, and embroidery, since Lady Sidney (Barbara Gamage) oversaw much of the building as the grounds were transformed and the edifice reshaped to accommodate spaces for women to embroider (the Solar Room) and for large-scale tapestries to be on display (the Queen Elizabeth Room).

Although we do not know whether or not Wroth herself dug in the dirt to plant the flowers and trees that adorned the Penshurst landscape, we do know that she appears to have shared her father's enthusiasm for gardens. The grounds at Penshurst were well known for their lush and ample fruit. In fact, Robert Sidney frequently mentions the Penshurst gardens in letters he wrote home to the family, and Mary Wroth reportedly brought him fruit from his orchards at home for comfort while he was away in London. On at least one occasion, it appears that Mary delivered apricots and cherries to her appreciative father in London (July, 1609) (*HMCD* 4: 138). Mary and her father were very close, as shown by a collection of correspondence between Sidney and his wife between 1608–1610, which reflect how Mary either visited him in London or the two planned to convene at Penshurst. Their mutual affection for one another seems to have extended to include a mutual love for the Penshurst estate and the gardens.

The "knotts" in Wroth's sequence are thus suggestive of the garden knots that decorated the grounds at the Sidney family estate where Wroth grew up, Penshurst, which further ties the gardening imagery in the sequence to Wroth's personal experience as a woman reared in a famous literary family. More than just the gardens, though, these "knotts" visible on the Penshurst grounds had a specific link to the room in the house where women retired after dinner and likely made their needlework designs as they spent hours in conversation together (Fig 5).

From the Solar Room window the women upstairs would have had one of the best views of the gardens to the south of the house, where parterres and knot gardens adorned the landscape. Given the immediacy of these gardens and their proximity to where women spent time at Penshurst, Wroth may well have associated the garden patterns that decorated her family home with those embroidered by the collectives of

---

especially from 1607–1613 show a real concern for setting his financial affairs in order, and he calls his condition "ruinous" (*HMCD* 2: 187).

Fig. 5   Penshurst Gardens (Solar Room, center window left of turret)

women inside.[16] While we have no clear way of knowing how much time Wroth spent in the Solar Room or whether she actually embroidered there, she more than likely spent time there and at least witnessed other women embroidering. After all, the Solar Room was an established place in the house for women to convene after dinner while men remained downstairs in the main banqueting room. And, since Penshurst was the home where she grew up, we might reasonably surmise that she wandered to the window from time to time and admired the elaborate patterns outside.

Among the women in the Solar Room, we can reasonably include Wroth's famous literary aunt, Mary Sidney. As a privileged member of the Sidney family, Mary Sidney would have spent many evenings at the Penshurst estate with her niece, Mary, and the rest of the family. Mary Sidney was well known for her embroidery and was, after all, commended by John Taylor in his manual, *The needle's excellency*, for her skill with a needle.[17] Taylor's commendation did not include, however, praise for Sidney's skill as a writer, a significant omission since Sidney was more renowned for her translation of the Psalms and other continental literature; and, Lanyer's

---

16   Tour books from Penshurst Place commonly describe the Solar Room as a more private, secluded space where women often retired and engaged in activities together, such as needlework or reading. To my knowledge, however, no other scholar has made the connection between the room often used by women and its visual proximity to the outside gardens. I discovered the link while visiting Penshurst in June, 2002.

17   Interestingly, Taylor includes in *The needle's excellency* a dedicatory poem to Mary Sidney, Countess of Pembroke, who was better known as a writer and translator than she was as a needleworker. In his poem, however, Taylor commends Sidney's virtue on the basis of her expertise with a needle, and says nothing about her skill with a pen.

commendation of Mary Sidney (discussed in Chapter 3) reminds us that Sidney was also known for her writing about settings that in many ways resemble the grounds outside and beyond the Solar Room at Penshurst. Using the word "knotts" in the sequence, then, points out the interfaces between the garden knots on the Penshurst grounds, the needlework knots the women made inside, and the way women were excluded from notoriety as published, original writers as well as the way their writing made them notable.

Looking for Love in All the Wrong Spaces

Just as Aemilia Lanyer's *Salve Deus* isolates an ideal for women in spatial terms, the Cooke-ham garden, so too does Wroth's *Pamphilia to Amphilanthus* suggest that the domains of needlework, gardening, and writing are more than figurative but are spatial as well. In fact, it is this "space" that Pamphilia seeks throughout the sequence, one in which she might articulate desire and, ideally, have that desire realized. In the absence of such a space, Pamphilia characterizes herself as alienated, marginalized, and indeed, "banish'd." On page 44, she asks,

> What pleasure can a banish'd creature have
> In all the pastimes that invented arr
> By witt or learning…
> Nor can I as those pleasant witts injoy
> My owne fram'd words, which I account the dross
> Of purer thoughts, or reckon them as moss
> While they (witt sick) themselves to breath imploy. (44 1–3, 45 5–8)

Pamphilia struggles to find locate her own "pleasures" among the "pastimes" she associates with "invention," "witt," and "learning." Like Sidney's Astrophil, the sources she seeks to situate her "pleasures" are contextualized in frameworks that call to mind male literary traditions, the conventions of being a desiring lover (in the case of Pamphilia and Astrophil) and of being a sonneteer (in the case of Sidney and Wroth).[18] Unlike Sidney's lover, although Pamphilia's "fram'd words" seem to come from a pure source, she finds it difficult to situate them within the already "invented" frameworks where others might hear them. Also unlike Sidney's would-be lover, whose Muse directs him to "look into thy heart and write," Wroth's Pamphilia receives no such consolation. Rather than looking inward, then, Pamphilia's struggle is directed outward, an externalized space where she might find acceptance. She sees herself not without the right words but rather without proper reception, like the Shepherdess of the first Song, or without the right space to express them, leaving her "banish'd" and alone.

This "banishment" conjoins Pamphilia's sense of frustration about how she might adequately express her "purer thoughts" and the possibility for women to be equal practitioners of "invented" literary frameworks. Pamphilia's "fram'd words" give her hope, and she finds companionship in her "thoughts," even if those words do not

---

18 See *Astrophil to Stella*, Sonnet 1.

meet with traditional modes of discourse: "When every one to pleasing pastime hies / Some hunt, some hauke, some play, while some delight / In sweet discourse, and musique showes joys might / Yett I my thoughts doe farr above these prise" (26, 1–4). Pamphilia's concern with "invention" emerges again, this time on page 69, as yet another option for self-expression, but one limited by those around her. She chides herself for being ruled by jealousy, which she concludes creates only "secret art," and she says, "Thou canst noe new invention frame butt part / I have allreddy seene, and felt with woe" (69, 2–4). Pamphilia's frustrated maneuvers within the structures of "invention" metaphorically evoke the way that women writers sought space for themselves in male-coded literary frameworks and call to mind Ann Rosalind Jones's assertion that women writers in this period were both "participants" in social change and "co-performers with the male poets they cite[d], revise[d], and challenge[d]" (3).

Early modern women writers like Wroth adapted male-coded literary frameworks, and their texts foregrounded, as Ann Rosalind Jones puts it, "strategies for maneuvering within restrictions and turning the contradictions among different discourses of femininity to their own advantage" (15). Adapting one such framework, pastoral, Wroth's sequence emphasizes this search for a "space" or "place," lending a spatial dimension to the issues of women's creativity raised throughout the sequence by the overlapping needlework, gardening, and writing imagery.[19] Pamphilia, for example, often laments her uncertain position in a "strang place," as she does on page 63:

> So ar my fortunes, bard from true delight
> Colde, and unsertaine, like to this strang place,
> Decreasing, changing in an instant space,…
> Where pleasure hath noe settled place of stay
> Butt turning still for our best hopes decay,
> And this (alas) wee lovers often gaine. (63, 5–7, 12–14)

Though she articulates her "true delight" and her "pleasure," both remain unrealized, constrained by the circumstances by which they *might be* realizable in the first place. Pamphilia is thus figuratively caught in the "strang place" somewhere between her desire to love and redefine constancy and her acknowledgment that such desire is always mediated by forces beyond her control, implying metaphorically that an ideal domain for women is mediated by the discourses and domains regulated by men, such as the pastoral genre itself. The image of the "strang place" becomes even more specific and confining, as it translates into a "strang cage" on page 66, when she says, "O in how strang a cage ame I kept in?" (66, 11). Therefore, Pamphilia's wandering never ceases, she remains in the "cage," because the modus operandi, the pastoral wanderings which her search exemplifies, limits the degree to which her love can ever fully be satisfied.

---

19   For good, general book-length studies of pastoral see Alpers, Empson, Toliver, and Poggioli. See also Montrose, "'Eliza'" and Patterson. Montrose and Patterson complicate the notions of pastoral in the aforementioned books to look instead at what kind of "work" pastoral texts might do.

Pamphilia's fruitless search among the "places" and the "ways" that already exist works as an effective metaphor for the way that women struggled to find identities for themselves as artists and agents in domains already claimed by men. Pamphilia seeks respite in the "sweet shades" on page 19: "Sweet shades, why doe you seeke to give delight / To mee who deeme delight in this vilde place" (P19, 1–2). And again, on page 34, she looks to the "blessed shades" which, as she says, "give mee silent rest" (P34, 1). Despite her attempts to find such a place, however, Pamphilia continues to lament that she cannot seem to find a way. On page 36, for example, she declares,

> After long trouble in a taedious way
> Of loves unrest, lay'd downe to ease my paine
> Hopeing for rest, new torments I did gaine
> Possessing me as if I ought t'obay. (36, 1–4)

And on page 53, she similarly concludes,

> Noe place for help have I left to invade,
> That show'de a face wher least ease might bee gain'd;
> Yett found I paine increase, and butt obtain'd
> That this noe way was to have love allay'd. (36, 1–4; 53, 5–8)

Pamphilia's undaunted attempts to proceed along the "taedious way" and find a "place" to express herself have, as she concludes, left her "Noe place" and "Noe way" left to go, only "new torments" and "pain[s] increase." These different "ways," like the pastimes she finds so dissatisfying, signal a connection between the places Pamphilia seeks and the different domains available to women like Wroth.

To Everything Turn, Turn, Turn

In the Crown of Sonnets approximately two-thirds the way through the sequence, Pamphilia's quest for a "place" or "space" abruptly halts, and the needlework, gardening, and writing imagery becomes concentrated and centrally focused on the most bounded, spatial image of the sequence, the labyrinth. Labyrinths have frequently appeared in literature—for example, the myth of Ariadne, Theseus, and the Minotaur, and in the *Romance of the Rose*. Wroth's use of the labyrinth has special significance in the context of the other needlework, gardening, and writing images elsewhere in the sequence, though. Garden labyrinths served as visual reminders of human art ordering the disorderly landscape; and yet when women made needlework labyrinths, they were a specifically female-appropriated art that imposed order and form over a blank canvas (Fig 6).

In Wroth's sequence, the labyrinth is an image that embodies all three artistic domains at once: it evokes actual garden labyrinths made of hedge material and the popular thread designs on women's canvases; it is a metaphor for Pamphilia'a wandering within spaces that leave her feeling trapped yet within which she exercises mobility and articulates desire; and, finally, it works as the most material, spatial representation of the search for an alternative space for women that pervades

Fig. 6   Garden labyrinth design, William Lawson's *The Country Hovsewife's Garden* (1623).

the sequence. Wroth asserts aesthetic control over the image as she composes the series of highly formalized interlocking sonnets. At the same time, even as a literary image, the labyrinth paradoxically suggests captivity within its maze-like structure *and* the potential for liberation if one reaches the center. Commonly used in both needlework and garden patterns, and a popular design in country house gardens in the period, labyrinth gardens dated back to Pre-Reformation churches and, later, monastic gardens and had their own spatial significance in relationship to the shift from ecclesiastical to private, secular land ownership.[20] Labyrinths were places of meditation and exercise, and they served as visual reminders of how humans imposed of order over the natural world. The garden labyrinth represents human art imposing order and form over nature; and the needlework labyrinth is a specifically female-appropriated art that imposes order and form over a blank canvas. By combining these meanings with her use of the labyrinth as a structure linked together by words, Wroth foregrounds the interconnections between them all. As a multiply-signifying image, the labyrinth thus unites the artistic domains in which Wroth—and, by extension, early modern women in general—could potentially speak, and it simultaneously

---

20   Strong discusses the significance of the labyrinth in the period, as he writes that gardens in the sixteenth and seventeenth centuries often consisted of a series of knots, mazes, and labyrinths, and that "The garden evolved into a series of separate yet interconnected intellectual and physical experiences which required the mental and physical co-operation of the visitor as he moved through them" (20). The interconnected experiences that Strong mentions as well as the "co-operation" between humans and the landscape they traverse in the garden space are precisely what Wroth's sonnet sequence presents. See also Girouard, 82–118, for a more detailed analysis of the architecture and landscape of English country houses in the Elizabethan and Jacobean periods.

represents the actual garden spaces where women worked and demonstrated how they, too, could use their art to stylize nature.[21]

The labyrinth in Wroth's sequence evokes a particularly spatial image related to these multiple domains, though. Labyrinths functioned much as architectural spaces did in literature and in early modern England. Shannon Miller has argued recently, as I do here, that Wroth "turns to spaces constructed by men—both architectural structures and literary traditions" in her *Urania* (to which *Pamphilia to Amphilanthus* was appended), in order "to provide an avenue for an expression of the female self" (Miller 142). Much as Miller argues for Pamphilia's attempts to vocalize her interior, female self within architectural "spaces constructed by men," I show here that the labyrinth, a spatially-oriented and highly-structured garden, needlework, *and* writing image, functions as the space where the potentially restrictive yet liberating conditions inherent to women's creativity in these different domains materializes in the clearest and most articulated way. In a sense, the labyrinth is the space Pamphilia has been looking for and that Wroth herself creates with words, making it the most tangible evidence of the way Wroth uses gardens to imagine making space for herself and other women to continue to do so as writers of original texts.

To find the labyrinth as such a central feature of *Pamphilia to Amphilanthus* is not surprising, since *The Countesse of Mountgomeries Urania* (1621), to which Wroth appended her sonnet sequence, features numerous scenes within gardens and garden-like spaces, including labyrinths.[22] In Book 2, Pamphilia asks to be delivered to a labyrinth for her comfort (61). One of the most developed of these garden scenes occurs at the end of Book 1, when the lovers must prove their constancy to gain entry into the Court of Love. Pamphilia and Amphilanthus pass through the first two towers at the Court of Love, Desire and Love, and approach the third and final one, Constancy, at which time

> Both then at once extremely loving, and love in extremity in them, made the Gate flie open to them, who passed to the last Tower, where Constancy stood holding the keyes, which Pamphilia tooke; at which instance Constancy vanished, as metamorphosing her self into her breast: then did the excellent Queene deliver them to Amphilanthus, who joyfully receiving them, opened the Gate; then passed they into the Gardens, where round about a curious Fountaine were fine seates of white Marble. (*Urania*, Book 1 169)

---

21 Hobhouse writes that gardens in the period were "organized by man's art so that the living plant's forms, colour, and texture became an integral part of the whole. Not only was nature itself seen as cosmically ordered so that the art of gardening required its imitation; it was also seen that nature could be improved upon if planted and cultivated in an ordered way" (140). Hobhouse articulates a sentiment that Wroth clearly contradicts here, which was that this improvement over nature was "man's art." Wroth draws on women's ability, too, to "imitate" the cosmic order of the landscape and improve on it with their art.

22 See Wroth, *The Countesse of Mountgomeries Urania* (1621), 41–42, which includes a brief scene in a garden, and pages 47–48, which includes a more extensive scene within a garden that looks ahead to the one at the end of Book 1, when Pamphilia and Amphilanthus enter the Court of Love and its interior garden. In this scene, too, they move "as in a labyrinth" (47). Pamphilia travels within gardens on pages 68–69 and 90–97, and Amphilanthus encounters gardens on pages 135–36 and 139. All of these scenes precede the culminating one at the Court of Love at the end of the Book, which I discuss later in this section.

One of the most significant bounded "places" in Wroth's prose pastoral, therefore, is part of a garden. In fact, the ultimate reward for constant love, their "love in extremity," is entry through the gates of the Court of Love into its promising gardens on the other side. This scene also foregrounds needlework, as Pamphilia appears in front of the three towers that precede the Court of Love "apparreld in a Gowne of light Tawny or Murrey, embroidered with the richest, and perfectest Pearle for roundnesse and whitenes, the work contrived into knots and Garlands" (*Urania* 169). Together, that is, needlework and gardens form the material base of the ritual reward for constancy.

The gardens in the Court of Love that figure as prominent spaces in the longer prose work, *Urania,* become incorporated into the Crown of Sonnets in *Pamphilia to Amphilanthus.* As if to emphasize further the importance of the garden space in the longer pastoral, the frontispiece to the *Urania* pictures the Court of Love, with its three towers for the lovers pass through, and beside them a formal garden like the one described at the end of Book One (Fig. 7). Picturing the gardens just to the right of the Court of Love in the frontispiece (bottom right side) impresses them into the visual memory of readers and frames them as significant. In the center of the frontispiece stands the Court of Love, its gardens to the right, which suggests a fundamental connection between the love shared by Pamphilia and Amphilanthus and the gardens as an ideal space for that love to be manifest and rewarded. Moreover, the knots and parterres in the walled garden (bottom right) in the frontispiece very much resemble the gardens at Penshurst, reinforcing the connection between Wroth's own familiarity with gardens and those she wrote about.

In the sonnet sequence appended to Wroth's long prose romance, *Pamphilia to Amphilanthus,* the Court of Love in the Crown of Sonnets similarly functions as the "place" Pamphilia is searching for where constant love prevails. On page 2, Pamphilia calls the Court of Love the "court of glory, wher Loves force was borne" and the "loved place of sought for triumphs neere" (2, 4, 3). In both texts, the Court of Love is the ideal place for lovers to convene, an isolated location where their constant and chaste love receives the recognition it lacks elsewhere. It is not a coincidence, then, that in the Crown of Sonnets the Court of Love (and its adjacent gardens central to the climactic moment when the lovers join) has a significant parallel with the space Wroth creates in her sonnet sequence.

Wroth's Court of Love (and its attendant gardens) serves as an earthly representation of heavenly perfection, much as early modern gardens were described as being in the period. In England earlier, the *Romance of the Rose* contained a garden described as an earthly paradise, and gardens later evolved out of the monastic gardening tradition and still bore its traces, the notion that the human art of gardening could reconstruct any flaws in the natural world from the Fall. During the sixteenth and seventeenth century, secular gardens were imagined as reconstructions of God's originally created Nature, Eden.[23] By offering "fruit" which "none repent," the Court of Love stands as a perfect (or perhaps perfected) version of the natural world, before Adam and Eve were thrust from Paradise, before repentance was a necessary remedy for sin. The court is, for example, the place where the "Light

---

23   See Strong, Thomas, and Hobhouse.

Fig. 7   Title Page, *Urania* (1621).

of true love, brings fruite which none repent / Butt constant lovers seeke, and wish to prove" and the heaven on earth where purity and innocence prevail over shame and affliction (78, 7–8, 79). The garden imagery here relates Pamphilia's desire to Adam and Eve's pure love and the purity of the landscape before the Fall. Like these ideal gardens, Wroth's ideal space in the Court of Love and its related garden space evoked by the labyrinth image in particular, becomes Wroth's own recreation of an earthly paradise.

Indeed, the very use of a "Crown" of Sonnets also carries with it connotations of both literary achievement and gardening. In *The Culture of Flowers* Jack Goody cites "crowns," or garlands, of flowers as having a special significance during different historical periods, including the early modern period. They were "awarded to the winners in popular games, in dances and for poetry," he writes, were associated with Petrarchan poetry, and figured in religious debates during the seventeenth century.[24] To call this series of poems a "Crown" is not surprising in and of itself, since other poets—notably John Donne and Wroth's father, Robert Sidney—used this poetic form, but Wroth's use of the Crown is particularly secular, unlike Donne's. Wroth's highly developed Crown draws attention yet again to her argument about uniting the artistic domains in which women can create art as well as women's demonstrated success in doing so. Wroth's Crown shows how a woman can shape Nature—in this case the flowers that make the garland—as well as claim poetic authority and earn the laurel crown for herself.

Women not only made labyrinths outside in the garden, but they also constructed labyrinths inside the house on fabric canvas. Although Penshurst apparently did not have a labyrinth on its grounds, Wroth frequented Hampton Court as one of Queen Anne's ladies in waiting, and there she probably took her turn navigating the labyrinth with others during court recreation. That Wroth might have associated the labyrinth with her experience at court also suggests a context for her depiction of Pamphilia's frustrated wandering through the labyrinth in the Crown of Sonnets. After all, by the time Wroth wrote *Pamphilia to Amphilanthus* she had been banished from the court following her scandalous relationship with William Herbert, with whom she had several children.[25] The labyrinth image may well have evoked for Wroth memories of festivities at court and her ties there as well as bitterness over being thrust from courtly circles.

The labyrinth is also associated with women's needlework in the Crown of Sonnets, since labyrinths were common needlework designs, too. The "thread" of love Pamphilia uses to guide her through the labyrinth unites the pleasure of creating something, a piece of needlework, and the potential freedom such creation makes possible. The "thread of love," Pamphilia claims, "leads unto the soules content" (78 1.1–2), and it links Pamphilia's hope to emerge from the labyrinth, Wroth's authorship, and the production of a piece of needlework. For Pamphilia, the

---

24   In *The Culture of Flowers,* Jack Goody explores the relationship between flowers, especially garlands, and religious debate: "The contrast persisted between the perishable garlands and enduring crowns, preferably spiritual" (201).

25   For more about Wroth's relationship with Herbert and this scandal, see Roberts's Introduction to Wroth's poems, pages 23–26.

"thread" to which she refers signifies both at the same time; the "thread," like her "bands," suggests both her bondage and her freedom. Pamphilia's claim to "take the thread of love," therefore, might call attention to the fact that women's embroidering reinforced prescriptive definitions of feminine behavior, but it also associates her work as author with the way women adapted men's designs in their own embroidery patterns.[26] These "patterns," evocative of both literary and domestic ones so important to the argument throughout Wroth's sequence, may seem to limit the extent to which Pamphilia can initiate and sustain her movement within the labyrinth. However, like the shepherdess earlier, and like Wroth herself, Pamphilia's experience within and use of the labyrinth space results in something new.

While Pamphilia might articulate her limitations, Wroth's sequence exemplifies the same kind of authority and social power women in early modern England found in employing their skills with the needle and thread, by making their own gardens, or by revising literary patterns to express themselves in distinct and effective ways. Pamphilia may defer to the authority of Love, saying that "*Love* is true vertu" and "Hee may our profitt, and out Tuter prove / In whom alone wee doe this power finde" (78, 13 my emphasis; 82, 1–2). And, she boldly proclaims, "His [Love's] flames ar joyes, his bands true lovers might / Noe staine is ther butt pure, as purest white, / Wher no clowde can appere to dimm his light, / Nor spott defile, butt shame will soone requite" (79, 1–4). In this case, Love's "bands" grant Pamphilia, and all lovers, strength. Love's "bands," as Pamphilia describes them, are "true lover's might," a sign that constancy equals power. Likewise, she associates this power with purity, since it is in the Love that "no spott defile." In so doing, Wroth questions the popular assertion that, as published writers of original texts, women compromised their chastity; the "bands" of Love and the power associated with them give Pamphilia the authority to proclaim her love and, by extension, they give Wroth the authority to write and publish her sonnets.[27] Rather than being purely restrictive, the "bands" that women worked in the domestic circles become the figurative means by which Wroth's own creative material is made public in her published poetry.

Such revision of traditional Petrarchan poetic discourse goes hand in hand with needlework imagery elsewhere, too, in the Crown.[28] Pamphilia's lovers share mutual

---

26 Waller identifies another specific "tracing" that Wroth executes as he writes that she is "tracing the ways both assigned and lived gender roles were under pressure in the seventeenth century" (*Sidney* 191).

27 Wall calls such original texts "gendered male" and argues that Wroth, in writing her own sequence, "inadvertently re-gendered herself when she published her ambitious, unmediated fictions" (*Imprint* 337).

28 While scholars have noted the Petrarchan elements in Wroth's sequence, I contend that Wroth does not so much follow the Petrarchan model but, as she does with other male literary frameworks, she revises it to make something unique. See Dubrow, who writes, for example, that Wroth's *Pamphilia to Amphilanthus* is "festooned and impelled by Petrarchan conventions" and that it "manifests the customary nostalgia of Petrarchanism and in so doing also signals her consciousness of the achievements of a dead father, a dead uncle, and a genre that many of her contemporaries considered moribund" (141–42). Dubrow also argues that Wroth is both "playing on a generic tradition as well as playing against it" (160). See also Roberts, "Introduction" and note for 77, line 1.

and reciprocal desire in the Court of Love, quite different from the unrequited frustration elaborated by traditional Petrarchan lovers: "Eyes which must to one deere object bind / Eares to each others speech as if above" (82, 5–6). Quite different from the Petrarchan blazon, which figures the female object of beauty by reducing her to a series of parts, the individual parts Pamphilia lists, the "Eyes" and the "Eares" here bind the lovers together. They are not simply a reduction of parts, but they are united as parts of a whole. Evocative of yet another reference to needlework, reciprocal love, a central tenet in the sequence and one which differentiates Wroth's sequence from her uncle's, is held together by the "frame" that binds lovers together: "To joine two harts as in one frame to move; / Two bodies, but one soule to rule the minde" (82, 3–4). As is true of the multiple signification of the "bands," the "thread of love," and the labyrinth, the "frame" here signifies both the lover's constancy that structures their relationship and the embroidery "frame" that women used to hold their fabric when working on a textile.[29]

Such multiple signification creates a tension between the conventional "frame" of the lover/beloved relationship in conventional (and male-authored) Petrarchan poetry and the way that women traditionally used frames to hold their work as they fashioned their own fictional tales of love on canvas. Wroth's Crown of Sonnets also calls attention to another kind of textual significance, the labyrinthian structure of the poems themselves. As a series of interconnected poems with such maze-like twists and turns, the Crown of Sonnets is structurally similar to a labyrinth, and it suggests that women can be active agents yet simultaneously limited by the poetic form they use for such self-expression. Pamphilia articulates her desire to make a mark for herself, to find her own way within the labyrinth's seemingly confined space, as she says, "In this strang labourinth how shall I turne? / Wayes are on all sides while the way I miss" (77, 1–2). Despite Pamphilia's attempts to find a way out, others' work has already marked the choices available to her, the "way" that she might proceed:

> If to the right hand, ther, in love I burne;
> Let mee goe forward, therein danger is;
> If to the left, suspition hinders bliss,
> Let mee turne back, shame cries I ought returne
> Nor fainte though crosses with my fortunes kiss;
> Stand still is harder, although sure to mourne;
> Thus let mee take the right, or left hand way;
> Goe forward, or stand still, or back retire. (77, 3–10)

Pamphilia is clearly limited by the structure within which she tries to move, but not by a lack of desire to move in the first place. We might read the various "way[s]" Pamphilia has to choose from to be analagous to the way that Wroth seeks a position for women within a male literary tradition. Like Pamphilia, Wroth's movement within the social and literary structures is limited not by her desire to assert herself as a woman writer but seemingly by the structures themselves. That both the sense

---

29 See Carvallo's Introduction for further explanation of the uses and pictures of these "frames."

of confinement and mobility in the labyrinth comes from Pamphilia's "turning" compounds the other imagery associated with negotiating the labyrinth and reinforces the textual structure, which makes Wroth's asserted mastery over these multiple art forms difficult to ignore and hard to imagine as arbitrary or accidental. Wroth creates a coherent textual labyrinth over which she claims authority and which reveals her poetic ability to rival any male poet who might challenge her.

Wroth repeatedly draws attention to the Crown of Sonnets as a whole and her metaphor of the labyrinth to show that her writing has redefined chastity, honor, and virtue as well as renegotiated the conditions under which those terms apply to women. She returns at the end of the Crown where she begins: "Soe now in Love I fervently doe burne, / In this strange labourinth how shall I turne?" (90, 13–14). This return completes the labyrinth that frames Wroth's Crown of Sonnets, and such a return would be inevitable in their maze-like structure; in the labyrinth one enacts a circular movement, emphasized by the return at the end of her Crown of Sonnets to the same question with which we begin. Such circularity further emphasizes the double bind that Wroth shows applies to women's active role in multiple artistic domains.

The sequence calls into question the gendered boundaries between art forms as she shows how women's use of any of these forms can equally and simultaneously embody chastity, purity, and constancy. Pamphilia explores new ways to define her "chaste art" as it applies to both writing and needlework. On page 83 Pamphilia describes "just desire" as the product of Love. She says,

> Love will a painter make you, such, as you
> Shall able bee to drawe your only deere
> More lively, parfett, lasting, and more true
> Then rarest woorkman, and to you more neere. (83, 9–12)

In this sonnet, Pamphilia has not only declared herself a desiring lover, but she has also declared her desire "just"; *her desire* licenses her power and authority to create art. However, the art that Pamphilia says that "just desire" makes possible is a type of art—painting—which was, like published texts, not typically produced by women in the period who wanted to avoid being stigmatized and declared unchaste. In this sonnet, as well as in the sequence as a whole, Wroth equates the production of art forms by men, such as painting and authorship, with the production of art forms by women, such as needlework; they are all, in other words, equally products of "just desire" and represented as the "chaste art" of Love.

By conjoining needlework and gardening imagery within a shaped, textual labyrinth, Wroth foregrounds her argument that women's writing is an appropriate art form for women, even if women struggle to find appropriate venues for their writing. The mobility Pamphilia gains as she negotiates within this space catalyzes her active challenge to the boundaries that seem so limiting. After all, Pamphilia continues to articulate this desire as she moves, not prevented by the obstacles she encounters. The "turning" she effects within the labyrinth-space actually grants her a kind of mobility and freedom, and it is reinforced by the Crown's structure itself, in which the interlocking lines create a sense of unity, despite Pamphilia's claims of feeling lost. This interconnecting framework further emphasizes how Wroth, too, is not entirely dissuaded by doubts or obstacles but instead challenges and negotiates the boundaries that seem to limit the extent to which her voice can or will be heard. And, while this negotiation does not necessarily mean that she will or even can successfully transcend such limitations, it does suggest that Wroth continues to speak and to assert her voice publicly as she pens and publishes her sonnets.

The various gardening, needlework, and writing images placed throughout the sequence tell us much about how a woman writer might imagine making space for herself and others like her in a man's world. Weaving these images together, Wroth draws on the experiences of early modern Englishwomen whose everyday domestic practices gave them opportunities for agency and establishes that women like Wroth might justify a claim to such agency in the print marketplace. But by aligning these three artistic domains, Wroth's sequence also looks ahead to the later seventeenth century when restrictions were lifted considerably and we find Hannah Woolley publishing *The accomplisht lady's delight* (1650). Included in a later edition of her book is a short section on gardening for women, written by Thomas Harris, *The Lady's Direction in Her Garden* (1675). Offering instruction for women in gardening and needlework (among other topics), this text is the first example of such concentrated instruction in a book by a woman, even if the section itself was penned by a man. In fact, it would seem that Harris was trying to capitalize on Woolley's success with previous editions of her book. Therefore, while Wroth's sonnet sequence shows us the imagined possibilities, Woolley's manual shows how women might be authorities in them all quite literally at the same time in print. Imagining the possibilities for women to negotiate positions in domains otherwise off limits means first looking at the domains in which they already occupied central positions, suggesting that social change begins with the imagination and what is imaginable is shaped by what is possible.

While Pamphilia emerges from the labyrinth asking the same question she asked upon entering it, she is hardly paralyzed or rendered immobile. Far from it, at the end of the Crown, Pamphilia continues to "burne[s]" as "fervently" as she did from the beginning, an undaunted passion that prevails despite her many moments of frustration (P90, 13–14). Wroth thus completes her labyrinth, weaving together in one image domestic and published artistic domains over which she demonstrates authority and control. Perhaps the most tangible sign of Wroth's unrelenting assertion of a public voice, however, is the fact that she did publish; even her promise to remove her books from circulation and prevent further sales is tempered by her insistence that she will only do so because others' have misrepresented and misconstrued her meaning.[30] Like Pamphilia, Wroth refuses to censor herself: "I shall with all cleernes and truth wittnes my innocency, and not now with words or submission (which I scorne) goe about to give any satisfaction, but [with] true and loyall faith prove and justifie what I have said."[31]

---

30 See "Lady Mary Wroth to the Duke of Buckingham" December 15, 1621 (Roberts, *Poems*, 236).

31 See "Lady Mary Wroth to Sir Edward Denny" February 27, 1621 (Roberts, *Poems* 240).

Epilogue:
Looking Ahead

"Every society…produces a space, its own space"
                                              Henri Lefebvre

If it is true, as Lefebvre suggests, that every society produces its own space, then the conclusions drawn here about the relationship between writing, gardening, and the gardens imagined and made apply specifically to the group and historical context of the gardens in question. By applying Lefebvre's theoretical model to a particular historical moment, the early modern period in England, this study answers critics of Lefebvre's work, who suggest that his theoretical framework does not provide enough historical specificity. The early modern English garden grew largely out of the contemporary, historical phenomena—an heightened sensitivity to fashioning the individual and the rise of the middling sort, to name but two that are deeply rooted in the gardening tradition (and its attendant changes) during this period. The gardens featured in this book grew out of a period of radical changes to the landscape that were directly related to social and economic reconfigurations in England, including Protestantism, nascent capitalism, and the transition from an independent female monarch to an absolutist male monarch. But the period that followed, from Charles I to the Commonwealth period to the Restoration reflect gardening that was radically divergent in its practice and representative efficacy. The gardens planted and written about from 1625–1660 were used as political tools and signified in ways quite different from those earlier. During a period of Civil War, the way men and women made garden spaces inherently linked them to questions of political subversion, religious dissent, and scientific discourse.

Focusing on a select group of texts and representative gardens, the work represented here can serve as a springboard for studying the triangulated interrelationship between gardening as a spatial practices, the social relationships represented in garden spaces, and representations of gardens in texts from other periods, too. Can we say the same things about gardens that came before or that followed? Or do these other gardens do something different? Are they different spaces altogether? One might reasonably argue that the period that followed, still considered "early modern" but markedly different in its attitudes (and rapidly changing ones) toward gardens, marks a different phase in its gardening practice and representation of gardens. To uncover these attitudes and practices would illuminate, as it did in this study, a broader understanding of how early modern English social space is not one thing but many, a product of different spatial practices and representations. When Charles I takes the throne, gardens serve as backdrops for court masques to reify the divine right of kingship in ways unprecedented under either Elizabeth or his father, James. The formal aristocratic garden increases in scale and further develops its use of Italianate gardening, with grottoes, statuary, and water automata, even as those in the middling sort establish themselves more than ever as players and practitioners in the "art" of gardening.

During the Civil War, however, aesthetic gardening takes on a different set of associations, as gardening becomes linked with the ostentation of the High Church and contrary to Puritan sensibilities. The Diggers, led by Gerrard Winstanley, literally dig up the ground in St. George's Park to plant a communal farm. Social leveling for Winstanley and the Diggers was equated with a leveling of the landscape and set in opposition to the kind of planting so popular through the early seventeenth century, in which rare and exotic flowers that depicted the owner's affluence were the rage. One might argue, then, that gardening during the Commonwealth period in England resembled something more akin to the subsistence planting popular in the early sixteenth century than the kind of planting popular among the middling and upper classes earlier in the seventeenth century. In 1660, however, when Charles II returned from France, he brought with him a fondness for and familiarity with French gardening, an even more formalized type of gardening than was popular in England earlier, and England began to develop what we now think of when we say, "English gardens."

Gardens as represented in literature throughout this period of radical changes to gardening practice follows suit. Robert Herrick's *Hesperides* (1648) reflect his Royalist sympathies; Andrew Marvell's "Upon Appleton House" (1650s) and his other garden poems indicate a poet struggling to articulate his ambivalent political allegiances; John Milton writes the Garden of Eden in *Paradise Lost* (1667) as a way of searching for a moment in England that is consistent with God's original creation; Francis Bacon and the Royal Society saw nature for its potential to be discovered by the empirical eye of the scientist, and gardens were the manifestation of nature's perfection. His "Of Gardens" (1625) describes a garden perfectly arranged and suited to apprehend all of its observers' senses, a garden for pleasure as well as scientific curiosity; but Margaret Cavendish, who was deeply interested in the new experimental science and the Royal Society, reframes not just the garden, but the entire world, under the empirical gaze and capable hands of the female scientist/ creator in *The New Blazing World* (1666). Texts that represent gardens in the second part of the seventeenth century seem concerned not so much with self-fashioning as with coming to terms with acute disruptions to the English political and physical landscape. That is, the scientific discourse of Bacon, Cavendish, and even Milton, suggests less an interest in shaping the self vis-à-vis English society than it does in situating the self's (or society's) place in a universe typified by but which extends beyond England. In short, there is still much terrain left unexplored, more gardens worth digging up.

Works Cited

Alpers, Paul, *What is Pastoral?* (Chicago and London: University of Chicago Press, 1996).

Amussen, Susan Dwyer, *An Ordered Society: Gender and Class in Early Modern England* (Oxford: Basil Blackwell, 1988).

Anonymous, *The Orchard and the Garden* (London: Printed by Adam Islip, 1594).

Bacon, Francis, "Of Gardens", in *The Essays* (1625) (Yorkshire: Scholar Press, 1971), pp. 266–79.

Baker, Alan R.H. and Gideon Biger, ed. *Ideology and Landscape in Historical Perspective* (Cambridge: Cambridge University Press, 1992).

Barroll, Leeds, "Looking for Patrons" In Marshall Grossman (ed.), *Aemilia Lanyer: Gender, Genre, and the Canon* (Lexington: University Press of Kentucky, 1993), pp. 29–48.

Beacon, Richard, *Solon his Follie, or a politique discourse, touching the reformation of common-weales* (Oxford: J. Barnes,1594), ed. Clare Carroll and Vincent Carey (Binghamton: Center for Medieval and Early Renaissance Studies, 1996).

Beck, Thomasina, *Embroidered Gardens* (London: Angus and Robertson Publishing, 1979).

Beilin, Elaine V., *Redeeming Eve: Women Writers of the English Renaissance* (Princeton: Princeton University Press, 1987).

Best, Michael, ed. *The English Housewife* (Gervase Markham. Kingston: McGill Queens University, 1986).

Bonnefons, Nicholas, *The French Gardiner* (London: Printed for John Crooke, 1658).

Bourdieu, Pierre, *Distinction: A Social Critique of the Judgment of Taste*, trans. Richard Nice (Cambridge: Harvard University Press, 1984).

_____*Outline of a Theory of Practice*, trans. Richard Nice (Cambridge: Cambridge University Press, 1977).

Bradshaw, Brendan, Andrew Hadfield, and Willy Maley (eds), *Representing Ireland: Literature and the Origin of Conflict, 1534–1660* (Cambridge: Cambridge University Press, 1993).

Brathwaite, Richard, *The English Gentlewoman* (1631), ed. Joan Klein, *Daughters, Wives, and Widows: Writings by Men about Women and Marriage in England, 1500–1640* (Chicago: University of Illinois Press, 1992).

Breen, John, "'Spenser's Imaginative Groundplot': *A View of the Present State of Ireland*' *Spenser Studies* 12(1998): 151–68.

Bright, Timothie, (*A treatise of melancholy* (London: Printed by Iohn Windet, 1586).

Burke, Mary E., Jane Donawerth, Linda L. Dove, and Karen Nelson (eds), *Women, Writing, and the Reproduction of Culture in Tudor and Stuart Britain* (New York: Syracuse University Press, 2000).

Burton, Robert, *Anatomy of Melancholy*, vol. 2, ed. Faulkner and Blair Reissling (Oxford: Oxford University Press, 1994).

Bushnell, Rebecca, *Green Desire: Imagining Early Modern English Gardens* (Ithaca and London: Cornell University Press, 2003).

Butler, Judith, *Bodies That Matter* (New York and London: Routledge, 1993).

———— *Gender Trouble* (New York and London: Routledge, 1990).

Cahn, Susan, *Industry of Devotion: The Transformation of Women's Work in England, 1500–1660* (New York: Columbia University Press, 1987).

Campbell, Mildred, *The English Yeoman Under Elizabeth and the Early Stuarts* (London: Merlin Press, 1967).

Canny, Nicholas, *Making Ireland British, 1580–1650* (Oxford: Oxford University Press, 2001).

Cantor, Leonard, *The Changing English Countryside, 1400–1700* (London and New York: Routledge and Kegan Paul, 1987).

Cavallo, Adolph S, *Needlework* (Washington D.C.: The Smithsonian Institute, 1979).

Cavanaugh, Sheila, "'The Fatal Destiny of that Land': Elizabethan Views of Ireland", ed. Bradshaw, Brendan, Andrew Hadfield, and Willy Maley, *Representing Ireland: Literature and the Origin of Conflict, 1534–1660* (Cambridge: Cambridge University Press, 1993), pp.116–31.

———— "'Licentious Barbarism': Spenser's View of the Irish and the *Faerie Queene*" *Irish University Review* 26(2) 1996: 268–80.

Chambers, Douglas, "'Storys of Plants': The Assembling of Mary Capel Somerset's Botanical Collection at Badminton," *Journal of the History of Collections* 9 (1997): 49–60.

Cheney, Patrick and Lauren Silberman, eds. *Worldmaking Spenser: Explorations in the Early Modern Age* (Lexington: The University Press of Kentucky, 2000).

Church of England, *The book of common praier* (London: Printed by Richard Iugge, 1559).

Coffin, David R., *The English Garden: Meditation and Memorial* (Princeton: Princeton University Press, 1994).

Coiro, Ann Baines, "Writing in Service: Sexual Politics and Class Position in the Poetry of Aemilia Lanyer," *Criticism* 25 (1993).

Comito, Terry, *The Idea of the Garden in the Renaissance* (New Brunswick: Rutgers University Press, 1978).

Cosgrove, Denis E., *Social Formation and Symbolic Landscape* (Madison: University of Wisconsin Press, 1998).

Dash, Mike, *Tulipomania* (New York: Three Rivers Press, 1999).

DeCerteau, Michel, *The Practice of Everyday Life,* trans. Steven F. Randall (Berkeley: University of California Press, 1984).

Derricke, John, *The Image of Irelande; with a Discoverie of Woodkarne* (1591), ed. John Small (Ediburgh: Adam and Charles Black, 1883).

Donne, John, "Twickenham Garden," John T. Shawcross, (ed.), *The Complete Poetry of John Donne* (Garden City, NY: Anchor Books, 1967).

Dove, Linda L., "Lady Mary Wroth and the Politics of the Household in 'Pamphilia to Amphilanthus.'" Ed. Mary E. Burke, Jane Donawerth, Linda L. Dove, and

Karen Nelson. *Women, Writing, and the Reproduction of Culture in Tudor and Stuart Britain* (New York: Syracuse University Press, 2000), pp. 141–56.

Dubrow, Heather, *Echoes of Desire: English Petrarchism and Its Counterdiscourses* (Ithaca: Cornell University Press, 1995).

Durant, David N., *Bess of Hardwick: Portrait of and Elizabethan Dynast* (London: Wiedenfield and Nicolson, 1977).

Duthie, Ruth, *Florists' Flowers and Societies* (Haverfordwest, Dyfed: C.I. Thomas and Sons, Ltd., 1988).

E.C.S. "The Government of Ireland Vnder the HONORABLE, IVST, and wife Gouernour Sir IOHN PERROT Knight, one of the Priuy Councell to Queene ELIZABETH, beginning in 1584. and ending in 1588," (London, for Thomas Walkley, 1626).

Eggert, Katherine, *Showing Like a Queen: Female Authority and Literary Experiment in Spenser, Shakespeare, and Milton* (Philadelphia: University of Pennsylvania Press, 2000).

Elizabeth I., "By the Queene," (London: Printed by Christopher Barker, 1578).

_____ "By the Queene: The Queenes Maiesties Proclamation declaring her princely resolution in sending ouer of her Army into the Realme of Ireland (London: Printed by the Deputies of Christopher Barker, 1599).

Empson, William, *Some Versions of Pastoral* (New York: New Directions Publishing Co, 1950; rpt. 1960, 1968).

Erickson, Amy Louise, *Women and Property in Early Modern England* (New York: Routledge, 1993).

Evelyn, John, *Sylva, or, a discourse of forest-trees* (London: Printed by Joseph Martyn and Ja. Allertry, 1664).

Ezell, Margaret, *Social Authorship and the Advent of Print* (Baltimore: Johns Hopkins UP, 1999).

Fisher, Will, *Materializing Gender in Early Modern Literature and Culture* (Cambridge; New York: Cambridge University Press, 2006).

Fitzherbert, John, *The boke of husbandry* (London: Thomas Berthelet, 1523?).

Fitzpatrick, Joan, "Spenser and Land: Political Conflict Resolved in Physical Topography," *Ben Jonson Journal* 7 (2000): 365–77.

_____ "Pastoral Idylls and Lawless Rebels: Sexual Politics in Books V and VI of Spenser's *Faerie Queene*," *Explorations in Renaissance Culture* 25 (1999): 87–111.

Foxe, John, *Acts and monuments* (London: Printed by Iohn Daye, 1583).

Freerick, Jean, "Spenser, Race, and Ire-land," *ELR* 31(1) 2002: 85–117.

Frye, Susan, "Sewing Connections," Ed. Susan Frye and Karen Robertson. *Maids and Mistresses, Cousins, and Queens: Women's Alliances in Early Modern England* (New York: Oxford University Press, 1999), pp. 165–82.

_____ and Karen Robertson (ed.), *Maids and Mistresses, Cousins, and Queens: Women's Alliances in Early Modern England* (New York: Oxford University Press, 1999).

_____ *Elizabeth I: The Competition for Representation* (Oxford: Oxford University Press , 1993).

Fumerton, Patricia and Simon Hunt, ed. *Renaissance Culture and the Everyday* (Philadelphia: University of Pennsylvania Press, 1999).

Fussell, G.E. and K.R., *The English Countrywoman: A Farmhouse Social History, A.D. 1500–1900* (London: Andrew Melrose, 1953).

Gardiner, Richard, *Profitable instructions for the manuring, sowing, and planting of kitchin gardens* (London: Edward Allde for E. White, 1599).

Gascoigne, George, *A Hundreth Sundrie Flowers* (London: Printed by Henry Bynneman and Henry Middleton for Richarde Smith, 1573).

Gerard, John, *The herbal or generall historie of plantes* (London: Printed by Edm. Bolliphant for Bonham Norton and Iohn Norton, 1597).

Girouard, Mark, *Life in the English Country House: A Social and Architectural History* (New Haven: Yale University Press, 1978).

Goody, Jack, *The Culture of Flowers* (Cambridge: Cambridge University Press, 1993).

Greenblatt, Stephen, *Renaissance Self-Fashioning: From More to Shakespeare* (Chicago: University of Chicago Press, 1980).

Grossman, Marshall, ed. *Aemilia Lanyer:, Gender, Genre, and the Canon* (Lexington: University Press of Kentucky, 1998).

Guibbory, Achsah, "The Gospel According to Aemilia: Women and the Sacred" Ed. Marshall Grossman. *Aemilia Lanyer: Gender, Genre, and the Canon* (Lexington: University Press of Kentucky, 1998), pp. 191–211.

Hadfield, Andrew, *Edmund Spenser's Irish Experience: Wilde Fruit and Salvage Soyl* (Oxford: Clarendon Press, 1997).

Halasz, Alexandra, *The Marketplace of Print: Pamphlets and the Public Sphere in Early Modern England* (Cambridge, New York: Cambridge UP, 1997).

Hannay, Margaret Patterson, ed. *Silent But for the Word: Tudor Women as Patrons, Translators, and Writers of Religious Works* (Kent: Kent State University Press, 1985).

Harris, Dianne, "Landscape in Context," Ed. Mirka Benes and Dianne Harris. *Villas and Gardens in Early Modern Italy and France* (Cambridge: Cambridge University Press, 2001), p.16.

———— "Cultivating Power: The Language of Feminism in Women's Garden Literature, 1870–1920," *Landscape Journal* 13.2 (1994): 113–24.

Harris, Tim, "Problematising Popular Culture," ed. Tim Harris. *Popular Culture in England, c. 1500–1850* (New York: St. Martin's Press, 1995), pp. 1–27.

Harrison, William, *The Description of England* (1587), ed. Georges Edelen (Ithaca: Cornell University Press, 1968).

Harvey, John, *Early Nurserymen* (London: Phillimore and Co., Ltd., 1974).

Hay, Millicent V., *The Life of Robert Sidney, Earl of Leicester (1563–1626)* (Washington: Folger Shakespeare Library, 1984).

Heffner, Ray, "Spenser's View of Ireland: Some Observations," *Modern Language Quarterly* 1942.3: 507–15.

Henrey, Blanche, *British Botanical and Horticultural Literature before 1800*, vol. 1 (London: Oxford University Press, 1975).

Heresbach, Conrad, *Foure bookes of husbandrie* (London: Printed for Iohn Wight, 1586).

Highley, Christopher, "The Royal Image in Elizabethan Ireland," ed. Julia M. Walker. *Dissing Elizabeth: Negative Representations of Gloriana* (Durham and London: Duke University Press, 1998), pp. 60–76.

Hill, Thomas, *A most briefe and pleasaunt treatise* (London: Iohn Daye, 1558).

_____*The gardeners labyrinth* (London: Printed by Henry Bynneman, 1577).

_____*The profittable arte of gardening* (London: Printed by Thomas Marshe, 1579).

Historical Manuscripts Commission. *Report on the Manuscripts of Lord De L'Isle and Dudley, Preserved at Penshurst Place,* vol. 3, ed. William A. Shaw (London: His Majesty's Stationery Office, 1936).

_____Vol. 4, ed. William A. Shaw (London: His Majesty's Stationery Office, 1942).

Hobhouse, Penelope, *Plants in Garden History* (London: Pavilion Books, 1992; 1997).

Hogrefe, Pearl, Tudor Women: Commoners and Queens (Ames: Iowa State University Press, 1975).

Howell, Martha C., *Women, Production, and Patriarchy in late medieval cities* (Chicago: Chicago University Press, 1986).

Humphrey, Carol, *Samplers* (New York: Cambridge University Press, 1997).

Hunt, John Dixon, "Paragone in paradise: translating the garden," *Comparative Criticism* 18 (1996): 55–70.

_____*Garden and Grove: The Italian Renaissance Garden in the English Imagination, 1600–1750* (Philadelphia: University of Pennsylvania Press, 1997).

_____ and Peter Willis, ed. *The Genius of the Place: The English Landscape Garden 1620–1820* (Cambridge, MA and London: The MIT Press, 1988).

James I. "By the King. A Proclamation touching the Earles of Tyrone and Tyrconnell" (London: Printed by Robert Barker, 1607).

Jones, Ann Rosalind, *The Currency of Eros: Women's Love Lyric in Europe, 1540–1620* (Bloomington: Indiana University Press, 1990).

Jonson, Ben, "To Penshurst," Hugh MacLean, ed. *Ben Jonson and the Cavalier Poets* (New York: W.W. Norton and Co., 1974).

Judson, Alexander C., *Spenser in Southern Ireland* (Bloomington, IN: The Principia Press, 1933).

Justice, George and Nathan Tinker, ed. *Women's Writing and the Circulation of Ideas: Manuscript Publication in England, 1550–1800* (Cambridge, NY: Cambridge University Press, 2002).

Keller, Evelyn Fox, *Reflections on Gender and Science* (New Haven: Yale University Press, 1985).

Klein, Bernhard, "The Lie of the Land: Surveyors, Irish Rebels, and *The Faerie Queene*," *Irish University Review* 26(2) 1996: 207–25.

Klein, Joan Larsen, *Daughters, Wives, and Widows: Writings by Men about Women and Marriage in England, 1500–1640* (Urbana: University of Illinois Press, 1992).

Lamb, Mary Ellen, *Gender and Authorship in the Sidney Circle* (Madison: University of Wisconsin Press, 1990).

Lanyer, Aemilia, *Salve Deus Rex Judaeorum*, ed. Suzanne Woods, *The Poems of Aemilia Lanyer, Salve Deus Rex Judaeorum* (Oxford: Oxford University Press, 1993).

Laurence, Anne, *Women in England, 1500–1750: A Social History* (New York: St. Martin's Press, 1994).

Lawson, William, *The Countrie Hovsewife's Garden* (London: Printed by B. Allsop for Roger Jackson, 1618).

_____ *A New Orchard and Garden* (London: Printed by B. Allsop for Roger Jackson, 1618).

Lazzaro, Claudia, "The Visual Language of Gender in Sixteenth-Century Garden Sculpture," ed. Marilyn Migiel and Juliana Schiesari. *Refiguring Women: Perspectives on Gender and the Italian Renaissance* (Ithaca and London, Cornell University Press, 1991), pp. 71–113.

Lefebvre, Henri, *The Production of Space*, trans. Donald Nicholson-Smith (Oxford: Blackwell, 1991).

Leslie, Michael, "Spenser, Sidney, and the Renaissance Garden," *ELR* 22(1) 1992: 3–36.

_____ and Timothy Raylor (ed.), *Culture and Cultivation in Early Modern England: Writing and the Land* (Leicester and London: Leicester University Press, 1992).

Lewalski, Barbara Kiefer, "Seizing Discourses and Reinventing Genres," Ed. Marshall Grossman. *Aemilia Lanyer: Gender, Genre, and the Canon* (Lexington: University Press of Kentucky, 1998).

_____ "Imagining Female Community: Aemilia Lanyer's Poems," ed. *Writing Women in Jacobean England* (Cambridge: Harvard University Press, 1993), pp. 212–41.

_____ "Claiming Patrimony and Constructing a Self: Anne Clifford and her *Diary*," ed. Barbara Kiefer Lewalski. *Writing Women in Jacobean England* (Cambridge: Harvard University Press, 1993), pp. 125–51.

_____ *Writing Women in Jacobean England* (Cambridge: Harvard University Press, 1993).

MacArthur, Janet H., "'A Sidney, though un-named': Lady Mary Wroth and her Poetical Progenitors," *English Studies in Canada*. 15(1): March 1989.

MacCarthy-Morrogh, Michael, *The Munster Plantation: English Migration to Southern Ireland, 1583–1641* (Oxford: Clarendon Press, 1986).

MacLean, Hugh, ed. *Ben Jonson and the Cavalier Poets* (New York: W.W. Norton and Co., 1974).

Maley, Willy. *Salvaging Spenser: Colonialism, Culture, and Identity* (London: Macmillan Press, 1997).

_____ *A Spenser Chronology* (Lanham, MD: Barnes and Noble Books, 1994).

Markham, Gervase, *The English Housewife* (1616), ed. Michael R. Best. Kingston and (Montreal: McGill-Queen's University Press, 1986).

_____ *The English Husbandman* (London: Printed by T. Snodham for J. Browne, 1635 ed.), p.192.

_____ *Maison Rustique, or the Countrie Farme* (London: Printed by Adam Islip for Iohn Bill, 1616).

Mascall, Leonard, *The Country-mans Recreation, or the Art of Planting, Grafting, and Gardening in Three Books* (1640).

Masden, Karen and John E. Furlong, "Women, Land, Design: Considering Connections," *Landscape Journal* 13.2 (1994): 89–101.

Masten, Jeff, "'Shall I turn blabb': Circulation, Gender, and Subjectivity in Mary Wroth's Sonnets." ed. Naomi J. Miller and Gary Waller. *Reading Mary Wroth: Representing Alternatives in Early Modern England* (Knoxville: University of Tennessee Press, 1991), pp. 67–87.

McBride, Kari Boyd, "Sacred Celebration: The Patronage Poems," ed. Marshall Grossman, *Aemilia Lanyer: Gender, Genre, and the Canon* (Lexington: University Press of Kentucky, 1998), pp. 60–82.

McGrath, Lynette, "'Let Us Have Our Libertie Againe': Amelia Lanier's Seventeeth Century Feminist Voice," *Women's Studies: An Interdisciplinary Journal* 20 (3–4) 1992: 331–48.

McGurk, John, *The Elizabethan Conquest of Ireland: The 1590s Crisis* (Manchester and New York: Manchester University Press, 1997).

McRae, Andrew, *God Speed the Plough: The Representation of Agrarian England, 1500–1660* (Cambridge: Cambridge University Press, 1996).

Meager, Leonard, *The English Gardener: or a Sure Guide to young Planters and Gardeners* (1670).

Melaney, William D., "Spenser's Allegory of Temperance," *Ben Jonson Journal* 4 (1997): 115–29.

Mendelson, Sara and Patricia Crawford, *Women in Early Modern England, 1550–1720* (Oxford: Clarendon Press, 1998).

Merchant, Caroline, *The Death of Nature: Women, Ecology, and the Scientific Revolution* (San Francisco, 1980).

Miller, Jacqueline T., "Lady Mary Wroth in the House of Busirane," ed. Patrick Cheney and Lauren Silberman, *Worldmaking Spenser: Explorations in the Early Modern Age* (Lexington: The University Press of Kentucky, 2000), pp. 115–24.

Miller, Naomi J. *Changing the Subject: Mary Wroth and Figurations of Gender in Early Modern England* (The University Press of Kentucky, 1997).

_____ "(M)Other Tongues: Maternity and Subjectivity," Ed. Marshall Grossman. *Aemilia Lanyer: Gender, Genre, and the Canon* (Lexington: University Press of Kentucky, 1998), pp. 143–66.

_____ and Gary Waller, ed., *Reading Mary Wroth: Representing Alternatives in Early Modern England* (Knoxville: University of Tennessee Press, 1991).

Miller, Shannon, "'Mirrours More Then One': Edmund Spenser and Female Authority in the Seventeenth Century," ed. Patrick Cheney and Lauren Silberman, *Worldmaking Spenser: Explorations in the Early Modern Age* (Lexington: The University Press of Kentucky, 2000), pp. 125–47.

_____ "Constructing the Female Self: Architectural Structures in Mary Wroth's *Urania*," Ed. Patricia Fumerton and Simon Hunt. *Renaissance Culture and the Everyday* (Philadelphia: University of Pennsylvania Press, 1999), pp. 139–61.

Mingay, G.E., *A Social History of the English* Countryside (London and New York: Routledge, 1990).

Montrose, Louis Adrian, "'Eliza, Queene of shepheardes' and the Pastoral of Power," *ELR* 10 (1980): 153–82.

_____ "*A Midsummer Night's Dream* and the Shaping Fantasies of Elizabethan Culture: Gender, Power, Form," ed. Margaret W. Ferguson, Maureen Quilligan, and Nancy J. Vickers, *Rewriting the Renaissance* (Chicago and London: Chicago University Press, 1986), pp. 65–87.

Moody, Joanna, ed. *The Private Life of an Elizabethan Lady: The Diary of Lady Margaret Hoby, 1599–1605* (Gloucestershire: Sutton Pub., 1998).

Mueller, Janel, "The Feminist Poetics of '*Salve Deus Rex Judaeorum*'," Ed. Marshall Grossman. *Aemilia Lanyer: Gender, Genre, and the Canon* (Lexington: University Press of Kentucky, 1998), pp. 99–127.

Mulcaster, Richard, *Positions Concerning the Training Up of Children* (1581), ed. William Barker (Toronto: University of Toronto Press, 1994).

Mullaney, Stephen, *The Place of the Stage: License, Play, and Power in Renaissance England* (Chicago and London: University of Chicago Press, 1988).

Murphy, Andrew, *But the Irish Sea Betwixt Us: Ireland, Colonialism, and Renaissance Literature* (Lexington: The University Press of Kentucky, 1999).

Newcomb, Lori Humphrey, *Reading Popular Romance in Early Modern England* (New York: Columbia University Press, 2002).

Orlin, Lena Cowen, ed. *Material London, ca. 1600* (Philadelphia: The University of Pennsylvania Press, 2000).

_____*Private Matters and Public Culture in Post-Reformation England* (Ithaca and London: Cornell University Press, 1994).

Overton, Mark, *Agricultural Revolution in England: the transformation of the agrarian economy, 1500–1850* (Cambridge: Cambridge University Press, 1996).

Palliser, D.M., *The Cambridge Urban History of Britain, Vol. I, c.600–c.1540* (Cambridge: Cambridge University Press, 2000).

Parker, Rozsika, *The Subversive Stitch: Embroidery and the Making of the Feminine* (London: The Women's Press, 1984).

Parkinson, John, *Paradisi en sole paradisus terrestris* (London: Printed by Humfrey Lownes and Robert Young, 1626).

Patterson, Annabelle, *Pastoral and Ideology* (Berkeley: University of California Press, 1987).

Payne, Robert, *A briefe description of Ireland: made in this yeare, 1589* (London: Printed by T. Dawson).

Perkins, William, *Christian Economy* (1609), ed. Joan Larsen Klein. *Daughters, Wives, and Widows: Writings by Men about Women in England, 1500–1640* (Urbana: University of Illinois Press, 1993).

Plat, Hugh, *Sundrie nevv and artificiall remedies against famine* (London: Printed by P. Short, 1596)._____*The nevve and admirable arte of setting corne* (London: Printed by P. Short, 1600).

_____*Delightes for Ladies* (London: Printed by Humfrey Lownes, 1609).

_____*The Garden of Eden: or, An accurate description of all flowers and fruits now growing in England* (Pt.1, 1652; Pt. 2, 1659) (London: Printed by William Leake).

Poggioli, Renato, *The Oaten Flute* (Cambridge: Harvard University Press, 1971).

Pollock, Linda, *With Faith and Physic: The Life of a Tudor Gentlewoman, Lady Grace Mildmay (1552–1620)* (New York: St. Martin's Press, 1995).

Puttenham, George, *The Art of English Poesie* (London: Printed by R. Field, 1589).

Quilligan, Maureen. "The Comedy of Female Authority in *The Faerie Queene*," *ELR* 17(2)1987: 156–71.

_____*Milton's Spenser: The Politics of Reading* (Ithaca: Cornell University Press, 1983.)

Rambuss, Richard, *Spenser's Secret Career* (Cambridge: Cambridge University Press, 1993).

Reynell, Carew, *A necessary companion or, The English interest discovered and promoted in the advancement of most trades and manufactures with infallible rules for the attainment thereof. Together with the emprovement of orchards, vineyards, medows, pasture lands, &c.* (1685).

Riley, Robert B., "Gender, Landscape, Culture: Sorting Out Some Questions," *Landscape Journal* 13.2 (1994): 153–63.

Roberts, Josephine, "The Biographical Problem of *Pamphilia to Amphilanthus*," *Tulsa Studies in Women's Literature* 1(1): Spring 1982.

Salter, Thomas, *The Mirrhor of Modestie* (1579), Ed. Suzanne Trill, Kate Chedgzoy, and Melanie Osborne, *Lay By Your Needles Ladies, Take the Pen: Women Writing in England, 1500–1700* (New York: St. Martin's Press, 1997).

Schlatter, Richard, *Private Property: The History of An Idea* (New York: Russell and Russell, 1973).

Schleiner, Louise, *Tudor and Stuart Women Writers* (Bloomington: Indiana University Press, 1994).

Scot, Reginald, *A perfite platforme of a hoppe garden.* London: Printed by Henry Denham for William Brome, 1574).

Shakespeare, William, *Sonnets* (1609), Ed. Stephen Booth (New Haven and London: Yale University Press, 1977).

Shepard, Alexandra, *Meanings of Manhood in Early Modern England* (Oxford: Oxford University Press, 2003).

Sherman, Sandra, "Printed Communities," *JEMCS* 3(2) 2003: 36–67.

Sidney, Sir Philip, *Astrophil and Stella* (1591), ed. Katherine Duncan-Jones, *Sir Philip Sidney: Selected Poems* (Oxford: Oxford University Press, 1984).

————*An Apology for Poetry, or the Defence of Poetry* (1595), ed. Geoffrey Shepherd (Oxford: Manchester University Press, 1973 [1965, first ed.]).

Silberman, Lauren, "*The Faerie Queene*, Book II and the Limitations of Temperance," *Modern Language Studies* 17(4) 1987: 9–22.

————"Singing Unsung Heroines," Ed. Margaret W. Ferguson, Maureen Quilligan, and Nancy J. Vickers, *Rewriting the Renaissance* (Chicago and London: Chicago University Press, 1986), pp. 259–71.

Sim, Alison, *The Tudor Housewife* (Gloucestershire: Sutton Pub., 1996).

Sinfield, Alan, *Faultlines: Cultural Materialism and the Politics of Dissident Reading* (Berkeley: University of California Press, 1992).

Spenser, Edmund, *The shepheardes calendar.* London: Printed by Henry Singleton, 1579).

————*The faerie queene* (London: John Wolfe for William Ponsonbie, 1590; 1596).

————*A View of the State of Ireland* (1596), ed. Andrew Hadfield and Willy Maley (Oxford: Blackwell Publishers, Ltd., 1997).

————*The Cantos of Mutabilitie* (London: Printed by Humfrey Lownes for M. Lownes, 1609).

Steele, Arnold F., *The Worshipful Company of Gardeners of London. A History of its Revival: 1890–1960* (London: The Worshipful Company of Gardeners of London, 1964).

Stewart, Stanley, *The Enclosed Garden: The Tradition and the Image in Seventeenth Century Poetry* (Madison: University of Wisconsin Press, 1966).

Strong, Roy, *The Renaissance Garden in England* (London: Thames and Hudson, 1998).

Stubbes, Philip, *The Anatomy of Abuses* (London: Printed by J. Kingston for Richard Jones, 1583).

Sullivan, Garrett, *The Drama of Landscape: Land, Property, and Social Relations on the Early Modern Stage* (Stanford: Stanford University Press, 1998).

Suzuki, Mihoko, *Subordinate Subjects: Gender, the Political Nation, and Literary Form in England, 1588–1688* (Aldershot, UK and Burlington, VT: Ashgate Press, 2003).

T.E., *The Law's Resolution of Women's Rights*, ed. Joan Larsen Klein, *Daughters, Wives, and Widows: Writings by Men about Women and Marriage in England, 1500–1640* (Urbana: University of Illinois Press, 1992).

Tawney, R.H. and Eileen Power (eds), *Tudor Economic Documents* (New York: Longman's Green and Co., 1924).

Tayler, Edward William, *Nature and Art in Renaissance Literature* (New York and London: Columbia University Press, 1964).

Taylor, John, "The Praise of the Needle," *The needles excellency* (London: T. Harper for J. Boler, 1631).

Thick, Malcolm, *The Neat House Gardens: Early Market Gardening Around London* (Devon: Prospect Books, 1998).

Thirsk, Joan, *The Rural Economy of England* (London: The Hambledon Press, 1984).

———"Tudor Enclosures," in *The Rural Economy of England* (London: Hambledon Press, 1984), pp. 65–83.

———"Making a Fresh Start: Sixteenth Century Agriculture and the Classical Inspiration," Ed. Michael Leslie and Timothy Raylor, *Culture and Cultivation in Early Modern England: Writing and the Land* (Leicester and London: Leicester University Press, 1992), pp. 15–34.

Thomas, Keith, *Man and the Natural World* (New York: Pantheon, 1983).

Toliver, Harold, *Pastoral Forms and Attitudes* (Berkeley: University of California Press, 1971).

Toller, Jane, *British Samplers: A Concise History* (Sussex: Phillimore & Co, Ltd., 1980).

Trevelyon, Thomas, (*Commonplace Book*. London: Thomas Trevelyon, 1608).

Trill, Suzanne, Kate Chedgzoy, and Melanie Osborne, Ed. *Lay By Your Needles Ladies, Take the Pen: Women Writing in England, 1500–1700* (New York: St. Martin's Press, 1997).

Tusser, Thomas, *A hundredth good pointes of husbandrie* (London: Printed by Richard Tottel, 1557).

———*Fiue hundreth points of good husbandry* vnited to as many of good huswiferie nowe lately augmented (London: Printed by Henry Denham for Richard Tottel, 1573).

Villeponteaux, Mary, "'Not as women wonted be': Spenser's Amazon Queen," ed. Julia M. Walker, *Dissing Elizabeth: Negative Representations of Gloriana* (Durham and London: Duke University Press, 1998), pp. 209–25.

Walker, Julia M. (ed.), *Dissing Elizabeth: Negative Representations of Gloriana* (Durham and London: Duke University Press, 1998).

Wall, Wendy, *The Imprint of Gender: Authorship and Publication in the English Renaissance* (Ithaca: Cornell University Press, 1993).

_____ "Renaissance National Husbandry," *Sixteenth Century Journal* 27 (3) 1996: 767–85.

_____ *Staging Domesticity* (Cambridge and New York: Cambridge University Press, 2002).

Waller, Gary, *The Sidney Family Romance: Mary Wroth, William Herbert, and the Early Modern Construction of Gender* (Detroit: Wayne State University Press, 1993).

_____ "Struggling Into Discourse: The Emergence of Renaissance Women's Writing," ed. Margaret Patterson Hannay, *Silent But for the Word: Tudor Women as Patrons, Translators, and Writers of Religious Works* (Kent: Kent State University Press, 1985), pp. 238–56.

Wheathill, Anne, *A handfull of holesome (though homelie) hearbs, gathered out of God's most holie word* (London: Printed by Henry Denham, 1584).

Whitney, Isabella, *A sweet Nosegay, gathered in a philosophical garden* (London: Printed by Richard Jones, 1573).

Wiffen, J.H., *Historical Memoirs of the House of Russell, vol. 2* (London: Longman, Rees, Orme, Brown, Green, and Longman, 1833).

Williams, Raymond, *The Country and the City* (New York: Oxford University Press, 1973).

_____ *Marxism and Literature* (Oxford: Oxford University Press, 1977).

Woods, Suzanne, *Lanyer: A Renaissance Woman Poet* (New York: Oxford, 1999).

_____ "Introduction" to *The Poems of Aemilia Lanyer, Salve Deus Rex Judaeorum* (Oxford: Oxford University Press, 1993).

_____ "Vocation and Authority: Born to Write," Ed. Marshall Grossman, *Aemilia Lanyer: Gender, Genre, and the Canon* (Lexington: University Press of Kentucky, 1998), pp. 83–98.

Woolley, Hannah, *The accomplisht ladys delight* (London: Printed by Benjamin Harris, 1675).

Worshipful Company of Gardeners, *Adam Armed* (London, 1700).

Wroth, Lady Mary, *The Poems of Lady Mary Wroth*, ed. Josephine Roberts (Baton Rouge: University of Louisiana Press, 1983).

_____ *The First Part of the Countesse of Mountgomeries Urania*, ed. Josephine Roberts (Binghampton: Center for Medieval and Early Renaissance Texts and Studies, 1995).

Youings, Joyce, Dissolution of the Monasteries (London: George Allen and Unwin Ltd., 1971).

Index